CRPYK

DE-SCRIBING EMPIRE

De-Scribing Empire examines the textual fabric of colonialism and its legacies. Starting from the premise that institutional colonialism was maintained by language as much as by guns, the book examines a range of textual strategies and their ramifications:

- the power of cartography to erase and dispossess

- the imperial role of nineteenth-century children's literature

- the place of the feminine in colonial power hierarchies

- the racial unease of early twentieth-century adventure fiction

- the meaning and implications of native 'authenticity'

- the technologies of containment in a racist state

- the ambiguities of teaching resistance literature in a Western university.

De-Scribing Empire also highlights the ambivalence of the Western academy in discussions of colonialism. As such it raises important questions for teachers and students of post-colonial literature.

Alan Lawson is a Senior Lecturer teaching Australian and Post-colonial Literatures at the University of Queensland, Australia. He has published widely on Australian and Canadian literatures, on post-colonial theory and on the institutionalization of national literatures and cultures in Canada and Australia. With Ken Goodwin, he edited *The Macmillan Anthology of Australian Literature*.

Chris Tiffin is also a Senior Lecturer in English at the University of Queensland. He is the editor of *South Pacific Images*, and author of *Rosa Praed: A Bibliography* and articles on Australian and post-colonial literatures.

DE-SCRIBING EMPIRE

EMPIRE

Post-colonialism and textuality

Edited by Chris Tiffin and Alan Lawson

London and New York

First published 1994
by Routledge
11 New Fetter Lane, London EC4P 4EE

Simultaneously published in the USA and Canada
by Routledge
29 West 35th Street, New York, NY 10001

Typeset in Bembo by
EXCEPT*detail* Ltd, Southport

Printed and bound in Great Britain by
Clays Ltd, St Ives plc

British Library Cataloguing in Publication Data

A catalogue record for this book is available from the British Library

Library of Congress Cataloging in Publication Data

De-scribing Empire: Post-colonialism and textuality/edited by
Chris Tiffin and Alan Lawson.
    p   cm.
Includes bibliographical references and index.
    1. Politics and literature. 2. Imperialism in literature.
3. Literature and society. I. Tiffin, Chris. II. Lawson, Alan.
PN51.D426   1994
808–dc20   93–44378

ISBN 0-415-10546-3 (hbk)
ISBN 0-415-10547-1 (pbk)

CONTENTS

CONTENTS

ILLUSTRATIONS

NOTES ON CONTRIBUTORS

Bill Ashcroft is Senior Lecturer in English at the University of New South Wales, Sydney, Australia.

J.M. Coetzee is Professor of English at the University of Cape Town, South Africa, and a well-known novelist.

Terry Collits, formerly Associate Professor and Head of English at the University of Melbourne, is now Director of Chisholm College, La Trobe University, Melbourne, Australia.

Robert Dixon, formerly Senior Lecturer in English at James Cook University, Townsville, is now Professor of Literature at the University of Southern Queensland, Toowoomba, Australia.

Helen Gilbert is Lecturer in English at Monash University, Melbourne, Australia.

Fiona Giles, formerly Lecturer in English at the University of New South Wales, is now a freelance writer in New York.

Gareth Griffiths is Professor and Head of English at the University of Western Australia, Perth, Australia.

Alan Lawson is Senior Lecturer in English at the University of Queensland, Brisbane, Australia.

Howard McNaughton is Associate Professor in English at the University of Canterbury, Christchurch, New Zealand.

Bridget Orr is Lecturer in English at the University of Auckland, New Zealand.

Chris Prentice is Lecturer in English at the University of Otago, Dunedin, New Zealand.

Simon Ryan is Lecturer in English at the Australian Catholic University, Brisbane.

Paul Sharrad is Senior Lecturer in English at the University of Wollongong, Australia.

Stephen Slemon is Associate Professor in English at the University of Alberta, Edmonton, Canada.

Sue Thomas is Senior Lecturer in English at La Trobe University, Melbourne, Australia.

Chris Tiffin is Senior Lecturer in English at the University of Queensland, Brisbane, Australia.

Jo-Ann Wallace is Associate Professor in English at the University of Alberta, Edmonton, Canada.

ACKNOWLEDGEMENTS

The essays in this volume are published for the first time except those by J. M. Coetzee, a version of which appeared in *Raritan* (1991), and by Robert Dixon, a version of which appeared in *Reconnoitres: Essays in Australian Literature in Honour of G.A. Wilkes* (1992), ed. Margaret Harris and Elizabeth Webby. We are grateful to the editors of *Raritan* and to Oxford University Press (Australia) and Sydney University Press for permission to reprint these essays.

For permission to quote other copyright materials we are grateful to the following: University of Minnesota Press for extracts from *Problems of Dostoevsky's Poetics* (1984) by M. Bakhtin, ed. C. Emerson; J.M. Meulenhoff for extracts from *Skryt* (1972) by Breyten Breytenbach; Breyten Breytenbach and Taurus Press for extracts from *Buffalo Bill* (1984); Zone Books for extracts from *The Accursed Share: An Essay on General Economy* (1967) by Georges Bataille; Currency Press for extracts from *Too Young for Ghosts* (1986) by Janis Balodis; Simon During and The Caxton Press for extracts from 'Postmodernism or postcolonialism?' in *Landfall* (1985); Farrar Straus & Giroux, Inc., and Wylie Aitken & Stone for extracts from 'Wingless' in *At the Bottom of the River* (1983) by Jamaica Kincaid; Oxford University Press for extracts from *The Collected Letters of Katherine Mansfield* (1984) ed. Vincent O'Sullivan and M. Scott; Oxford University Press (New Zealand) for extracts from *The Urewera Notebook* (1978) by Katherine Mansfield, ed. I. Gordon; Columbia University Press for extracts from *Subject to Change: Reading Feminist Writing* (1988) by N.K. Miller; Curtis Brown & John Farquharson for extracts from *Cambridge* (1991) by Caryl Phillips; Harvard University Press for extracts from 'Passions of the Renaissance' by J. Revel in *A History of Private Life* (1989) ed. R. Chartier; Penguin Books for extracts from *Tigers Are Better Looking*

(1968) by Jean Rhys; Harvester Wheatsheaf for extracts from 'Modernism's last post' by Stephen Slemon in *Past the Last Post* (1991) ed. Ian Adam and Helen Tiffin; Pluto Press for extracts from *Antarctica: Private Property or Public Heritage* (1991) by K. Suter; University of Chicago Press for extracts from *Shamanism, Colonialism and the Wild Man: A Study in Terror and Healing* (1987) by M. Taussig; Chatto & Windus for extracts from *The Spectacle of Women* (1987) by L. Tickner; Hans Zell, an imprint of Bowker-Sauer, for extracts from 'Post-colonialism, post-modernism and the rehabilitation of post-colonial history' by Helen Tiffin in *The Journal of Commonwealth Literature* (1988); West Australian Newspapers Limited for extracts from an article from the *West Australian* on 12 August 1991.

For permission to reproduce materials from their collections we gratefully acknowledge: The Huntington Library, San Marino, California; The Newberry Library, Chicago; The Bodleian Library, Oxford; The Museum of London; Stiftsbibliothek, Einsiedeln, Switzerland; and the Fryer Library, Brisbane.

We are grateful to Christy Collis for the swift performance of many nameless, unrecorded acts associated with the editing of this volume, and to Elizabeth Mitchell for cheerful and efficient clerical assistance.

Versions of the papers were originally presented at a symposium convened by Helen Tiffin, assisted by Leigh Dale and Glen Thomas. This book both records and extends the discussions at that stimulating event.

INTRODUCTION
The textuality of Empire
Chris Tiffin and Alan Lawson

On 1 June 1953 news reached England that Tensing Norgay and a New Zealand companion, Hillary, had climbed the world's highest mountain, Chomolungma. England, preoccupied with preparations for the coronation of the new Queen Elizabeth, had not been following the previous movements of Mr Tensing very closely, but was still quick to proclaim the significance of the event as an omen for a new and glorious Elizabethan age. Next morning the *News Chronicle* devoted an ecstatic front page to the story, not so much pushing aside the regal preparations, as inscribing the ascent of the mountain as a paroxysm of tributary loyalty and an unofficial part of the investiture.

THE CROWNING GLORY

EVEREST IS CLIMBED

TREMENDOUS NEWS FOR THE QUEEN

HILLARY DOES IT

Glorious Coronation Day news! Everest – Everest the unconquerable – has been conquered. And conquered by men of British blood and breed.

The news came late last night Edmund Hillary and the Sherpa guide, Bhotia Tensing, of Colonel John Hunt's expedition, had climbed the summit of Earth's highest peak, 29,002 feet high.

New Zealand's deputy Premier announced it at a Coronation Day ceremony at Wellington – and within seconds it flashed round the world.

Queen Elizabeth the Second, resting on the eve of her crowning, was immediately told that this brightest jewel of courage and endurance had been added to the Crown of

1

British endeavour. It is understood that a message of royal congratulation is being sent to the climbers. . . .

The New Elizabethan
[*photo of Hillary*]

Edmund Hillary, whose conquest of Everest sets the seal on a new Elizabethan age, is a 34–year-old bee farmer from New Zealand.

He learned his mountaineering in the Alps of the little Dominion of two million people, and was a pioneer in introducing winter skiing there. . . .

Told of Hillary's achievement, New Zealand's Prime Minister, Mr. Sidney Holland, said:

'What a grand achievement on the eve of the Coronation! I hope this terrific example of tenacity, endurance and fortitude, in this our Coronation year may be regarded as a symbol that there are no heights or difficulties which the British people cannot overcome.'

The event is complexly incorporated into imperial discourse. Both the start and end of the item assert a frame of the coronation. The successful ascent is a 'conquest' of a foreign and 'unknown' geographical space – a stubborn enemy overcome. The conqueror is of British (in the Greater Britain sense) birth and breeding. The nineteenth-century figure of the Empire as crown (with India as its principal jewel) is redeployed as a new crown constituted by the courageous deeds of the sons and daughters of Empire. The Queen receives the tribute of her subjects and returns gracious acknowledgment to her brave but insignificant people (a 'bee farmer' from a 'little dominion'). The event is commended by middle management (the New Zealand Prime Minister) who gives a moral exhortation which links the idea of the new monarch to the indomitability of British endeavour.

The hierarchies of the Empire are also preserved. Although Tensing and Hillary both reached the top, it is Hillary who is declared 'the new Elizabethan'. This exemplifies the recurrent pattern in accounts of imperial explorations for which indigenous guides were co-opted. The guide, by definition, has knowledge or travelling skills which enable the exploration to proceed. Nevertheless, the paradigmatic account of such voyages has the guide leading the European to some place or some thing which the European then 'discovers'. But the European can discover the place only if it is not already known, so the indigenous guide must know and yet not know. This paradox is implicitly resolved in textualizing the event by rendering the guide's knowledge pragmatic rather than conceptual and strategic. The guide has the practical knowledge to reach the goal, but not the conceptual knowledge to see its 'true' significance and thereby pre-empt the European discovery. Tensing's knowledge of the route and his experience in the conditions may be necessary for the Europeans to arrive at the summit, but he cannot 'conquer' the mountain in the comprehensive way the European can. He can never be 'the new Elizabethan'.

The event is appropriated to the imperial occasion, the players are established in their hierarchy, and a further hortatory text is written from the event to inspire other endeavours which can in turn be appropriated to the British Crown. In fact, any ascent of Everest would already be inscribed within a colonial framework since the English name for the mountain commemorates Sir George Everest, who for twenty years served the Empire as Surveyor-General of India.

This process of textualizing events for transmission and consumption is an ever-present one, and as Howard McNaughton shows in his essay in this volume, the potential inscriptions of any event, whether actualized or negated, are bewilderingly diverse. The 'successful' inscriptions are not randomly propagated, of course, but like the arcs of iron filings effortlessly induced by a magnet on a piece of paper, the actualized ones reflect the power structures and desires of the dominant discourse. Names and codes of naming are obvious, basic ways of curving the account to indicate who matters and who is subordinate, as the realigning in our opening sentence suggests.

Imperial relations may have been established initially by guns, guile and disease, but they were maintained in their interpellative phase largely by textuality, both institutionally as scholars like Gauri Viswanathan (1989) have shown, and informally. Colonialism (like its counterpart, racism), then, is an operation of discourse, and as an operation of discourse it interpellates colonial subjects by incorporating them in a system of representation. They are always already written by that system of representation. As Peter Hulme formulates it, colonialist discourse is 'an ensemble of linguistically-based practices unified by their common deployment in the management of colonial relationships' (Hulme 1986: 2). The children who read *The Water-Babies* in England in the 1860s were, as Jo-Ann Wallace argues in this volume, not just being entertained with a pleasing fantasy narrative, but being instructed in the 'innate' hierarchies of race and nation. This laying out the ground plan of the universe is, if anything, even more evident in the adventure fiction discussed by Robert Dixon. It is when the children (in both senses) of the colonies read such texts and internalize their own subjection that the true work of colonial textuality is done.

Language is an opaque medium whose ability to obscure can be deployed just as readily as its ability to express (as politicians and administrators know). When the Nixon administration, caught out in yet another lie, announced that the previous day's press statement was now 'inoperative', language was being chosen to obscure, rather than convey, meaning. Chinua Achebe shows a cognate process at work in an episode in his 1964 novel, *Arrow of God*. When the British administrators want to appoint Ezeulu as Paramount Chief, a sort of puppet headman, they first summon him, and when he declines to come, decide to arrest him. But on what charge, since they were actually seeking to honour him? The experienced Winterbottom who understands the opacity of language, and who 'enjoyed mystifying other Europeans with words from the Ibo language which he claimed to speak fluently' (Achebe 1964: 184) quickly announces: 'Leave him inside until he learns to cooperate with the Administration' (ibid.: 218). The young officer, Clarke, goes off admiring the linguistic resourcefulness which could find such a highsounding phrase to justify an action which has been worrying him because of its clear clash with the justice he is supposed to administer. Ultimately the resolving power lies with the phrase. It is language, not law, which creates the mechanism for detaining Ezeulu.

Used in that way, language and textuality are oppressive and sinister, but, as J. M. Coetzee shows, language becomes obscene when it proceeds from an imperium or power base so secure that it can abandon even the pretence of referentiality or the negotiation of truth. 'When the police explain a prisoner's death by saying that he slipped on a bar of soap, the unstated continuation is: and we defy any court in the land to reject that explanation' (p.87). Language itself then becomes an insulting taunt, not just a vehicle for taunting. Instead of seeking to obscure (which implies a recognition of the weakness of one's position), it offers the studied

4

arrogance of a palpable lie, knowing that its position is impregnable.

A particular form of the obscuring function of language and textuality is the process of erasure by which the obscurity is transferred from the language to the field being inscribed. Colonialism, like other dominant discourses, alternately fetishized and feared its Others – both race and place – depending on its sense of the threat posed by the Other. As Kay Schaffer has argued, the American Indian could be portrayed as a good character, a 'helper of the white destiny in America' (Schaffer 1993: 4), a native cultural and ethical guide, cousin to the geographical one. He could also, however, be portrayed as guilty of much evil culminating in human sacrifice and cannibalism. Colonialism conceptually depopulated countries either by acknowledging the native but relegating him or her to the category of the subhuman, or simply by looking through the native and denying his/her existence. These were necessary practices for invoking the claim of *terra nullius* upon which the now-disputed legality of imperial settlement (as opposed to 'invasion') was based. Only empty spaces can be settled, so the space had to be made empty by ignoring or dehumanizing the inhabitants. 'The topic of land [was] dissimulated in the topic of savagery, this move being characteristic of all narratives of the colonial encounter', as Peter Hulme (1986: 3) has pointed out. Both these strategies are analysed by Simon Ryan as he explores the evacuating power of maps and mapping. The blankness of the map is not an innocent ignorance because it enables, and therefore bears responsibility for, the subsequent practices of dispossession and annihilation.

Inscribing the natives as primitive and unable to make use of the natural resources around them allowed first the biblical parable of the ten talents, and then the Darwinian theory of natural selection to justify their dispossession as part of the plan of Destiny. Resistance was interpreted as malignant treachery and a justification for brutal suppression and even annihilation. But such a hectic policy did nothing for the labour force. If labour was required in the coffee plantations or on cattle stations to exploit the 'natural' wealth of the seemingly limitless tracts of land, a new way of encoding the native had to be arrived at. The solution was to see the native as, in Kipling's phrase, 'half savage and half child'. (This line of thinking underpins one type of post-1918 colony, the 'Protectorates'.) Childhood itself, though, as Jo-Ann Wallace demonstrates, was not a primordial concept in the Anglo-Saxon archive, but one which had been comparatively recently developed. It is almost, she argues, as though the idea of childhood was a necessary conceptual precursor of Empire.

Imperial textuality appropriates, distorts, erases, but it also *contains*. J.M. Coetzee finds perhaps the ultimate image of this containment in his discussion of the prison poems of Breyten Breytenbach. Imprisoned for publishing a poem attacking the Prime Minister, John Vorster (a crime of text), Breytenbach was granted permission to write in prison on condition that the poems were submitted exclusively to his gaoler. 'Exclusively' meant that the poems were to be shown to no-one else, and that all notes and drafts were to be destroyed. The position of voice that results is deeply paradoxical. The voice is *licensed* in the double sense of being allowed, but remaining under the control of the licensor. Breytenbach may write poems – subversive textuality is enabled – but only because the imperium is confident of its technologies of control. If we isolate that moment we have a totally closed system: a voice that cannot be heard, protest which can be articulated only from a position of total vulnerability to a position of impregnable strength. This is a paradigm of the total control of the subaltern that has been envisioned in recent colonial discourse studies. But the moment is not, perhaps never can be, isolated. The mere knowledge by outsiders of the existence of the poems invades the totality of control, a control which was never in fact absolute, for the stipulation that no poems were to be smuggled out acknowledges that poems *could* be smuggled out – that the technology of control might not be perfect. The control is complete only up to the moment of its announcement; once enunciated it can never again be total, since the circulation of the knowledge loosens it.

AMBIGUITY, AMBIVALENCE, AND TEXTUALITY

Post-colonial critics and theorists have found it difficult to postulate a way for the colonized to circumvent the cognitive patterns by which their world has been structured. The quest to defeat, escape or circumvent the pattern of binaries which has been identified as foundational to Western thought, for example, is seldom, if ever, attained. But theoretically, just as historically, the lines of colonial division were transgressed and at times became blurred. The situation of the settler colonies, for example, problematizes the nature of the self/Other dichotomy, as does the situation of a modern country which is simultaneously colonized and colonizer. As Anne McClintock (1992: 88–9) points out, the patterns of political and economic independence, colonization and recolonization are enormously complicated. The boundary between European self and colonized Other was not always maintained, and as Homi Bhabha has argued in a series of papers, the whole estate of colonialism is a breeding ground for fractures and flaws and a series of anxieties within European modernity itself that are taking longer to recognize than those within the forever-altered world of the Other. Only as the contradictions within the foundation (of these) texts of Empire and the surprising texts of colonial reaction are finally 'read out' is the full extent of colonial power intelligible. Colonial power then becomes intelligible as the energy *in potentia* in the always problematic negotiation between the epistemology of European modernity-in-imperium and that of its troublesome Other in its full agonistic utterance, that Other which always threatens to expose the knowledge of itself as plural and complete and outside the discourses of Europe. Despite their homogenizing vectors, colonial structures are not seamless. The sites they create are, in Howard McNaughton's oxymoronic tag, only 'impossible possibles'; both the ambiguity or liminality of place (the fringes of Empire where self startlingly meets Other) and the innate subversion of sex (refusing the prohibitions on contact with Other) coalesce possible with impossible. Europe's establishment of Empire never eliminated shadows and grey areas which post-colonial critics recognize and explore.

The difficult boundaries between European self and colonized Other are illustrated in the constitution of the very field of post-colonial studies itself. Stephen Slemon has made the point that, in the competition for the suddenly valorized term 'post-colonial', the Anglo-American critical coalition (and its politics of citation) may have been in danger of foreclosing on a particularly valuable locus of critical reading and textual resistance by finding resistance to be located either (deconstructively) within the texts of Empire themselves or in the oppositional 'valency of subjectivity specifically within Third- and Fourth-World cultures'. As Slemon sharply observes, this practice unreflectingly reinscribes the familiar 'binarism of Europe and its Others, of colonizer and colonized, of the West and the Rest, of the vocal and the silent' (Slemon 1990: 32, 34). By archaically resubscribing the binary which *preserves* colonial power, this habit effects a careful forgetting, not only of one of the sites of resistance, but also of the possibility of interrogating that binarist critical practice itself as an operation of power/knowledge. Benita Parry (1987), Jenny Sharpe (1989), and others have observed in critiques of post-colonial theory that the location of textual resistance either in the contradictions of the colonialist text or in an essentialist Third World consciousness serves to veil the actual operations of resistance. One might further argue, though, that this continues to recirculate the self-serving Eurocentricity (or US imperialism) of the binary operation of power in the overarching reductionist conception of the world as, once again, Europe and its Other. This overlooking effectively *oversees* Europe's other Others. 'Does this not', Alice Jardine says in another context, 'run the danger of (belatedly) developing nothing but the negative of the Great Western Photograph?' (Jardine 1985: 35).

RACE AND EMPIRE

In most, if not all, colonial situations, the obvious and immediate marker of difference was race. From the early debates about the doubtful humanity of the Africans, to nineteenth-century discussion about whether the British themselves would mutate into a new race in the different climates to which they were exposed, to the twentieth-century phenomena of national institutions of racism (like segregation in the US, the White Australia Policy or South African apartheid), legal, social and literary structures have fore-grounded the notion of race.

But what is the purchase of 'race' on a discourse which tries to eschew racism? Can it be an energizing and enabling position allowing articulation? Essays in this book take different views on this question. Gareth Griffiths warns that a reformative programme based upon essentializing race can be subverted, and that auth-enticity can become a weapon of reaction. Given that many of the most articulate political and literary activists are of mixed race, the demands for a truly authentic speaker and the rejection of anyone who is not so designated as 'authentic' can be a way of resisting any attempt to change the status quo. Helen Gilbert points out, however, that Australian Aboriginal dramatists have been particu-larly successful at adapting the forms of Western theatre to de-scriptive practices, and that strategies of diffused authorship, mimicry, and orality all help to generate a hybrid and powerful performance practice. Sue Thomas instances moments when the dream of perfect social symmetry, a classless, raceless, sexless society collides with the fact of its own impossible nostalgia. Just as the claim of sexual discrimination was not legally 'available' to the suffragettes, so the great Caribbean cricketer, Learie Constantine, was to discover in the early 1950s that 'race' was not a legal category upon which a case of discriminatory behaviour could be brought against a London hotel for excluding him (Pilkington 1988: 47). Only when difference can be spoken legally can it become possible to speak difference illegally. So, as Terry Collits reminds us, it is a question of 'speaking position'. 'Who,' he asks, 'is it that is to name the racist?'; indeed how, within the increasingly urgent sense of our own multi-constituted selves, do we name our own subject-positions? The urgency ultimately turns upon that same troublesome question of authenticity and its disturbing tendency to collapse into authority. The argument about race, then, reconnects with the arguments about the nature of imperial textuality itself; each is a 'dense system of ideological practices entwined over time' (Collits p.64, below) or 'an ensemble of linguistically-based practices' (Hulme 1986: 2). It is the multi-vectored nature of these phenomena that makes them so resistant to theoretical demobilization.

DE-SCRIBING EMPIRE

Robert Young notes that one of the major achievements of colonial discourse studies has been to demonstrate 'the extent to which colonialism, in the British example, was not simply a marginal activity on the edges of English civilization, but fundamental in its own cultural self-representation' (Young 1990: 174). The first stage of a process of de-scribing Empire is to analyse where and how our view of things is inflected (or infected) by colonialism and its constituent elements of racism, over-categorization, and deferral to the centre. The processes of history and of European historicizing continue to warrant attention, but they should not seduce us into believing that de-scribing Empire is a project simply of historical recuperation. The hegemony of Europe did not end with the raising of a hundred national flags, and as both Gareth Griffiths and Terry Collits show, its legacy of division and racism are alive and well in political, media and legal domains.

Just as fire can be fought with fire, textual control can be fought with textuality. As Ross Chambers has observed 'there is no stopping *texts*: in their readability lies their potential for oppositional resilience' (Chambers 1990: 3). The post-colonial is especially and pressingly concerned with the power that resides in discourse and textuality; its resistance, then, quite appropriately takes place in – and from – the domain of textuality, in (among other things) motivated acts of reading. The contestation of post-colonialism is a contest of representation.

T.S. Eliot proposed that each new significant work of literature necessitated a reassessment of all previous ones in the tradition. Paul Sharrad's essay imports that idea into a post-colonial space by asking what we learn about a Dickens novel by reframing it with a modern novel of roughly comparable setting which explicitly acknowledges the Empire not only as a simultaneously flourishing society, but one in which England had a deep economic and moral investment. This investment, Sharrad finds, passes virtually unacknowledged by Dickens, and he goes on to explore the implications of this erasure. Such reading strategies are fruitful, for the insights they reveal have powerful implications for education, for publication, and for the continued reframing of literary tradition.

Whether or not the subaltern can ever speak is obviously a profound and perplexing question which justifies the lengthy and subtle discussion it has provoked. But the curious thing about the debate is that it is being conducted by non-subalterns, people with voice, institutional power, and unlimited access to the technologies of textuality. A second curious thing is that they seem largely not to have noticed that the subalterns, meanwhile, *are* speaking. Post-colonial writers are declaring their spaces, engaging with canonical texts, rewriting not just the tradition but the episteme which underpins it. It may not be a pure or unrefracted discourse, but it is a vigorous and inventive one which is far removed from the inescapable closure predicted (though surely not observed) by that debate. In any case, we cannot wait until the last philosophical 'i' has been dotted. As Martin Green observed:

> In intellectual discourse we often assume that to ignore anything is a sin of irresponsibility; but in the context of action, ignorance can be a very positive and constructive policy – to turn away from *x* and concentrate on *y* is perhaps

your most effective way of expressing your judgment of the two.

(Green 1980: 343)

We are not suggesting that there are not genuine, even pressing, theoretical issues requiring resolution around the sites of the colonial and the post-colonial. But we are saying that a post-colonial discourse which ignores the recuperative and imaginatively syncretic writing currently appearing in post-colonial societies around the English-speaking world is not likely to arrive at very satisfying resolutions of those issues.

Part I

POST-COLONIAL THEORY

1

THE SCRAMBLE FOR POST-COLONIALISM

Stephen Slemon

It is scarcely news to readers of this volume that the heterogeneous field of 'post-colonial studies' is reproducing itself at present as a spectacle of disorderly conduct. Perhaps this is as it should be for a field which takes for its academic objective a wholesale refashioning of the Western project of the traditional 'humanities'; but I think it is clear that the institutionalized field of post-colonial studies, at least, has arrived at a point of multiple intersections, of ruptures, of territoriality – and this suggests that the field has arrived at a point that really matters in its history. In this essay, I want to try to think through the dis/order imbricated in the post-colonial academic field, and in part to respond to the ways in which a policing energy seems to carry itself across a variety of articulations within the post-colonial problematic. The policing energy which interests me here is in the final instance an internalized apparatus for control and regulation, an effect of ideology, and I am not about to argue that 'out there' in post-colonialdom there are double agents, neo-colonialist conspirators, wolves-in-sheep's-clothing, whom 'we' must resist through some vigorous form of oppositional collectivity. But I am going to suggest that as the field of post-colonial studies is becoming professionalized as an institution for social critique and as an apparatus for producing cultural knowledge, it is beginning to perform within itself a regulating operation which has no necessary relation to, or investment in, a politics of anti-colonialism. This article, consequently, is an attempt to carry out some (ideological) refereeing in this structure of professionalized or disciplinary regulation: I want to address the question of who gets to play on the post-colonial field, who is asked to sit on the bench, who plays on the farm team, how and when a player is, or ought to be, called 'out'. Now obviously, I am in no

15

sense outside of these questions; I too have an institutional stake in this game and am part of the disciplinary scramble. My refereeing persona here must necessarily be ambivalent, compromised by a double articulation in meta-regulation and in wager. Nevertheless, for the purposes of this exercise, I want to pretend to stand somehow outside the 'field'.

My thesis here is that in one register, the scramble now taking place within critical theory over the valency of the 'post-colonial' marker is at heart an institutional scramble, a debate whose specific provenance is an emerging critical and pedagogical field within the apparatus of the Western 'humanities'. My general argument is that the site of rupture for post-colonial studies is, in fact, predicated by a set of possibly unresolvable debates in the related field of colonial discourse theory, and more distantly in 'humanities'; and the conclusion I will be reaching for is a highly personal and I suspect ungeneralizable credo that has to do with the practice of anti-colonialist empowerment. But the question I will be pursuing on the way to this conclusion is why it is – and why it should be – that some radically differential, and in fact methodologically hostile, critical and teaching practices seek a grounding in something called 'post-colonialism' in order to de-scribe their various Empires and engage in an emancipatory and local institutional politics.

1

'Post-colonialism', as it is now used in its various fields, de-scribes a remarkably heterogeneous set of subject positions, professional fields, and critical enterprises. It has been used as a way of ordering a critique of totalizing forms of Western historicism; as a portmanteau term for a retooled notion of 'class', as a subset of both postmodernism and post-structuralism (and conversely, as the condition from which those two structures of cultural logic and cultural critique themselves are seen to emerge); as the name for a condition of nativist longing in post-independence national group-ings; as a cultural marker of non-residency for a Third World intellectual cadre; as the inevitable underside of a fractured and ambivalent discourse of colonialist power; as an oppositional form of 'reading practice'; and – and this was my first encounter with the term – as the name for a category of 'literary' activity which sprang from a new and welcome political energy going on within what used to be called 'Commonwealth' literary studies. The obvious tendency, in the face of this heterogeneity, is to understand 'post-colonialism' mostly as an object of desire for critical practice: as a shimmering talisman that in itself has the power to confer political legitimacy onto specific forms of institutionalized labour, especially on ones that are troubled by their mediated position within the apparatus of institutional power. I think, however, that this heterogeneity in the concept of the 'post-colonial' – and here I mean within the university institution – comes about for much more pragmatic reasons, and these have to do with a very real problem in securing the concept of 'colonialism' itself, as Western theories of subjectification and its resistances continue to develop in sophistication and complexity.

The nature of colonialism as an economic and political structure of cross-cultural domination has of course occasioned a set of debates, but it is not really on this level that the 'question' of European colonialism has troubled the various post-colonial fields of study. The problem, rather, is with the concept of colonialism as an ideological or discursive formation: that is, with the ways in which colonialism is viewed as an apparatus for constituting subject positions through the field of representation. In a way – and of course this is an extreme oversimplification – the debate over a description of colonialism's multiple strategies for regulating Europe's others can be expressed diagramatically (see Figure 1.1).

The general understanding in Figure 1.1 is that colonialism works on a left-to-right order of domination, with line 'A' representing various theories of how colonialism oppresses through direct political and economic control, and lines 'BC' and 'DE' representing differing concepts of the ideological regulation of colonial subjects, of subordination through the manufacture of consent. Theories that recognize an efficacy to colonialism that proceeds only along line 'A' are in essence 'brute force' or 'direct political' theories of colonialist oppression: that is, they reject the basic thesis that power manages social contradiction partly through the strategic production of specific ideas of the 'self', which subordinated groups then internalize as being 'real'. Theories, however, that examine the trajectory of colonialist power primarily along line 'BC' – a line representing an ideological flanking for the economic colonialism running along line 'A' – focus on the constitutive power of state apparatuses like education, and the constitutive power of professional fields of knowledge within those apparatuses, in the

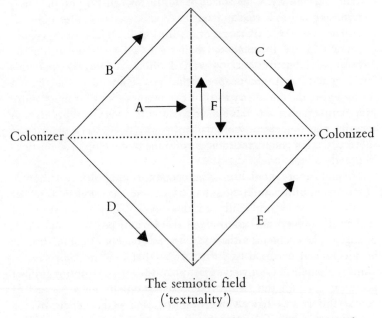

Figure 1.1 Diagram representing the debate over the nature of colonialism.

production of colonialist relations. Along this line, Edward Said (1979) examines the political efficacy of 'orientalism' within colonialism; Talal Asad (1973) and many others examine the role of anthropology in reproducing colonial relations; Alan Bishop (1990) examines the deployment of Western concepts of 'mathematics' against African school-children, Timothy Mitchell (1988) examines how the professional field of 'political science' came into being through a European colonialist engagement with the cultures of Egypt; Gauri Viswanathan (1989) examines the foundations of 'English' literary studies within a structure of colonialist management in India. This work keeps coming in, and the list of radically compromised professional fields within the Western syllabus of 'humanities' options grows daily longer. Theories that focus primarily on line 'DE' in this diagram examine the ways in which ideology reproduces colonialist relations through the strategic deployment of a vast semiotic field of representations – in literary works, in advertising, in sculpture, in travelogues, in exploration documents, in maps, in pornography, and so on.

This pattern, as I have laid it out so far, does not seem especially controversial or problematic, but the difficulties arise at the moment of conceptualizing the *relation* between colonialist professional fields and institutions (at the top of the diagram) and the whole field of representation (at the bottom of the diagram) – the field of 'textuality' and its investment in reproducing and naturalizing the structures of power. To take up one example of this paradigmatically: in Edward Said's work on Orientalism, colonialist power is seen to operate through a complex relationship between apparatuses placed on line 'F', where in the first instance a scholarly educational apparatus called 'Orientalism' – at the top of the line – appropriates textual representations of 'the Orient' in order to consolidate itself as a discipline and to reproduce 'the Orient' as a deployable unit of knowledge. So, in the first instance, colonialist power in Said's argument runs not just through the middle ground of this diagram but through a complex set of relations happening along line 'F'; and since Said's thesis is that a function at the top of this line is employing those representations created at the bottom of the line in order to make up 'knowledges' that have an ideological function, you can say that the vector of motion along line 'F' is an upward one, and that this upward motion is part of the whole complex, discursive structure whereby 'Orientalism' manufactures the 'Orient' and thus helps to regulate colonialist relations. That is Said's first position: that under Orientalism the vector of line 'F' is upward. But in Said's analysis, colonialist power also runs through line 'F' in a downward movement, where the scholarly apparatus of Orientalism is understood to be at work in the production of a purely fantastic and entirely projected idea of the 'Orient'. The point is that in the process of understanding the multivalent nature of colonialist discourse in terms of the historical specific of 'Orientalism', Said's model becomes structurally ambivalent – under 'Orientalism', the 'Orient' turns out to be something produced both as an object of scholarly knowledge and as a location for psychic projection.[1] I have graphed this ambivalence as a double movement or vector along line 'F'. For Said, the mechanism that produces this 'Orient', then, has to be understood as something capable of deploying an ambivalent structure of relations along line 'F', and deploying that structure towards a unified end. And so Said (and here I'm following Robert

Young's analysis of the problem) ends up referring the whole structure of colonialist discourse back to a single and monolithic originating intention within colonialism, the intention of colonialist power to possess the terrain of its Others. That assumption of intention is basically where Said's theory has proven to be most controversial.

Said's text is an important one here, for as Robert Young has shown, Said's work stands at the headwaters of colonial discourse theory, and this ambivalence in Said's model may in fact initiate a *foundational* ambivalence in the critical work which comes out of this field. This ambivalence sets the terms for what are now the two central debates within colonial discourse theory: the debate over historical specificity, and the debate over agency.

The first debate – the debate over the problem of historical specificity in the model – concerns the inconclusive relation between actual historical moments in the colonialist enterprise and the larger, possibly trans-historical discursive formation that colonial discourse theory posits in its attempt to understand the multivalent strategies at work in colonialist power. Can you look at 'colonial discourse' only by examining what are taken to be paradigmatic moments within colonialist history? If so, can you extrapolate a modality of 'colonialism' from one historical moment to the next? Does discursive colonialism always look structurally the same, or do the specifics of its textual or semiotic or representational manoeuvres shift registers at different historical times and in different kinds of colonial encounters? And what would it mean to think of colonial discourse as a set of exchanges that function in a similar way for all sorts of colonialist strategies in a vastly different set of cultural locations? These questions of historical specificity, though always a problem for social theory, are especially difficult ones for colonialist discourse theory, and the reason for this is that this theory quite appropriately refuses to articulate a simplistic structure of social causality in the relation between colonialist institutions and the field of representations. In other words, colonial discourse theory recognizes a radical ambivalence at work in colonialist power, and that is the ambivalence I have attempted to show in Figure 1.1 as a double movement in vector at the level of line 'F'.

To clarify this, I want to make use of Gauri Viswanathan's important work on Britain's ideological control of colonized people through the deployment of colonialist educational strategies in nineteenth-century India. Obviously, the question of what happens along line 'F' in Figure 1.1 can only be addressed by specific reference to immediate historical conditions, and every piece of archaeological work on colonialist power will want to formulate the vector of action here with particular sensitivity to the local conditions under analysis. Viswanathan researches this part of the puzzle with exemplary attention to history, and at heart her argument is that colonialist education in India (which would stand in as the ideological apparatus at the top of the diagram) strategically and intentionally deployed the vast field of canonical English 'literature' (the field of representations at the bottom of the diagram) in order to construct a cadre of 'native' mediators between the British Raj and the actual producers of wealth. The point here is that Viswanathan's analysis employs a purely upward vector of motion to characterize the specifics of how power is at work along line 'F' in the diagram, and what secures this vector is Viswanathan's scrupulous attention to the immediate conditions that apply within British and Indian colonial relations.

The problem, though – and here I mean the problem for colonial discourse theory – is that the foundational ambivalence or double movement that Said's work inserts into the model of colonialist discourse analysis always seems to return to the field; and it does so through critical work that on its own terms suggests a counter-flow along line 'F' at the same moment of colonialist history. That is, the residual ambivalence in the vector of line 'F' within colonial discourse theory seems to invite the fusion of Viswanathan's kind of analysis with critical readings that would articulate a downward movement at this place in the diagram; and one of the areas such work is now entering is the analysis of how English literary activity of the period (at the bottom of line 'F') suddenly turned to the *representation* of educational processes (at the top of the line), and why this literature should so immediately concern itself with the investments of educational representations in the colonialist scene. In examining the place of English literary activity within this moment of colonialist history, that is, a critic such as Patrick Brantlinger would want to argue for the valency of texts such as *Jane Eyre* or *Tom Brown's School Days* within colonialist discursive power, and colonialist discourse theory would want to understand how both kinds of discursive regulation, both vectors of movement along line 'F', are at work in a specific historical moment of colonialist relations. Because of Said's ambivalence in charting out the complex of Orientalism along line 'F', I am arguing, the field of colonialist discourse theory carries that sense of ambivalence forward, and looks to an extraordinary valency of movement within its articulation of colonialist power. The ambivalence makes our understanding of colonial operations a great deal clearer for historical periods, but it also upsets the positivism of highly specific analyses of colonialist power going on *within* a period.

The basic project of colonial discourse theory is to push out from line 'A', and try to define colonialism both as a set of political relations and as a signifying system, one with ambivalent structural relations. It is remarkably clarifying in its articulation of the productive relations between seemingly disparate moments in colonialist power (the structure of literary education in India, the literary practice of representing educational control in Britain), but because it recognizes an ambivalence in colonialist power, colonial discourse theory results in a concept of colonialism that cannot be historicized modally, and that ends up being tilted towards a description of all kinds of social oppression and discursive control. For some critics, this ambivalence bankrupts the field. But for others, the concept of 'colonialism' – like the concept of 'patriarchy' for feminism, which shares this structure of transhistoricality and lack of specificity – remains an indispensable conceptual category of critical analysis, and an indispensable tool in securing our understanding of ideological domination under colonialism to the level of political economy.

The first big debate going on within colonialist discourse theory, then, is a debate over what happens when a model of 'colonial discourse' is carried beyond its scattered moments of archaeological research and is taken up as a general structure of oppression. I want now to turn to the second big debate going on between theorists of colonialist discourse; and that is the debate over the question of *agency* under colonialist power. Basically, the question of agency can be restated as a question of who or what acts oppositionally when ideology or discourse or psychic processes of some kind construct human subjects, and the question of specifying agency is becoming an extremely complex one in all forms of critical theory at present. Again, however, this debate has especial urgency within colonial discourse theory and, again, that is because this theory recognizes foundationally that the vector of line 'F' in Figure 1.1 remains ambivalent at every moment of colonialist discursive control.

I tried to explain the first debate – the debate over historical specificity – by demonstrating just how slippery the colonial discourse model becomes when two different orders of archaeological work on the same historical period were conflated by the theory. For this second debate, however, the debate over agency, I think I can more effectively suggest the essential difficulty of this problem by tracing very briefly how one theorist, Homi Bhabha, attempts to address this ambivalence.

In his analysis of Bhabha's critical work, Robert Young suggests that the place of beginning for Bhabha is Said's radical ambivalence over the 'topic' of Orientalism. Orientalism is a discovery in Said's analysis; it is a discipline; but it is also a projection, a myth of desire or of disavowal. Said refers this ambivalence back to a single originating intention in Orientalism, but as Young sees it, this is where Bhabha makes his most important intervention into the field of colonial discourse theory, and begins to extrapolate ambivalence away from a term within the colonialist equation to a notion of flaw in the articulation of colonialist administration itself (Young 1990: 143). Colonial discourse, Bhabha will go on to argue, is *itself* an ambivalent discourse; as Young puts it, 'the representation may appear to be hegemonic, but it carries within it a hidden flaw invisible at home but increasingly apparent abroad when it is away from the safety of the West. The representation of the colonial subject . . . is not so much proved or disproved . . . as disarticulated' (ibid. 143) in the way it actually *works* at specific moments of colonialist history.

In the language of the diagram I have been using, what Bhabha is saying is this: that the recognition of a fundamental ambivalence along line 'F' within colonialist ('orientalist') power simply cannot be 'managed' at the level of intentions, but rather needs to be taken seriously; and when this happens, the recognition of ambivalence at line 'F' begins to crack open the foundational assumption that this diagram moves in an entirely left-to-right direction, where the colonized subject is simply *made* by colonialist power: a subject without agency. Bhabha's counter-move, therefore, is to *develop* the ambivalence in this structure of colonialist discourse and to expose it as a radical ambivalence – an ambivalence working not just up and down line 'F' but also back and forward across all the lines on the left–right axis of the diagram. Bhabha's basic argument is that ambivalence is everywhere in the model, as an effect of colonialist discourse. This means not only that there must always be resistance to power within any moment of colonialist articulation; it means also that there must always be an agency to colonialist resistance, not because colonized people simply intend oppositional actions but because colonialist representations are always overdeterminations, and are always ambivalent. This fracture of the monolithic left-to-right direction of colonial discourse is examined everywhere in Bhabha's work, and the genealogy he supplies for this fracture varies. But one of the ways in which Bhahba articulates this fracture is to show how the subject-forming strategies of Colonialist Self onto Colonized Other produce an 'impossible object', an impossible subject-position for both the colonizer and the colonized, because a purely 'colonial identity' is always already radically overwritten by the differential play of colonialist ambivalence. Since it is impossible to claim an origin for either colonizer or colonized 'within a tradition of representation that conceives of identity as the satisfaction of totalizing, plenitudinous object of vision', Bhabha argues, the construction of subjectivities within colonialist relations must always return as a 'persistent *questioning* of the frame' (1990c: 190, 189) – which on one level is the 'space of representation', and on another level is the frame of Western modernity itself. This space of questioning – itself an effect of colonialist discourse – is for Bhabha the space where colonial subjects become agents of resistance and of change. It is the space within which Bhabha locates the condition of post-coloniality itself.

2

As I said at the beginning, this paper is an attempt to understand the specificity of 'post-colonialism' within the frame of a professionalization of the field, and the problem I am about to address is the way in which a scramble over this field is threatening to disperse it into heterogeneous, in fact contradictory, ends. I think the motives behind this scramble for the territory of post-colonialism are grounded in the unresolved debates that trouble colonial discourse theory at present, and are predicated on the conceptual slipperiness of 'discursive colonialism' in terms of historical specificity and of agency. I am now going to try to unpack this institutional scramble for post-colonialism, this balkanization of the post-colonial field, in terms of these two problematic areas in colonial discourse theory, but I am aware that the spatial purchase of my analysis in the preceding section is not in itself entirely proof against exactly the kind of critique that students of colonialist discourse are training themselves to carry out. And so a critique could go forward that would say, in effect, that the diagram I have just articulated in Figure 1.1 is an example of critical Orientalism at the level of the conceptual frame. You could point out how a framing device such as this one offers the ruse of 'knowledge' only by reifying a set of binary oppositions and by containing a disruptive field and the play of difference within it; you could critique this diagram as a spatialization that covertly reiterates a north–south axis to cross-cultural relations and thus conflates power with the West and powerlessness with the East; you could read the whole thing as a metaphor whose real power lies in its naturalization of a left-to-right reading flow at precisely the moment it permits the question of agency for the colonized, at the right side of the map, to be raised as both a possibility and a problem.

I want to use this mapping device, however, because it allows some kind of purchase on what I take to be the central problem, at present, in academic constructions of the 'post-colonial' marker, and because it keeps alive the central metaphor I have been moving towards here: the metaphor of post-colonialism as a geographical area, and one that is at present being carved up by critical methodologies which are seeking forms of absolute control over the terrain. For as I see it, the terrain of conceptual post-colonialism is especially vulnerable at present precisely because genuinely post- or anti-colonialist forms of academic work need to image themselves *differently* in relation to this diagram: sometimes they need to focus on the extraction of the colonized out of the field of this diagram (as in the work of Benita Parry); sometimes they will want to relativize the diagram by positioning it within a much longer history of relations which both precedes and exceeds colonialist contact; sometimes, as in the work of Homi Bhabha, they will attempt a wholesale reconfiguration of this diagram towards a renewed conceptualization of colonialist subjectivity and of agency on the part of the colonized. What I am saying, in other words, is that 'post-colonialism' – whatever else it is – functions in the academy as a political analysis of *what to do* about the 'problem' of colonialism both as a structure of historical power and as a debate within 'theory', and, because the nature of colonialism as a social apparatus is so vigorously under debate at present within colonial discourse analysis, the field of post-colonial critical activity cannot help recapitulating the debates which trouble the field of colonial discourse theory at its present moment of development within the university.

For example, the ambivalence in vector within colonial discourse theory is likely to suggest two different forms of literary critical work which – in their model for a genuine 'post'-colonialism – seek to understand what happens politically when the colonized 'write'. One form of this critical work will assume the mantle of post-coloniality by seeking to retrieve the colonized from the hegemonic left-to-right flow of this historical moment, and to read on that place the figurations of an enduring cultural script. This form of work is likely to be archaeological, and will attempt to bracket the left side of this diagram from what it will call the 'real', the 'unwritten', history, that obtains on the site of the colonized. And this form of work – at least in terms of the Western academy – will also be seen as expressivist, as recuperative, as nationalist or culturalist, and as founded on liberal humanist notions of individuality. While this is going on, another form of literary critical work will posit a recursive vector to the politics of writing on the site of the colonized, and will articulate the ways in which anti-colonialist figuration runs along line 'CB' or line 'ED': the Empire writes *back*. In turn, this form of reading will be seen by the first school as occlusive in relation to the extra-colonialist purchase of the writing, and as championing a reactive as opposed to pro-active facet of Third World representations.

The methodological opposition here is of course institutionally predicated: it goes back to a long debate that continues to play itself out within the Western humanities. But because this opposition within post-colonialism is also, and more proximately, predicated upon another field – colonial discourse theory – two specific principles of organization are likely to structure methodological conflict that takes place within post-colonial critical work itself. First, the debate between oppositional schools of post-colonial criticism is likely to play itself out in the first instance as an academic debate – that is, as a struggle for academic terrain – where critical methodology stands in for cultural politics, and where 'post-colonialism' figures itself as an attempt to contain an interest in writing by colonized or ex-colonized peoples within very particular and specific strategies for textual reading. Second, the debate between oppositional forms of post-colonial analysis is likely to produce gestures of affiliation towards powerful articulations that take place within colonial discourse theory and its debates, so that the big names in colonial discourse theory (Bhabha, Gates, Spivak, and so on) will find themselves continually deployed as champions of representation for cultural formations which they neither know nor work on, and for literary tactics in which they have taken no professional interest. In this second register, the most successful expressions of post-colonial agonism will tend to be located not randomly across what would technically comprise the possible points of difference within the field, but rather, precisely upon the pressure points that structure the debates within colonial discourse theory. Thus the problem of historical specificity for post-colonialism, and the question of tenor for a post-colonial concept of agency, will carry an echo within them as they organize debate within post-colonial studies, and will carry this organizing purchase into the scramble for post-colonialism within the institutional terrain.

Arun Mukherjee (1991) has quite rightly pointed out, for example, that my own work along the 'ED' line of the diagram I have drawn overlooks the mode of literary realism in India – in this she sees the lineaments of a neo-colonialist methodological return. In a similar vein, Vijay Mishra and Bob Hodge (1991) have criticized the authors of *The Empire Writes Back* for supplying a plenitude to recursive work along the 'ED' axis by conflating too many types of presumably 'colonized' subjects at the right hand side of the diagram – an orientalism, they argue, at the level of methodology. The methodological issue here, at heart, is the question of historical adequacy, but it is noteworthy that methodological disagreement within the field comes loaded with the charge of unconscious neo-colonialism at play within the work of the opposing critical practice. This has to do, I think, with the peculiar historical positioning of the post-colonial critical field, and in a moment I will return to this phenomenon.

First, however, I want to comment on the other pole in this conflict, and on the other privileged debate going on at the foundations of colonial discourse theory – the debate over agency. In this context, those critical schools which interrogate the subject-making apparatuses of dominant ideology are, institutionally at least, unlikely to smile upon critical work which buys into expressivist notions either of cultural existence or of resistance and opposition, since the theory behind this expressivism is one which would call down the theory of subject formation upon which they depend. And so a vociferous debate springs up in the scramble for post-colonialism between two avowedly anti-colonialist critical forms – ones which, taken on their own, are exemplary in their commitment to political resistance to the forms of colonialist power. Critics like Barbara Christian, Barbara Harlow, and Benita Parry, for example, have consistently sought an identity-based notion of anti-colonialist opposition on the theory of alter/native voices and of intentional resistance in representation; and their work has quite visibly enabled all sorts of emancipatory critical activity in Third World and colonized locations. It has also run into some very sharp criticism from Gayatri Spivak, who has pointed out that the desire to recuperate those 'authentic' subaltern voices that colonialism has silenced necessarily buys into colonialist notions of expressive subjectivity which enable power by promulgating the concept of voice as articulation of full individuality. Under col-onialism, Spivak argues, the colonized speaks only through speaking positions which imperial and other powers permit to its Others (Young 1990: 165); under colonialism, the subaltern *cannot* speak in the authentic voice of the colonized. Criticism which argues otherwise necessarily participates in an inherently neo-colonialist function whose contemporary home is the Western university institution itself.

These, of course, are important debates in their own right, and within post-colonial studies I usually find myself in sympathy with both sides of the argument. But the point I want to make here is that the groundwork for this set of quarrels is established, first, by colonial discourse theory's debate over the crisis in historical specificity, and second, by an institutionalized debate within the Western humanities: a debate between proponents of nationalist literary groupings and proponents of literary theory, between historical forms of criticism and process-based structures of critical pedagogy, between theories of the subject (or of the construction of subjectivity) and expressivist schools of reading. This quarrel in the field of post-colonial critical work, that is, can at least partly be read as a consequence of these foundational debates within colonial discourse theory and within the 'humanities' institution, and so we should not perhaps be overly surprised if the terms for resolving these debates do not seem available to us only from within the frame of the post-colonial field, or only in the name of a political post-colonial resistance. Indeed, if my analysis is correct, this kind of debate within post-colonial studies need have no necessary relation at all to the question of a post- or anti-colonial tactical efficacy.

What interests me about these debates in terms of the crisis I am describing in the post-colonial critical field is the tenor, and I think the effect, of accusation and reply over the question of methodological difference. At heart, what seems to structure these oppositions is a pattern in which proponents of post-colonial archaeological work are trained to criticize anti-colonialist articulations of counter-discourse theory for a residual neo-colonialism, and in return find themselves criticized by anti-humanist post-colonialists who have trained themselves to link that form of research to a neo-colonialist function through an allegorization of methodology. The general tenor of the rhetoric in this pattern of accusation and counter-accusation – the figurations by which basic methodological differences are subject to disciplinary policing strategies – is peculiar to post-colonial studies, and I think it is significant: the Other is always neo-colonialist: the voice of the colonizer in renewed function and in institutionalized form. But the question of whose apparent anti-colonialism turns out in fact to be neo-colonialism in disguise remains for post-colonial studies an open one – and if I am right, it remains an unresolvable one in strictly post-colonial or anti-colonial terms. This means that the question of anti-colonial work returning in the ghostly mask of neo-colonialist discursive practice remains also an abiding and lurking threat for future researchers, and for all those new students who might be turning to post-colonial studies precisely because of its political grounding in anti-colonial work.

3

I want to stress the presuppositional location of this post-colonial scramble – I want to articulate its foundations within the problematic of colonial discourse theory and within an unresolved debate within the Western humanities institution – because I suspect that at times workers in various orders of post-colonial analysis are made to feel a disempowering energy at work in their field – a disempowerment which stems from their sense that these debates ought to be resolved within post-colonial studies itself. And I also raise the question of an effect to these debates, not because I want to suggest they are anything other than crucial ones for the field, but because I think the terrain of post-colonial studies remains in danger of becoming colonized by competing academic methodologies, and being reparcelled into institutional pursuits that have no abiding interest in the specifics of either colonialist history or post-colonial agency. One of the most exciting research projects now going on in colonial discourse analysis, for example, is Homi Bhabha's theorizing of colonialist ambivalence, and his attempt to carry that analysis forward to a wholesale critique of Western modernity. It is possibly instructive, therefore, that in the process of expressing admiration for his work, the post-structuralist critic Robert Young (1990) inserts Bhabha's project into a narrative of unpackaging whose terms of reference are entirely European in origin: the radical restructuring of European historiography, and the allocation of alterity to the theatre of the European postmodern.

Along parallel lines, it is also instructive that Henry Louis Gates Jr. notes in Spivak's deconstructive brilliance a remarkable conflation between colonial discourse and Derrida's concept of writing itself – an argument that there is '*nothing* outside of (the discourse of) colonialism' (Gates 1991: 466) and that all discourse must be nothing other than colonial discourse itself. Gates warns of a hidden consequence in this elevation in ascendancy of the colonial paradigm by questioning what happens when we elide, for example, 'the distance between political repression and individual neurosis: the positional distance between Steve Biko and, say, Woody Allen?' His argument is that academic interest in this history and the discourse of colonialism bids fair to become the last bastion for the project of global theory and for European universalism itself, and he asks us whether we really need to choose between oppositional critics whose articulations of the post-colonial institutionalize themselves as agonistic struggles over a thoroughly disciplined terrain.

I would like to echo Gates's sentiments in the face of this balkanization; and in the absence of any real solutions to this crisis in the field I'd like to offer a two-part credo towards post-colonial work as it takes place within the Western academic institution. First, I think, post-colonial studies, if nothing else, needs to become more tolerant of methodological difference, at least when that difference is articulated towards emancipatory anti-colonialist ends. I am reminded that the great war within the Western 'humanities' is carried on the back of critical methodology and its competing orders, and that in many ways the subject-making function of the humanities is effected precisely in that debate. I have seen no evidence that the humanities carry any special brief for the global project of decolonization, and so I would desperately want to preserve this function of decolonizing commitment for post-colonial studies, despite its necessary investment in and ironic relation to the humanities complex. I am suspicious of the kind of argument that would insist on the necessary conflation of the diagram I put forward in this essay with a colonialist allegorical function, but I can see how the argument could be made. The tools for conceptual disempowerment in the struggle over method are going to remain available within post-colonial studies, but I remain suspicious of ahistorical and, I think, intolerant calls for homogeneity in a field of study which embraces radically different forms and functions of colonialist oppression and radically different notions of anti-colonialist agency.

Tolerance is never simply passive and, ironically, the area of institutionalized post-colonial studies is finding itself increasingly invested in an academic star system of astonishing proportions, and through that star system it is learning to seek its instruction in oppositional tactics along lines that run increasingly and monolithically backward towards the centres of Western power. I cannot help noticing, for example, that, in what Hortense Spillers (1990) calls the 'politics of mention', our theoretical masters in Paris or Oxford or New Haven are read and referenced by exemplary theorists of the local – the critic J. Michael Dash at the Mona campus of the University of the West Indies is an example – but those metropolitan theorists seldom reference these cultural and theoretical mediators in return. Post-colonial studies should have an investment in open talk across cultural locations, however, and across methodological dynasties; and I think we do damage to the idea of post-coloniality at an immediate political level when that investment in cross-talk runs only one way.

As for the second part of this credo, I believe that post-colonial studies needs always to remember that its referent in the real world is a form of political, economic, and discursive oppression whose name, first and last, is *colonialism*. The forms of colonialist power differ radically across cultural locations, and its intersections with other orders of oppression are always complex and multivalent. But, wherever a globalized theory of the colonial might lead us, we need to remember that resistances to colonialist power always find material presence at the level of the local, and so the research and training we carry out in the field of post-colonialism, whatever else it does, must always find ways to address the local, if only on the order of material applications. If we overlook the local, and the political applications of the research we produce, we risk turning the work of our field into the playful operations of an academic glass-bead game, whose project will remain at best a description of global relations, and not a script for their change. There is never a necessary politics to the study of political actions and reactions; but at the level of the local, and at the level of material applications, post-colonialism must address the material exigencies of colonialism and neo-colonialism, including the neo-colonialism of Western academic institutions themselves.

If the field of post-colonial critical studies resembles a geographical terrain upon which discordant methodologies scramble agonistically for purchase, it also remains the one institutional location upon which the idea of anti-colonialist human agency can trouble the monologic droning of Western self-reference, and can insert within that drone-note the babble of cultural alterity. I have no investment in any single or privileged location for that alterity, and I distrust that moment of institutional self-presence which convinces the anti-colonialist worker that the vectors of tactical methodology are either linear or isolationist. I like the noisy discordance of post-colonial differences, and I welcome its clarity. But I worry about a moment when the concept of the post-colonial becomes so thoroughly generalized that the specificity of colonialist relations simply drops out of the equation. And I worry about a moment when the concept of the post-colonial becomes so thoroughly specialized that within the Western humanities the clamour of that discord simply quiets, and then completely dies away.

NOTES

1 For its articulation of this residual ambivalence in Said's *Orientalism*, I am grateful to Robert Young's important analysis of colonialist discourse theory in *White Mythologies* (1990).

2

EXCESS

Post-colonialism and the verandahs of meaning

Bill Ashcroft

I will begin, with a word: 'Too': Too much, too long, too many, too subversive, too voluble, too insistent, too loud, too strident, too much-too-much, too complex, too hybrid, too convoluted, too disrespectful, too antagonistic, too insistent, too insistent, too insistent, too repetitive, too paranoid, too . . . excessive.

The beauty of the word 'excess' is that, like language itself, it is always in 'excess' of its definition. It can never be cornered by meaning, so to speak. Writing, in its attempt to grasp something not evident in the material of experience, may also be said to be a manifestation and function of excess. But the concept of excess with which I begin comes from a conversation between Edward Said and Salman Rushdie about Said's book on the Palestinians called *After the Last Sky* (Said 1989). Said mentions, at Rushdie's prompting, the excess with which the Palestinian, and particularly Palestinians together, insist upon the reality and autonomy of the Palestinian experience. It is an excess which can reveal itself in many other ways too, such as parody and mimicry, but it always seems, according to Said, 'too much'. The reason for this is obvious. In Said's words the Palestinian is riven by incompletion, marginality, fragmented in a world in which the individual Palestinian is both self and other. Excess performs the function of shouldering a space for oneself in the world.

Excess as a lived experience, therefore, seems a good place to start to talk about the position of post-colonialism in relation to the postmodern octopus. 'Excess', says Georges Bataille 'is no other than that whereby the being is firstly and above all else conveyed beyond all circumscribing restrictions' (Bataille 1956: 145). While shouldering a space in the world post-colonialism distinguishes itself from all those discourses which threaten to engulf it.

33

MODES OF EXCESS

It does not take us long to find an excess of discussions of excess; but they are generally surplus to our requirements.[1] The work of my conversants, Said's representations of the Palestinians and Rushdie's own irrepressible fictional exuberance present at least two significant examples of post-colonial excess. But I want to identify three interrelated modes of this phenomenon in post-colonialism: the excess of insistence, the excess of supplementarity, and the excess of hybridity. These must remain heuristic, of course, because just as excess resists definition, so it resists structure. The literature of excess is obviously not limited to the post-colonial, neither is all post-colonial literature what we could call 'literature of excess'. But at least one of these modes of excess is usually present in post-colonial writing, both 'creative' and 'theoretical' (although excess subverts this distinction).

Insistence

The energy of insistence is clearly demonstrated in that excessive and voluble affirmation of Palestinian experience about which Said speaks. But this has its clear correlative in post-colonial theory. How many times must we insist that post-colonialism does not mean 'after colonialism', that it begins from the moment of colonization? Indeed, how often must we insist that post-colonialism *exists*? How often must we wrestle with the octopus of postmodernism and insist that post-colonialism is not postmodernism?[2] How often must we wait for the occasional applause attending post-colonial theory to be matched by some small textual application by the applauders?

Of course, the excess of insistence must always be the lot of the marginal and displaced. As the Palestinian example forcibly reveals, excess can become the *place* in which the post-colonial is located.[3] Curiously, in a discourse which can be prone to several kinds of excess, this insistence is an insistence upon *reality*, the reality of post-colonial experience, and *hence* an insistence upon questions of representation. The 'real' is always a site of contestation; insistence upon the real is curiously a strategic insistence upon the *marginality* of all experience. And the 'marginal' place in which the post-colonial is located is in language itself, not the 'edges' of the colonial real but the shifting site of an insistent semantic indeterminacy which continually actualizes the possibilities of language. The notion of excess, therefore, helps post-colonialism to position itself between the endlessness of the 'signifying chain' on the one hand, and the socialist-realist dream on the other – the dream that the gap between the signifier and signified can be closed by an act of political will.

The political territory of post-colonialism is something like that surveyed by J.M. Charcot when he noticed that 'Theory is good, but it doesn't prevent things from existing'. The definition of the post-colonial reality is located ultimately not so much in existence as in death itself. We could detail the history of oppression and death that has attended much post-colonial writing to elaborate this. But we need go no further than one of our conversants – Salman Rushdie. In an immense contemporary tragedy of reading, the literature of excess is faced with the pristine judgement of totalitarianism – the terrorism of absolute meaning – and finds itself sitting on the thin clear denominating line of post-colonial reality: the author's death.

The irony of this is deeply symptomatic. The Ayatollah's absolute judgement is based on a *misreading*.[4] And the irony doesn't end there. How is it that 'Islam', the oriental 'Other' of the European self, generates this imperial character? The reason lies simply in its totalist monocentrism. The 'monoglossic' oppression of the system is a symmetrical binary of the imperial centre. And this, of course, is the ultimate constriction. The hegemony of the absolute always falls short of the continual supplement, the excess, which is the real. Rushdie's final signified, the catastrophic final linking of the signifier and signified, will only occur at the end of all signification.

We are all familiar now with Foucault's discussion of the emergence of the author-function in 'What is an author' (Foucault 1969). Authors emerged when owners needed to be found for texts, to validate their status as property and to be held accountable for their possible transgression. Foucault asks: 'How can one reduce the great peril, the great danger with which fiction threatens our world?' 'The answer is: One can reduce it with the author' (ibid.: 158). In his connecting of writing and death we find a precise moment in which the real and the deferred coincide. Foucault points out that writing leads to death: 'The work, which once had the duty of providing immortality, now possesses the right to kill, to be its author's murderer, as in the cases of Flaubert, Proust, and Kafka' (ibid.: 142). And then he says:

> That is not all, however: this relationship between writing
> and death is also manifested in the effacement of the writing
> subject's individual characteristics . . . the mark of the writer
> is reduced to nothing more than the singularity of his absence;
> he must assume the role of a dead man in the game of writing.
> (Foucault 1969: 142–3)

That is all well and good, we might say. But we must add a
supplement to it; we must say to Foucault: 'and yet . . .' – and with
this insistence the post-colonial defines itself – 'and yet . . . Rushdie
may die!' Theory cannot prevent people from existing. Neither can
it prevent them from being killed by an interpretation. Rushdie's
possible death has meaning in a number of possible discourses. It is
metonymic rather than metaphoric in the way Foucault uses the
term. The author's death becomes the synecdoche of post-colonial
writing itself, an abstraction which cannot be separated from the
material reality of an actual death; a discursive trope which cannot
avoid the insistence of referentiality. 'Nevertheless', we insist,
'Rushdie may die!'

The point I want to make about this is that the dream of the real
as a world uninflected by ideology, or the pure and pristine dream
of the socialist real is just as constricting and imperialist as the
Ayatollah's dream of absolute meaning. Post-colonial exuberance
dances away from this closure just as surely as it dances away from
the Ayatollah. While the excess of post-colonial reality resists the
imperial cementing of the sign, it is a reality which is conditioned
by the final surplus, the excess of death. In this way it balances itself
between the postmodern dream of infinity and the realist dream of
closure.

Supplementarity

Another mode of post-colonial excess is one I want to call
'supplementarity'. In his book *The Accursed Share* (1967), Bataille
proposes a theory of excess which stems from a general economy of
energy. Thus 'if the demands of the life of beings (or groups)
detached from life's immensity defines an interest to which every
operation is referred, the *general* movement of life is nevertheless
accomplished beyond the demands of individuals' (Bataille 1967:
74). Bataille's economy hinges on the need for a system to use up
that excess energy which cannot be used for its growth. Thus the

unproductiveness of *luxury* itself; the apparently meaningless expenditure of *sacrifice*; the tradition of gift giving called 'potlatch' which demands the maintenance of honour by the return of a greater gift, all maintain a system's balance by using up surplus wealth. Within this general economy the sexual act is a pre-eminent form of non-utilitarian expenditure of energy, war is almost essential, while death itself is the ultimate moment of 'luxury' in the system. Bataille summed up his general economy with the resonant statement that '*the sexual act is in time what the tiger is in space*' (Bataille 1967: 12).

If we accept at least the general proposition of this trans-phenomenal and trans-discursive movement of energy, we discover something very revealing about the imperial process. Imperial power expends its excess wealth through war (that is, military force such as that employed in colonial expansion) to create greater wealth which is then diffused as luxury, further military expansion and so on. Though it is a centred system, it is never a closed system: the dissipation of the excess always increases wealth.

But when we look at the colonial world we see that the excess of 'luxury' is ideally exported as high culture. Culture, and the non-productive superstructure which it supports is an extremely prodigal expenditure of surplus energy originally accumulated as wealth. As post-colonial theory has long known, the expenditure of surplus energy through cultural hegemony long outlasts the 'luxury' of war, invasion, and annexation, and maintains the production of wealth which is always distributed centripetally. In other words, cultural hegemony maintains the economy of wealth distribution.

This process of transformation maintains the system of imperial hegemony intact. An instance of this hegemony can be seen in the export of theory, and this of course works on its own momentum long after the official end of imperialism. Thus, whereas surplus value creates wealth for the centre in a fairly obvious way, so the cultural surplus works to the same end. Even when manifested in apparently subversive and heterogeneous formations such as post-structuralism (with its own ironic doctrine of the surplus of the sign), this cultural surplus works through language to defuse opposition and preserve the system of wealth creation. The middle term in this startling congruence of culture and wealth is discourse itself because the *idea* of wealth, despite its very obvious materiality, is a discursive formation, a production of language. Thus the general economy of imperialism is an economy of discourse. The oppositionality of the post-colonial finds its greatest material success in the counter-discursive.

The point to be emphasized here is that cultural hegemony is not simply an effect of economic control. As 'luxury', cultural formations are a part of the actual mechanism of that control. As Stephen Slemon has argued (1989: 5), this explains the contradiction ('paradox') which Linda Hutcheon sees in postmodern 'subversion' as it both inscribes and contests culturally certified codes of recognition and representation (Hutcheon 1988: x, xii). Postmodern culture, art and theory 'uses and abuses, installs and then subverts' (3), the 'conventions of discourse' (xiii) which it sets out to challenge. When we see postmodernism as a luxury which actually maintains the general economy of neo-colonial (or 'late capitalist') hegemony, we begin to understand the contradiction of its dependence on, and independence from, that which made it possible.

According to Bataille, true opposition is best effected by the one who spurns the very system in which wealth has its meaning. This is of crucial significance to post-colonialism since, whatever else it is, it manifests itself as *opposition* from the beginning of colonialism.

> The true luxury . . . of our times falls to the poverty-stricken, that is, to the individual who lies down and scoffs. A genuine luxury requires the complete contempt for riches, the sombre indifference of the individual who refuses work and makes his life on the one hand an infinitely ruined splendour, and on the other, a silent insult to the laborious lie of the rich. . . . henceforth no one can rediscover the meaning of wealth, the explosiveness that it heralds, unless it is in the splendour of rags and the sombre challenge of indifference. One might say, finally, that the lie destines life's exuberance to revolt.
>
> (Bataille 1967: 76–7)

Post-colonial excess is quintessentially the exuberance of life which is destined to revolt. But the most effective revolt is the one which denies the system its power over representation. The implication of this is an economy of discourse, and specifically, the discursive production of wealth. The irony of the individual who refuses to work, making his life 'an infinitely ruined splendour' is not a consolation for the poor but a strategy for resisting the very process of representation in which the binarism of wealth and poverty is created. The option of 'lying down poverty stricken to scoff' is not an invitation to accept defeat but to dismantle the binarism itself.

This 'unproductiveness' which denies the very system that classifies it as unproductive is indeed a 'genuine luxury' as Bataille says, but paradoxically one which resists the mechanism of control. Where postmodernism may fail because it continually installs that which it attempts to subvert, the post-colonial may successfully resist when it simply ignores, refuses, or sidesteps the system of representation which constitutes it as subject. Wilson Harris does this, for instance, when he persistently refuses to be called a 'theorist' – he simply sidesteps that discourse into which the practice of articulation itself can be so easily incorporated. However, such an end may also be accomplished less cataclysmically in the strategy of appropriation (Ashcroft, Griffiths, and Tiffin 1989: 38). This customarily describes the process of language adaptation but it also applies to theory itself; the post-colonial subject is not only given a voice but the medium itself is changed in the process. The appropriation of that surplus wealth represented by theory is therefore not just a cunning strategy, but one of a quite limited number of ways to recirculate the energy stolen from the colonized world in the first place.

Post-colonial discourse appropriates the cultural surplus, whether as language, genre, form, style or theory itself, and redistributes it as excess. This means that the appropriated form of life or language game is immediately 'blown apart' so to speak, by the perpetual supplement of hybridity, marginality, supplementarity, the open horizon of post-colonial ontology. In a sense this can be the option of the poverty stricken to 'lie down and scoff' because the selective mimicry of appropriation mocks the riches of the system. Excess is, in this sense, the continual supplement of the surplus (that is, a surplus can be finite, but excess is not).

There are many ways of conceiving this, of course. The selective mimicry of appropriation is a transgression in which the bandit post-colonial mounts raids across the porous borders of discourse. This poverty and transgression in the gaze of the centre puts post-colonial discourse beyond the apparent riches of an alternate but symmetrical centre. Such scoffing rejects the system itself, and with it the hope of resurrecting some seamless and unproblematic cultural identity. Indeed, the very opposite is the case; post-colonial 'ontology' itself is located in the excess of hybridity.[5]

But also available to post-colonialism is a programme of recuperation, in which the immense wealth of 'theory' generated in the post-colonial creative text is recovered (the 'excess' of this essay is itself a supplement to a conversation). Such a recuperation of theory could enhance the construction of a non-symmetrical and non-reactive oppositional system which hinged on a kind of hybrid excess of theoretical profusion. In this way post-colonial theory might be better able to avoid an 'opposition' that is simply a response to the 'position' of Eurocentric theory and invoke a 'resistance' which changed the nature of theory itself.

Nevertheless, the *centripetal* impetus of hegemony works feverishly against the exuberance of post-colonial life in many ways, both from without and from within. The Rushdie sanction is the grimmest example of the issues at stake in the struggle over representation. But the centripetal impetus operates much more subtly when writers such as the Nigerian Wole Soyinka, the West Indian V.S. Naipaul, or the Irishman W.B. Yeats are expropriated into the canon of 'English literature' by a process of apparently 'disinterested' approbation. But the same principle works 'from within' so to speak, when Joseph Furphy or Robbie Burns, say, are incorporated by a nationalist ideology. Opposition can itself be a form of luxury which merely maintains the energy of the total system by conserving a symmetry of oppositions. It is the excess of post-colonialism which avoids this symmetry.

Horizon

While excess is important to a theory of writing it also suggests a theory of reading. Excess resists the closure of the name 'post-colonial' because it continually intimates something more; it continually offers the surplus. The excess of repetition and insistence is therefore linked to the supplementarity of the real because each insistence, each repetition, rewrites itself on the palimpsest of being. This process becomes one in which post-colonial hybridity itself is located. Such a rewriting occurs from what we might call the verandahs of being, the verandahs which are being. How, then, does this implied deferment implicit in the term 'verandahs' differ from heterology? The difference may be located, I think, in the concept of *horizon*.

It is satisfying to recuperate this term *horizon* from Husserl's phenomenology, so clearly the bête noir of Derridean deconstruction. While the project of phenomenology to isolate the irreducible, eidetic features of experience becomes one of the great manifestations of logocentrism to Derrida, it also provides the concept of horizon, which prefigures Heidegger's destruction of metaphysics and Derrida's own deconstruction of presence.

The notion of horizon first appears in Husserl's *Ideen* (1913) and refers to the circumference in which all things, real and imaginable are bound to appear 'spread out in space endlessly, and in time becoming and become, without end' (Husserl 1913: 101). Just as post-colonial excess identifies the real as an ever-emerging supplement, so reality itself is the horizon of horizons, that is the intimation of possibility which locates any object of consciousness. In one sense this notion of horizon is a far more satisfactory definition of that order of experience which Lacan terms the Real. That which for Lacan is the order of the unknowable (because beyond the symbolic order of language) is transferred by horizon into the order of possibility. Fredric Jameson regards the Real as the realm of History itself. But if History is located on the horizon, it is not the order of the unknowable so much as the continually recuperable verandah of possible representation.

Crucially, the horizon itself is created in language. As Wittgenstein (1976: 56) says, '*the limits of my language* mean the limits of my world' (*Tractatus* 5.6). The object, determined by its relation to a horizon, a context, is therefore an object determined in language, as is the very notion of objectivity. The model of the horizon also links space and time because the contextual horizon initiates a *process* of traversal by the act of consciousness. This linking of space and time leads to the further conclusion that consciousness *is* language.[6]

Horizon is useful for post-colonialism for a number of reasons. First, it sends the gaze outwards. It operates from a reference point and that reference point is place, indeed the most localized place – the body. But because horizon links the spatial and the temporal it confirms the fact that both place and body are themselves a process within language. Take a simple example: if arms, legs, hands, fingers, and feet were all replaced by the single word 'appendages' our bodies would not be the bodies we know. David Malouf discusses the way the body has changed in time in *12 Edmonstone Street* (1985), which is a curious conjunction, because this book also discusses the importance of verandahs. Confirming the crucial importance of verandahs to the developing consciousness, he says:

> A verandah is not part of the house. Even a child knows this. It is what allows travelling salesmen, with one foot on the step

to heave their cases over the threshold and show their wares with no embarrassment on either side, no sense of privacy violated. . . . Verandahs are no-man's-land, border zones that keep contact with the house and its activities on one face but are open on the other to the street, the night and all the vast, unknown areas beyond.

(Malouf 1985: 20)

It is the bi-focal orientation of the verandah which gives it its resonance. While faced towards the house it also faces the 'vast, unknown areas beyond' and it is precisely this ability to maintain the ambivalent link between the 'house' and the unknown which gives post-colonial language its peculiar agency.

In post-colonial discourse the body, place, language, the house of being itself are all 'verandahs'. That is, they are a process in which the marginal, the excess, is becoming the actual. The verandah is not the surplus of the building but the excess which redefines the building itself. The verandah is that penumbral space in which articulation takes form, where representation is contested, where language is supplemented. The post-colonial lives on the verandah because this is the space where the provisionality of language and the reality of experience can coincide. Our story here comes full circle, for if excess is the place in which the Palestinian is located, the post-colonial place is itself 'excess'; an excess which changes the nature of discourse – a verandah.

A growing dissatisfaction with the idea of marginality lies perhaps in its apparent reinstallation of the imperial binarism of centre/margin. But the margin, the verandah, is the region of 'luxury' in Bataille's sense, it is the region where the control of representation can be contested. For instance, in resisting the idea of a 'standard language', the perspective from the verandah shows us that all language is an interwoven fabric of 'marginal' practices. It is in this space that the post-colonial also resists the centripetal impetus of nationalism. The nationalist view of language, for instance, might suggest that certain words are inherently applicable to place in a way that the imperial language is not. As writers sought to challenge inherited names in Australia, words such as 'creek', 'bush' and 'gully' were coined for topographical features which appeared to have no comparison in the European landscape. But the word 'creek', for instance, is not a more inherently appropriate description of an Australian watercourse than 'brook' or 'stream'. It is above all a sign of difference, a metonym of location. The post-colonial construction of language is not a simple binary contestation but a centrifugal process. Through the creation of such words, place is continually in the process of coming into being. Our great grandchildren's place will be different from the one we know because it will be differently – more complexly, more intricately – named.[7]

The theory of the text this initiates is therefore bound up in the tautology: the horizon of excess. Horizon adumbrates the continual excess, the surplus of meaning but at the same time provides a limit to the endless signifying chain of the world. This is the limit of the gaze which brings the relation between the object and its horizon into being. This is not the reference point of a transcendental subject but a tension in which the world is held intact, the tension of the gaze itself, much like the tension between the centre and margin, a tension in which both centre and margin are always marginal. When we turn from the verandah to survey the house, we find that it, too, is a verandah.

NOTES

1 American critics such as Weiss (1989) and LeClair (1989) investigate the aesthetics of excess in the work of writers like Thomas Pynchon, Joseph Heller, John Barth, Robert Coover. For Tom LeClair (*The Art of Excess*, Urbana, University of Illinois Press, 1989), excess is a feature of those writers who demonstrate 'mastery' – 'a combination of quality and cultural significance' (1). Since this engaging phrase occurs on page one of LeClair's book, post-colonialists not interested in systems theory need read no further.

  The work of Georges Bataille (*The Accursed Share*, trans. R. Hurley, New York, Zone Books, 1988; and *Visions of Excess: Selected Writings 1927–1939*, ed. A. Stoekl and trans. A. Stoekl *et al.*, Minneapolis, University of Minnesota Press, 1985) is more useful for this discussion. In Bataille, excess takes many forms. Mostly the excess is an excess of the iconoclastic, the taboo, the breaking of restrictions to the realization of full being.

2 By postmodernism I do not necessarily mean a set of methods and practices but a name (really a proper noun) which stands for closure, and, in the inevitable canonical processes of English departments, a name that comes, increasingly, to stand for power.

  This, of course, can be the case for any discourse in the academy, and remains an issue about which post-colonial critics need to remain alert.

3 And where else is this place but in language? The word *Instanz* in Freud is translated as 'agency', as in 'the agency of the ego in the unconscious'. But Lacan mimics this word with the homonym *instance* which in French

means 'insistence'. Thus the term metonymically joined by the homonym in Lacan's text links insistence and agency in the signifying chain. His paper 'The insistence of the letter in the unconscious', is also translated as 'The agency of the letter in the unconscious'. Similarly, by a process of metonymic abutment, we can say that the excess of *insistence* in post-colonial discourse is a strategic site of agency for the post-colonial subject.

4 How can one use such a word these days? 'A reading' would work just as well. But a reading which can kill a man is a misreading! This is the point at which the combative irony of the term 'misreading' merges with the desire for political agency.

5 Since quite enough has been written about hybridity by post-colonial critics, I will not elaborate on this third, and perhaps most crucial, mode of excess.

6 The point is that this is all available through the concept of horizon and is very different from the notion of transcendental subjectivity by which phenomenology is usually characterized and for which it is rejected by deconstruction.

7 The aboriginal word *walu* is one which has no correlation, yet, in English. It refers to that sensation of the crunchiness of bark and leaves underfoot, of bark stripping off trees and is vastly different from that notion of order implied in the word 'garden'. The appropriation of such a word would lead to the more subtle and intricate construction of place through language in Australian English. That is, 'place' would become different.

3

SOME PROBLEMS OF RESPONSE TO EMPIRE IN SETTLER POST-COLONIAL SOCIETIES

Chris Prentice

It has become a commonplace of descriptions of Imperial–colonial relations to invoke familial and bodily metaphors, while more recently their function in 'naturalizing' such relations has been exposed. Nevertheless, I believe it is necessary to address questions of the *power* of these metaphors, noting, for instance, their relevance in describing real political relations in 'settler' post-colonial societies such as Australia, Canada, and New Zealand. Having acknowledged them we may interrogate them, and work towards de-scribing some less obvious aspects of their ideological bases. Specifically, I suggest that what is missing from these bodily-relational analogies is precisely any *body*, let alone relations *between* bodies. In other words, it is not the body which is problematic, but the metaphor. Further, the omission of the body is consistent with the gendered structuring of what Luce Irigaray has termed 'the empire of phallocratism' (Irigaray 1985b: 136).[1]

Although my central concern is with post-colonialism as a response to Empire, I will approach it somewhat circuitously, beginning by suggesting that in settler post-colonial societies, it is useful provisionally to separate Nation and post-colonialism as two distinct moments in that response. Of course, this is not strictly a chronological separation.[2] Nevertheless, I would argue that in white-settler societies which quickly established numerical, cultural, and institutional dominance of British forms over indigenous populations and cultures, nationalism, as a response to Empire, rather than constituting a clear movement of decolonization, has been doubly implicated in that same Empire.

This can be explained with reference to the Lacanian psycho-

45

analytic account of subjectivity, with some Kristevan amendments, an account whose blind-spots are as useful to an analysis of post-colonialism as its analogic function. The analogy itself is invoked by the prevalence, in historical, political, and cultural discourses, of references to the Imperial Mother, to daughter-colonies, and to the manhood of Nation. This family group (which is really only a mother–infant pair) suggests the process of maturation which is not only consistent with descriptions of the way in which Australia, Canada, and New Zealand gained nationhood (e.g. Price 1945: 139–40; Morton 1972: 39, 58–9), as opposed, for example, to the United States, but with a process of *psychical* development as represented in the theory of oedipalization. Indeed the problem of its status as a naturalistic account of maturation is indicated when, for example, dutiful daughter colonies announced their manhood on the slopes of Gallipoli (Sinclair 1969: 232). Again, this points to a moment in the psychoanalytic account to be explored rather than simply deplored.

The appearance, in the following argument, of a one-sided focus on the point of view of what Simon During would term the 'post-colonizers' (1985: 369) is a deliberate acknowledgement of what I believe to be the actual one-sidedness of post-colonial discourses, including those of contestation, in terms which are isomorphic with the imperial epistemological and ontological legacy. That is, rather than expressing *difference*, the positions of 'self' and 'other' represent, in Paul Smith's formulation, 'a foreshortened idealist dialectic still attending to the yet-to-come possibility of its own resolution' (1988: 88). It is not until this commensal dyad is acknowledged and analysed – de-scribed – that voices of unassimilated difference may really be heard, and power relations changed.

Colonial status names the ideal of an undifferentiated relation with the Imperial Mother, a kind of pre-Imaginary total absorption in and by the Mother, such as is suggested in Julia Kristeva's notion of the semiotic *chora* (1984: 40). Nevertheless, this absorption involves its own element of threat, requiring the colonial struggle to expel the excess of the *real* body upon which the colony is dependent – that is, the *otherness* of the colonial *land* – in order to attain the ideal, Western, white body of Empire. The emergence of Nation can be likened to the erection of the phallic 'I', the Self whose passage through an historical-cultural mirror-stage confers the image of autonomy, unity, integrity, and identity. In other words, it reflects the separation from the Maternal Continent, and projects a narcissistic investment in images of the whole and unique Self – images of national identity. However, just as it has been shown, for example by Irigaray, that the Lacanian mirror is, in its very morphology, phallocentric, privileging images of the One and the Same, producing and valorizing that which may be *seen* (Irigaray 1985a: 47–50), so is the morphology of the national 'mirror' both phallocentric and imperialist. The image it produces is valued as autonomous, but it is valued on the basis of its specular similarity to British cultural and institutional *models*.

The cost of such narcissistic investment is the repression into the National Self – by which I mean a discursive, imaged Self – of its bodily debt, to the Imperial Mother, of cultural specificity. It requires also the repression of the excess of Nation's libidinal self, those haunting Others which cannot be reconciled to the image of National Sameness. Nevertheless, if identification with the Father's Law which enables identity to be articulated also requires relinquishment of maternal desire, compensating access is gained through another, a mother-substitute, the feminine Other. However, because the mirror only recognizes and values the image of the Same, otherness is not 'itself', but rather the not-Same. In other words, the feminine is simply the negative reflection of the masculine, whose 'lack' confirms masculine wholeness. I would argue, then, that these acts of repression in the passage through the cultural mirror-stage into Nationhood hold disturbing implications for post-colonial discourses of identity-in-resistance.

In their valorization of the body of the land, of the authenticity of origins, of cultural continuity and belonging, post-colonial counter-discourses offer to Nation that promise of *origin*-al desire (for the Mother, for origins) about which Nation had been anxious since its Symbolic alienation raised the spectre of uncertain legitimacy. Indeed, these Others are constructs of the founding delineation of the National Self through a phallocentric, Imperialist, Imaginary order. They represent less the detumescence of the phallic Nation than its confirmation, the response to the spectacle of its desire. For example, the preface to a volume of essays entitled *Culture and Identity in New Zealand*, contained the apology that

> There are some glaring gaps in this book. We regret the absence of chapters on Maori-Pakeha relations, on working-class culture . . . and contributions from Maori women, from

Pacific Islanders, from lesbian feminists, all of which were originally planned for inclusion.

(Willmott 1989: ix)

What is remarkable here is the security with which these 'absences' are identified as absent 'presences'; as if the whole were knowable in terms of the desire of the part. Further, the image of the 'glaring gap' points to the perception of the feminine 'nothing-to-be-seen' which activates masculine anxiety regarding castration. In other words, such ideal completion would provide Nation with its feminine object of desire, and in perceiving the feminine desire for, or lack of, the phallus of signification or Symbolization, would confirm Nation's status as possessor of the phallus.

Therefore, *post-colonial* national discourse strengthens its claim to legitimacy through 'fuller' representation, and to ethical integrity through the self-representation of its constituent Others. However, its integrity is also located in the fact that these identities belong to the order of the Same, determined by the phallocentric Imperial-National Imaginary. For example, it is that order which projects and reflects identities of race, colour, gender, sexuality, class and so on, founded on its perception of the unitary Self, and the negative but also unified Other. It would appear, then, that the failure of inclusion is more troubling to a discourse of nation seeking redemption, than what would amount to the flattery of its narcissistic gaze by enabling it to reflect a fuller, more desirable self.

The new, redeemed post-colonial nation, where the post-colonized are represented and the post-colonizers are authenticated, speaks for identity, integrity, autonomy, self-representation, the value of the specific and the local, and the value of history, as that narrative of progress(iveness) towards the just inclusion of previously omitted identities. Post-colonial discourse stands for the delimitation of the boundaries of legitimate cultural activity. In order to assert its own security of identity, threats to that identity are necessarily projected as external. This could be termed the 'paranoid' moment of post-colonial discourse, the 'dual passage between self-affirmation and self-defence' (Smith 1988: 87).[3] For example, Laura Mulvey has argued that:

The question of Canadian national identity is political in the most direct sense of the word, and it brings the political together with cultural and ideological issues immediately and inevitably. For the Canada delineated by multinational, international finance, U.S. economic and political imperialism, national identity is a point of resistance, defining the border fortifications against exterior colonial penetration.

(Mulvey 1986: 10)

Similarly in the Introduction to *Culture and Identity in New Zealand*, referred to earlier, it is argued that New Zealand 'can either succumb to increasing economic and cultural dependence . . . or it can begin to develop a sense of autonomous identity that unites our people in opposing internal exploitation of the disadvantaged and external exploitation by the mighty' (Willmott 1989: 19). While the external threat to identity is figured in political and economic terms as neo-imperialism, postmodernism is frequently identified as its cultural moment. During has argued that 'The play of passions that we call postcolonial . . . . wish once and for all to name and disclaim postmodernism as neo-imperialist' (During 1985: 368–9)[4].

Relations between post-colonialism and postmodernism have been expressed in terms of radical spatial and strategic separateness. Stephen Slemon refers to 'the major fault-lines that run between them' (1991: 1–2), while Helen Tiffin locates them in terms of '*European* post-modernism and *Euro-American* post-structuralism' as opposed to post-colonial 'cultures and texts *outside Europe*' (Tiffin 1988: 170; my emphases). Along with spatial or geographic separation, post-colonial critics refer to those of strategy. Slemon claims that 'post-modernist theory and post-colonial criticism have remained more or less separate in their strategies and foundational assumptions' (1991: 1), while Arun Mukherjee, who identifies postmodernism as 'largely a white European cultural phenomenon' (1990: 3), argues that 'the postmodernist label does not apply to texts of native and African-American women' (4). Thus in post-colonial discourse (about post-colonialism) a certain morphology of the Self is suggested: post-colonialism is bounded, whole, unique, and autonomous. It represents here, inside, and identity, while postmodernism belongs there, outside, and is a threat to identity *from outside*.

The unnegotiable closure of the borders between 'self' and 'other' has been described by Smith in terms of the 'claustrophilic' tendencies of paranoia. However he goes on to note that 'the importance of these symptoms . . . is that they absolutely depend upon an initial opening of those spheres, an opening which is the threat they themselves are designated to ward off' (Smith 1988: 97).

Such an initial opening may be posited at the moment of the colonial encounter, when the very constitution of 'self' and 'other' is inseparable from their mutual contamination by each other, producing colonial cultural *hybridity* (Bhabha 1985b). Further, and more specifically in relation to settler post-colonialism, it could be suggested that the cultural scene was opened to postmodernism from the moment of emergence of a dominant capitalist order which, from the modern project of national development through to the postmodern elision of national boundaries as effective economic and cultural designators of identity, projected the impossibility of retaining such economic and cultural separateness from the centres of trade and military power. Thus the post-colonial insistence on the postmodern as 'not-self' may be seen as a defence or disavowal of the 'self's' implication in it.

Therefore, there are moments in post-colonial discourse in which postmodernism may also be recognized as *abject* for post-colonialism. To describe it thus is to invoke Kristeva's description of abjection as, for instance, 'what disturbs identity, system, order. What does not respect borders, positions, rules. The in-between, the ambiguous, the composite' (Kristeva 1982: 4). Further, she explains,

> The abjection of self would be the culminating form of that experience of the subject to which it is revealed that all its objects are based merely on the inaugural loss that laid the foundations of its own being. . . . [A]ll abjection is in fact recognition of the *want* on which any being, meaning, language, or desire is founded.
>
> (ibid.)

It can be shown in relation to post-colonialism that the 'loss' and the 'want' are those of the *body* upon whose exclusion phallocentric/ Imperial subjectivity is predicated.

At this point it becomes necessary to acknowledge those abject moments in the debate, including within the terms of specific contributions, which indicate an *encounter*, one which cannot be so clearly or cleanly contained – or prevented – by oppositional structures. Linda Hutcheon refers to the 'problematic site of interaction' (1991: 170) between the postmodern and the post-colonial, naming this site variously a 'playground' and a 'battlefield' (179). Similarly, Slemon acknowledges 'an on-going critical struggle' between them with regard to the 'political terrain of textual interpretation' (1991: 2).[5] Even During's suggestion that 'postcolonialism is to be viewed quite simply as a resistance to postmodernism' (1985: 372) suggests the persistence of a relation (in which postmodernism is logically prior, and post-colonialism relegated to the status of reaction) determined by the abject fact that (the issue of) postmodernism keeps returning, threatening the 'clean and proper' self of post-colonialism with its excess(iveness). Therefore, its expulsion becomes a matter of continual process, rather than a once-and-for-all event. Further, this compromises the claim to autonomy of post-colonialism; rather, its status as the Ideal Symbolic body must be viewed as the effect of its repeated assertion.

The site of interaction between post-colonialism and postmodernism is problematic because it consists of ambiguously inside/outside 'rims' on the 'body' of post-colonial nations, cultures, discourses, or texts. These 'rims' are the sites of expulsion of threatening excess, but also – because they will constitute the body's erotogenic zones, in relation to which *desire* functions – the sites of introjection. The expulsions of the postmodern confirm the permeability of its boundaries and the inefficacy of their existing formulation. For example, Tiffin argues that

> Given the extent to which European postmodernism and Euro-American post-structuralism have increasingly invested in cultural relativity as a term in some of their most radical insights, it is ironic that the label of 'post-modern' is increasingly being applied hegemonically to cultures and texts outside Europe, assimilating post-colonial works whose political orientations and experimental formations have been deliberately designed to counteract such European appropriation.
>
> (1988: 170)

Along with spatial oppositions, we have here the defensive/offensive oppositions of post-colonial victim and postmodern aggressor. Yet the argument continues with the suggestion that these post-colonial works 'have themselves provided the cultural base and formative colonial experience on which European philosophers have drawn in their apparent radicalization of linguistic philosophy' (Tiffin 1988: 170–1). It is therefore necessary to examine the source of apparent failure of the defences (intentions, strategies) suggested here. What may be found, I suggest, is a complicity of the *structuring* of the post-colonial Self in its vulner-ability to the incursions of the postmodern Other.

Four discursive 'rims' which compromise the integrity of post-colonial discourse and identity (whether of an entire culture or, for example, a specific text), four discursive points of the incursion and expulsion of the abject represented by postmodernism, and *in* post-colonial discourse *about* postmodernism, are the notions of desire, seduction, appearance, and strategy. Post-colonial discourse is at its most abject when located on, or faced with, these rims of undecidability.

First, as Tiffin argues, 'while Euro-American post-structuralist theories offer exciting possibilities to post-colonial theoreticians, it would be dangerous if they were accepted without rigorous interrogation from post-colonial perspectives' (1988: 171). While there is clearly a need for such interrogation, I would want to interrogate just as rigorously the source of desirability or attraction held by such theories, and also the structuring of post-colonial perspectives themselves. For example, in this construction of the post-colonial subject or theoretician as the desiring (and thus incomplete and non-autonomous) subject, are we directed towards recognition of the legacy of separation from a 'cultural' *chora* of un-Self-conscious undifferentiation? Do post-structuralist theories evoke more primal or original desires, reaching back to a cultural plenitude and heterogeneity, and the tension of their loss in the construction of the unitary subject? Is the desire the *dependence* of the subject on the recognition of the Other? On the other hand, the desiring subject is an active subject and thus less amenable to description as passive victim.

Second, however, there have been a number of expressions of postmodern *seduction* of post-colonialism. In one explicit example, it has been claimed from a New Zealand perspective, that 'For many people in the world, the American way of life, even with all its inequalities, is highly attractive – one may say seductive' (Willmott 1989: 19). As Jane Gallop argues, 'as with all seductions, the question of complicity poses itself. The dichotomy active/passive is always equivocal in seduction' (1982: 56). Initially, it may seem scandalous to suggest post-colonial complicity. After all, there are so many assertions of post-colonial propriety, resistance, and boundaries *against* postmodern incursion (or 'penetration' as Mulvey put it). Arun Mukherjee expresses her support for 'the objections raised by the post-colonial critics against post-modernist readings of non-European texts' (Mukherjee 1990: 1). She points out that post-colonial writers 'want us to believe the truth claims of the history they themselves are providing' (4), a point also made by Slemon, who differentiates the 'mimetic or referential purchase' of [post-colonial] textuality from – and against – ungrounded postmodern claims of the 'constructedness of *all* textuality' (Slemon 1991: 5). However, it may be suggested that post-colonial discourse is seductive to postmodernism precisely because of the closed, innocent body it presents; that, to cite Slemon again, 'post-modernism *needs* its (post-)colonial Others in order to constitute or to frame its narrative of referential fracture' (ibid.: 9). At the same time, though, post-colonialism asserts its purity and innocence in relation to the advances of postmodernism, and so there is a mutuality in which post-colonialism must at least concede that it displays the very terms – history, representation, truth – that postmodernism most consistently violates.

Third, discussions of the relation between post-colonial and postmodern textuality are often forced to acknowledge the appearance of similarity in their strategies. Mukherjee refers to 'antirealist representation, parody, auto-referentiality, problematizing of history' (Mukherjee 1990: 3), but warns that 'surface similarities may turn out to be deceptive since the semiotic codes of cultures are often not interchangeable. . . . [W]hat may seem postmodernist and new to cultural outsiders may seem quite ordinary and traditional to those from within a culture' (ibid.: 4). In this case, while she suggests an undecidable quality of textuality, amenable to different readings, the recourse is to a cultural insider whose authorial intentions or privileged reading casts others as intrusive or invasive. Yet we have already seen the apparent inefficacy of intentions and deliberate strategies in preventing such transgressive readings. Slemon makes the similar observation that

> Hutcheon's framing of the postmodern field is important, for the general textual practice she defines . . . resembles – at least on the surface – the kind of reiterative textual energy which . . . marks out an especially interesting moment within a broadly post-colonial literary activity.
>
> (1991: 3)

Thus he is required to call on depths or intentions to differentiate them. Again I would stress the need to interrogate the epistemological position from which that which looks the same may be revealed as different. Although it requires a securely centred identity, I would want to investigate the entrapment, or possibly even complicity of that identity in the terms of the Symbolic field of the Other from which it is articulated. As During has noted,

> the postcolonial self knows itself in universal terms, that is, in terms of the international centres of a colonial past. Yet the images and texts it produces as 'its own' can affect it as if they have passed through no 'external detour', no world which is not their own.

(1985: 369)

The implications of this may be clarified by moving on to the fourth of these 'rims of abjection'.

Post-colonial discourses variously characterize postmodernism as totalizing, assimilative, appropriative, neo-universalizing, and neo-imperialist, while post-colonial cultural authenticity and specificity are posited as target-objects and victims of such energies. However, Mukherjee complains of post-colonial replication of these very energies when she states that she finds 'the proprietary tendencies of the post-colonial critics with regard to "post-colonial work" equally problematic' (1990: 1).[6] As well as differentiating *between* post-colonial societies, she points to differences *within*, such as those between 'the experiences of white and non-white post-colonials' (ibid.: 2),[7] and argues that 'post-colonial societies . . . have their own internal centres and peripheries, their own dominants and marginals' (ibid.: 6). She specifies race, class, gender, language, religion, ethnicity and political affiliation. However, while such identities or positions constitute the basis of exploitation and oppression, as sites of resistance, they may function to circumscribe or limit the possibilities of forging truly decolonized relations. They may concentrate critical and activist energies into themselves as if they were natural, original identities, and not the *products* of an Imaginary order which constructed the dominant National subject they contest. It is therefore worth considering the *appeal* of post-colonial counter-discourses to post-colonizing institutions, the way in which they are often too easily appropriated and assimilated by the very structures and discourses they seek to challenge.

It could be argued that, like postmodernism, post-colonial discourse has its own moments of neo-universalizing, not so much in the application of the term 'post-colonial' to a range of different cultural contexts and products, but rather in the positing of one true post-colonial voice, the authentic post-colonial subject, thus eliding both the complexity of subjectivity in settler post-colonial cultures, and the multiplicity of subject-*positions* in relation to their histories of colonization (Hutcheon 1991: 172; Mukherjee 1990: 2). On the other hand, it is necessary to acknowledge that settler post-colonial discourses of resistance to the structures of power and subjectivity that informed nationalism tend, in their attempts to recuperate 'nation' as a viable cultural and political structure, to replicate – or at least supplement – the discursive structures they putatively oppose. There is the danger that, through the commodification of discourses or symbols of identity and authenticity, these 'values' are lent to the project of post-colonizing cultural legitimation; they are emptied of specificity and circulated as signifiers in an exchange of indifference. This may even be the result of sincere intentions to include previously unrepresented otherness. For example, During argues with regard to the rapturous reception in New Zealand of Keri Hulme's *The Bone People* (1983), and 'the desire of New Zealand to see a reconciliation of its postcolonizing and postcolonized discourses', that 'The reconciliation *is* achieved, but the price of that success is that the otherness of the Maori is destroyed' (During 1985: 374). Therefore, when Tiffin suggests that the indigenous writers of, for example, Australia and New Zealand 'are able to challenge European perspectives with their own metaphysical systems', while the non-indigenous writers may enact 'subversive manoeuvres from within European positions' (1988: 173), it is necessary to acknowledge both the efficacy of the specification of these *positionalities*, and the inextricable mutual implication of each in the other in the settler post-colonial cultural context.

Linda Hutcheon may be wrong in her apparently persuasive argument that

> The current post-structuralist/postmodern challenges to the coherent, autonomous subject have to be put on hold in feminist and post-colonial discourses, for both must work first to assert and affirm a denied or alienated subjectivity: those radical post-modern challenges are in many ways the luxury of the dominant order which can afford to challenge what it securely possesses.
>
> (1991: 168)

I concur with Diana Brydon's critique of this position, particularly in the suggestion that part of the appeal of such an argument lies in its isomorphism with dominant historical narratives of continuous progress, in which each 'stage' is both 'self-evident' and supposedly indispensable, toward a commonly agreed goal. Instead, as Brydon implies, post-colonial and feminist discourses are in a position to expose the alienation – from the body, its heterogeneity and desire – of *all* subjectivity founded in the dominant Western-humanist valorization of identity. They are in a position to infiltrate phallic Sameness with their disruptive difference. Rather than erecting and reasserting more and more defensive boundaries against transgressive desires, it would be useful to extend Tiffin's formulation of a clearly unacceptable position for post-colonial cultures as 'a peripheral term in Europe's self-questioning' (Tiffin 1988: 171), to discover the opportunity for actively using postmodern challenges in post-colonialism's Self-questioning. By retaining a perspective on post-colonialism which names the difference within the self which refuses to be unified and absorbed, which will always exceed totalizing impulses, post-colonialism will more successfully resist the absorption of a promised, redemptive difference into the same, emptying it into the mere signifier of that difference. In other words, if a post-colonial culture or text is not the same as itself, it resists being made the same as its Other.

As Gallop argues, 'Perhaps any text can be read as either body (site of contradictory drives and heterogeneous matter) or Law' (1982: 62), and I believe that many current formulations of postcolonial discourse are grounded in Law. The question then becomes, 'whose Law is it?', and further, 'what is lost in the "tendency to accept a traditional, unified, rational, puritanical self – a self supposedly free from the violence of desire"?' (Gallop 1982: xii). What is lost is the body – the specificity and difference which post-colonialism claims to name – in the 'clean and proper . . . fully symbolic' body which bears 'no trace of its debt to nature' (Kristeva 1982: 4).

I would like to see in post-colonial theory and discourse a working towards a formulation of subjectivity which problematizes the assumption of epistemological innocence of the 'self', and which negotiates the necessity of foregrounding the site of enunciation as constitutive of meaning – in other words which harnesses the efficacy of a politics of identity – but which relinquishes its dependence upon a belief in the purity of its discourse. This would point to a relation between subjectivity and discourse grounded not in the flat, Lacanian mirror of specularization, mimesis and representation (an inherently aggressive notion), but in terms of Irigaray's concave, self-touching, speculum (Irigaray 1985a: 143–6); discourse in contiguity with the multiplicity and specificity of the socio-cultural body.

NOTES

1 Of course, this is not to argue that there is access to a 'pure body' outside of ideological mediation, but rather that there are specific political implications of ideologically specific inscriptions/de-scriptions of the body according to a morphology of One-ness. Further, I do not mean that 'Nation' may be understood in some redeemed way which incorporates previously excluded or marginalized subjectivities. The point is precisely that the idea of Nation is predicated upon the exclusion of the excess upon which it is founded and out of which it emerges. The metaphor refers not to uninscribed bodies 'in nature', but to power relations between elements of ideologically inscribed anatomies.
2 For example, Stephen Slemon has noted that we may recognize 'a specifically anti- or *post*-colonial *discursive* purchase in culture, one which begins in the moment that colonial power inscribes itself onto the body and space of its Others' (1991: 3).
3 Smith states that 'what is crucial to the paranoiac is the dual ability to objectify or realize a reality and yet to proclaim the "subject's innocence of its formation" (Smith 1988: 87). However, it should also be emphasized that I use this term in order to suggest certain (privileged) socially-produced discursive structures and patterns, *not* a clinical diagnosis of individuals associated with, or implicated in, such discourses.
4 In the context of the following discussion of post-colonialism and postmodernism, I am not at all concerned with the various understandings of postmodernism itself, but rather with the terms of the debate, principally from the post-colonial perspective, and solely in terms of its implications for self-representation in and of post-colonialism.
5 Arun Mukherjee also refers to the 'contested terrain' between them, suggesting even more clearly the tensions between post-colonialism and postmodernism (Mukherjee 1990: 1).
6 This is not to agree with Mukherjee's point. She argues it in relation to attempts to 'create a post-colonial theory that can be applied to "all" . . . post-colonial writing, regardless of the differences of gender, race, class, caste, ethnicity, and sexual orientation' (1990: 2). However, this seems to be founded on a misreading of statements, for example, in Ashcroft, Griffiths, and Tiffin (1989) that 'We use the term "post-colonial" . . . to cover all the culture affected by the imperial process from the moment of colonization to the present day', and that

> the literatures of African countries, Australia, Bangladesh, Canada, Caribbean countries, India, Malaysia, Malta, New Zealand, Pakistan, Singapore, South Pacific Island countries, and

Sri Lanka are all post-colonial literatures. The literature of the U.S.A. should also be placed in this category.

(Ashcroft, Griffiths, and Tiffin 1989: 2)

Such statements address the relevance and efficacy of the term 'post-colonial', and do not in any way imply the development of a single, totalizing theory to cover all situations, eliding specificities. Nevertheless, the importance of Mukherjee's argument here is in its positing of a strategic parallel between postmodernism and post-colonialism which problematizes their (more commonly expressed) 'oppositional' relation.

7 On the other hand, Brydon has argued that 'discussions of Canadian post-colonialism do not usually equate the settler with the native experience' (1991: 194).

Part II

RACE AND REPRESENTATION

4

THEORIZING RACISM

Terry Collits

> Only the Southerner is competent to discuss slavery, because
> he alone knows the Negro . . .
>
> > (Memmi 1965: xxi)

With this dictum, Jean-Paul Sartre began his introduction to Albert
Memmi's (now neglected) classic of the anti-colonial movement,
The Colonizer and the Colonized. He went on to recommend Memmi
to 'those intimidated by this criminal line of reasoning' (Memmi
1965: xxi).

And yet, even now, if I get into an argument about the Australian
Black 'Question' (it is *still* a question) with someone from Darwin
or Western Australia, or even with someone who has just visited
there, at a deep and instinctual level I am effaced by the voice of
authentic experience. This familiar, personal difficulty can be
translated into the god-like question: who is it that is to name the
racist? If it is also true that wearing a badge proclaiming 'I am not a
racist' might well, in its Manichean assertion of differences, signify
'I am a racist', the difficulty is further compounded. In academic
terms, this is the problem of the speaking position, of the post-
colonial critic and the ethnographer alike. It is not a problem that
arises in, nor is restricted to, the academy.

SPEAKING PERSONALLY AND ACADEMICALLY

I should introduce myself and declare my interest.

I am an eighth generation Australian, or more precisely in
current Australian parlance an 'Anglo-Celtic Australian'. In my
case, this hybrid label is reasonably accurate, but in relating me to
the oldest type of Australianness (some believe, to authentic

61

Australianness) the label represses a lot in Australian cultural history. My oldest known forebear was certainly English, transported to Botany Bay as a convict in 1803; but the dominant strain in my genealogy is Irish Catholic. In the 1940s, mainstream Australia was Protestant in name, but already secular, and the large Catholic minority was anything but secular: aggressively separatist, we attended our own schools to be taught religion by nuns, wore distinguishing uniforms, practised medieval religious ceremonies in Latin and ate fish on Fridays. For one such ceremony, at the age of 6 I was dressed in a white silk blouse and pantaloons with a silk purse full of rose petals around my neck, these to be kissed then floated before a processing statue of the Virgin Mary, as I slowly walked backwards down the church aisle. Inside the church this was fine; but outside, walking a mile along a public highway dressed in this fashion, I did feel distinctly different. Our difference was often expressed as a strong but ambivalent anti-Englishness; less rationally, in an attitude of being at once embattled and spiritually superior. The family seemed to thrive on unquestioning loyalty to a forever losing Labor Party, which nevertheless had its own heroes, Prime Ministers past and gone. Non-Catholic religious services were forbidden, including civil services such as Anzac Day; you saw them from a distance but they were taboo. One effect of this is that the following verse is *not* ingrained in my memory:

> God of our fathers, known of old,
> Lord of our far-flung battle-line,
> Beneath whose awful Hand we hold
> Dominion over palm and pine –
> Lord God of Hosts, be with us yet,
> Lest we forget – lest we forget!

Of course, such an anecdote won't really identify me or define my speaking position in a volume such as this, though it may have an oblique relevance. What I hope it does do, partially, is lightly to underline the impossibility inherent in one of the most prominent elements of current post-colonial theory: its necessary preoccupation with specifying the subject-positioning of the post-colonial cultural critic. The impossibility and the necessity of this new problem are such that, while 'imperialism' and 'racism' must go on meaning 'Western imperialism' and 'white racism' in this context, the ground on which the older oppositions rest (colonizer/colonized, centre/periphery, European/native) becomes increasingly more contestable. Are Rushdie or Achebe to be thought of as Third World writers or First World intellectuals or internationalist hybrids? Gayatri Spivak's important question, 'Can the subaltern speak?' (1985a) might be matched by another: 'Should the Western post-colonial academic stop speaking?' Similarly, Benita Parry (1987) challenges post-structuralist analysers of colonialism such as Spivak herself or Homi Bhabha on the grounds that their deconstructionist practices deny the political potency of an earlier anticolonialist polemics. Parry herself has been charged in turn with a nostalgic hankering for the authentic native voice; but Parry could also be read as looking for the lost political clarity and authority apparently available to a Fanon in the 1960s which she feels all but disappears in the subtleties of our current moment.

Within the Western academy, the 1980s witnessed a sharp intensification of attention on the question of racism. Yet this was not so much a new academic interest as a relocation. An early sign of the change that is still happening was that the first edition of Raymond Williams' influential *Keywords* (1976) did not include 'race' or 'racism' in its lexicon, whereas the 'revised and expanded' edition (1983) included under 'racial' a detailed and lengthy genealogy of the whole cluster of 'race' terms. Noting the historical nexus between the scientific study of racial differences and the ideological practices of racism, Williams shows himself still locked into older discursive assumptions when he regrets the compromising of such legitimate inquiry by 'proponents of racial superiority or *discrimination*' (Williams 1983: 250). In contrast with this implicit belief in the possibility of an objective, non-exclusive mode of inquiry is one of the main insights of a recent anthology of essays on the subject, David Goldberg's collection entitled *Anatomy of Racism*: 'rather than supporting the widespread presumption that racism is inherently a set of irrational prejudices, *Anatomy of Racism* ultimately demonstrates that it has assumed in normal course the mantle of scientific theory, philosophical rationality, and "morality"' (Goldberg 1990: blurb). The radical relocation of 'race/ racism' in the 1980s is no less than an absolute challenge to and displacement of older taxonomies and what Williams calls their 'important and productive' work. One watershed moment in this story (as it can now be told) was the work of the psychologists Eysenck and Jensen on intelligence differentials between the races, work that managed to be scientific, objective and offensive all at once: their project may well have foundered not so much on buried racist assumptions as because it unwittingly drifted beyond the limits of its older scientific paradigm.

Older attempts to theorize 'race' notoriously were used to support racist and not anti-racist discourses, almost the reverse situation from that obtaining in the case of 'class' and 'gender'. The contemporary full-blown address to the panoply of questions related to racial difference has found its place of enunciation not in genetics or psychology but in new forms of cultural studies fed by (among other things) linguistics, literary theory, revisionist anthropology and French-inspired philosophy. Racism is no longer examined as a thing-in-itself but as a dense system of ideological practices over time entwined with history, language, gender and class relations, and problems of representation and interpretation, to name but a few of the relevant keywords of the new field. It is neither discreet nor discrete, strongly proclaiming a political agenda of liberation and emancipation, while consorting freely with feminism, colonial discourse analysis and, somewhat more nervously, new forms of marxism. It relentlessly tracks down and exposes racism, not in the name of the older liberalism, morality or truth (all of which are shown to be disablingly compromised, part of the problem and not the solution), nor even of a Eurocentric marxism or Third World nationalism; if it owns affinities with a Frantz Fanon, it is Fanon (1986) as re-presented by the Derridean/Foucauldian/Lacanian Homi Bhabha.

In the 1980s a number of earlier anti-racist analyses of racism were reissued whose authors were practitioners in the social sciences: Ruth Benedict's *Race and Racism* (1983) in anthropology; Frantz Fanon's *Black Skin, White Masks* (1986) in psychiatry; and Joel Kovel's *White Racism* (1988) in psychoanalysis. Even these books, however, involved a movement away from the particular disciplinary training of their authors towards a wider, not yet existent, discursive space, one not afforded by the most tolerant liberalism. Goldberg's *Anatomy*, for example, includes selections from a somewhat earlier generation of writers who pointed to the need for a non-scientistic, rigorous discourse for the adequate confrontation of racism (Fanon, Barthes, Kristeva, Balibar: the group testifies to the power of the French connection) along with new names of the 1980s, gurus of post-colonial studies (Appiah, Bhabha, Said, Henry Louis Gates, Jr.: this group shows the importance of non-European and 'hybrid' life-experience in the constitution of the new).

At the simplest level, one challenge for the post-colonial critic, 'white' or 'black', is to overcome the traditional bland tone and comfortable closure of academic discourse, now that the objects of academic analysis (colonial and post-colonial texts) quite obviously relate to questions of human happiness and misery on a global scale. An older desideratum of value-neutral objectivity as the sign of the academic must now be put in question in terms of the supposed innocence or transparency of the post-colonial analyst. The world-historical importance of the subject-matter seems an automatic guarantee of political commitment for left academics disenfranchized since the early 1970s; at the same time, the often arcane diction and manoeuvres of the emergent discourse, along with a sneaking suspicion that the new-found politics might be no more than an *academic* politics, concerned with syllabuses, appointments and promotions, while the immiseration of the greater post-colonial world goes on, carries with it a self-doubt that could easily prove fatal.

NEW SPACES

Political struggles, in the academy and in its fictitious Other, 'the real world', will not be won through an excess of fastidiousness: the place of hybridity[1] must inevitably be messy. One kind of fastidious-ness is the misplaced fear of ideological unsoundness, of inauth-enticity, as though their opposites are remotely attainable or even desirable. The futile, forever retrospective, search for the auth-entic, the pure origin (whether it be the garden of Eden, the Organic Society, or the Noble Savage in a world not yet visited by the depredations of capitalism: I refer to Milton, Leavis, and Jameson respectively) must remain doggedly pre-libertarian and purist; worse, it can no longer grab the hearts and minds of the young. The new churches that will thrive will coexist with a good deal of heresy.

And yet, does not that wonderfully suggestive title of Fanon's book, *Black Skin, White Masks*, recall just such a violated auth-enticity? That will depend on whether the phrase is thought of as an oxymoron or as a chiasmus; of course, it must be read both ways at once. The binarisms involved remind us that 'race' itself depends on a series of differences, of contrasts, sharing this much as a concept with 'class' and 'gender'. Racial categories are meaningless in isolation, its markers of difference always serving the function of identification, drawing borders, operating at the interface in a dangerous and messy confusion of attractions and refusals. We now know vividly that the sheer cultural opposites of Black and White are nothing more than powerful constructs, mind-forged masks in fact. But does not Fanon's title also describe an *essence*? Skin is not just assumed like a mask: it is god-given even if its meanings are social, discursive. What skin and masks have in common is that they mark the interface between the self and the world; they are the border. And it is this spatial positioning that both share with language: all three work together in the theatre.

Both skin and masks can identify and they can hide. It is the mask in Greek Tragedy that tells us that it is the hero of the mask and not the face of the nondescript Athenian actor beneath which is the important identification; but it is the mask of the gunman which conceals the dangerous identification of the face. Skin also both identifies and masks: while, in the Eurocentric world, skin-colour carries an automatic cultural content, it nevertheless masks 'true' identity. It is, at most, an element in the formation of subjectivity, and will not reveal subjectivity. The frustrated desire to make skin-colour *identify* (which is racism) was a linchpin of colonial authority, sustaining the cohesiveness of the ruling group, those included by Conrad's insistent phrase, 'One of us'. The anxiety of that insistence is met by the dizzying dislocations in Fanon's title: black/white, skin/masks; white skin/black masks. It is all relative to where you are standing in the strange order of the colonial world: white masks, there, can indicate the hapless plight of the native, forever condemned not to know his rulers. But if, in the colonial world, the native cannot know the 'true Englishman', that lack is destined to be repeated in the sad quest of E.M. Forster's heroine for the 'real India'.

ACHEBE AND CONRAD

Where does all this muddying of the clear waters of meaning get us? To be practical for a moment: are we now better placed to judge whether Achebe was right to call Conrad a 'bloody racist' (Achebe 1975)? Can we now say with confidence (what three hundred years of Shakespearian criticism elided) that *Othello*, far from being the dramatization of 'motiveless malignity', is an early exposure of European racism and its deep source, the fear and fascination of miscegenation?[2] Should we celebrate or condemn the messy novels of Salman Rushdie, after all that has been said and done in their name? I shall try to answer briefly the first of these questions.

The embarrassment of Achebe's tendentious attack on Conrad is partly that he argued a powerful and unexpected case, one which exposed a problem in Conrad's writing elided even in political analyses of his novels, just as the 'political' itself was all but forgotten by the academic criticism of Conrad for forty years after the author's death (years not untouched by ongoing European imperialism). A second source of embarrassment is that the attack was made in a manner that transgressed fundamental academic assumptions of politeness (strategies of containment) at a moment when Western academics were not yet ready to deal with such a transgression (in the first instance, it was largely left to Third World intellectuals to thrash out the ensuing debate). Finally, one suspects, the embarrassment related to an uneasy sense that this blunt, cogent and passionate accusation of a racism embedded in the language of the great tradition of English fiction might just have a special validity: the authentic voice of protest coming from a highly respected, internationally acclaimed African writer.

Authentic or not, Achebe's challenge represents an ongoing problem area for First World intellectuals, either directly in the terms in which it was then cast, or in the current anxiety about what might constitute progressive political efficacy through interventions that remain, by and large, academic. To make it personal once again: in what terms do I, inhabiting an arguably European body and employed by an English department in a 'Western' university, correct Achebe's passionate misreading of *Heart of Darkness* without reinforcing what hardly needs reinforcing – the hegemony of Western discourse? And that especially if the necessary correction is made by an appeal to the second dominant strain of post-colonial theory today, the post-structuralist concern with the instability of the text and the relative insignificance of authorial control? For Achebe's error was not so much that he misread Conrad's attitude to blacks as that he took *Heart of Darkness* for a stable and unproblematic embodiment of its author's beliefs in the first place. And yet: if Conrad has produced in *Heart of Darkness* a text so slippery that it can never be pinned down, locked into the play of an inconclusive ironic meditation which leads no more to the need for political action than to a quietist awareness of the philosophical absurd, what has such a text to do with political change? It is at least arguable that Conrad's description of the Belgian Congo, much later in his life, as 'the vilest scramble for loot that ever disfigured the history of human conscience and geographical exploration' (Conrad 1924: 17) has a sharper political edge than Marlow's narrative in *Heart of Darkness*.

Part of Achebe's charge is that the Africans in *Heart of Darkness* are 'dehumanized' (denied that fuller human presence and individuality given the Europeans) not so much through mis-representation as under-representation. But the greater sophistication of *Heart of Darkness* over the early Conrad derives precisely from the text's very refusal to represent African life 'directly': what looks reductive to Achebe, reading this European's account of his own grandparents' generation of Africans, can be seen from a different perspective as a deep challenge to the old colonial novel's claim to cosmopolitan omniscience. Hence the limited, prejudice-ridden liberalism of the Marlow character-narrator. *Heart of Darkness* encloses within its own strict limits the liberal-humanist ideology underpinning European imperialism at the end of the nineteenth century (the mission, the work ethic, the superiority of civilized man) and faces it with its inbuilt contradictions. To this extent, it can be read as an overcoming of colonial discourse, while appearing unable to imagine anything beyond the colonialist nexus but a limitless darkness (into which presumably Kurtz – though not Marlow or the reader – is permitted to peer).

Yet Achebe is also right: when he shocked his academic audience at Amherst early in 1975,[3] he too was marking a break. In the then pervasive New Critical practices in the United States academy, negative depictions of Blacks passed without a comment. Achebe's attack can be seen in retrospect as both a call for equal space, for representation, and for the implicit recognition of the necessary deconstruction of critical orthodoxy that must attend the moment of hybridization.

The consistent refusal of *Heart of Darkness* to represent 'fully' its non-Europeans (even to give them names) leaves the text open to the charge of making its Africans appear as less than human. But Conrad shows us the Congo at an early moment of colonialist intervention; he makes no attempt to include or even offer informed speculation about pre-colonialist Africa, prior to this 'fantastic invasion'. The story frames that moment of disruption at a fairly advanced stage, and meditates on its present and future implications:

We two whites stood over him, and his lustrous and inquiring glance enveloped us both. I declare it looked as though he would presently put to us some question in an understandable language; but he died without uttering a sound, without moving a limb, without twitching a muscle. Only in the very last moment, as though in response to some sign we could not see, to some whisper we could not hear, he frowned heavily, and that frown gave to his black death-mask an inconceivably sombre, brooding, and menacing expression.

(Conrad 1902: 112–13)

Shakespeare's Iago didn't have to explain to his audience why he 'hated the Moor': the sentence was surely self-explanatory, even if it has taken us a further three hundred years to take it in. Interrupted and deferred, conjured up and gossiped over in the raciest terms, the precise moment of the Moor's penetration of the fair Desdemona is tantalizingly held just beyond our gaze, while the forestage is occupied by rioting, drunken Venetians (*Othello* II.iii). The disturbing silence of the dying helmsman's mute judgement, like the strange interface of race and sexuality in Othello's repressed passion for Desdemona, are moments that indicate the new space which we may now be approaching belatedly.

NOTES

1 For the strong sense of this word, which needs to be maintained even as it passes into fashion, see Homi Bhabha (1985c) and throughout Bhabha's work. A recent discussion of Bhabha's specialized lexicon is in 'The postcolonial critic: Homi Bhabha interviewed by David Bennett and Terry Collits', *Arena* 96, Spring, 1991: 47–63.
2 For one such discussion of racism in Shakespeare's *Othello*, see Karen Newman (1987).
3 I am indebted to Lyn Innes for a vivid first-hand account of this exciting, scandalous occasion; and for a timely reminder of the specific construction of the text that prevailed at that moment, against which Achebe's intervention needs to be read. I would only note, in passing, that, in moving from the initial polemical public lecture to the latest printed version in Norton, Achebe has modified the terms of his attack on Conrad from 'bloody racist' to 'thorough-going racist'.

5

THE MYTH OF AUTHENTICITY

Representation, discourse and social practice

Gareth Griffiths

There are real dangers in recent representations of indigenous peoples in popular discourse, especially in the media, which stress claims to an 'authentic' voice. For these claims may be a form of overwriting the complex actuality of difference equal but opposite to the more overt writing out of that voice in earlier oppressive discourses of reportage; in fact it may well be the same process at work, and the result may be just as crippling to the efforts of indigenous peoples to evolve an effective strategy of recuperation and resistance.

For example, in the recent dispute over mining at Yakabindie in Western Australia both sides of the dispute invoked the sign of the authentic in defence of their position. The 'liberal' tone of modern journalism, its claim to even-handedness, is possible partly because of the way in which certain signs have been fetishized within popular discourse, in this case that of the 'authentic', the traditional and the local. A report in the *West Australian* can stand as an encapsulation of this problem, as it represents two images of the authentic, both inscribed under such legitimating signs as the 'elder', the local, and the tribal, and both counterposed by the signs of the illegitimate outsider – the southerner, the fringe-dweller, whose representative in the article is the Perth political activist Robert Bropho. Let me quote the relevant paragraphs.

> Wiluna resident Tony Green, 89, said he was born less than 8 km. from Yakabindie. He had spent most of his life in the area and had never heard of a sacred site near the proposed mine.
>
> 'What about the future?' he said. 'We need the jobs for the people. I'd give that land to the mining people.'

But community elder Dusty Stevens highlighted the feelings which have divided the region's Aborigines.

'Some of these fellahs just wouldn't know,' he said. 'There are a lot of sites in there.'

The appearance of Mr Bropho and members of the Swan Valley Fringe Dwellers at the meeting was attacked by Goldfields Aboriginal spokesman Aubrey Lynch, who said the southerners had nothing to do with the issue.

(Duffy 1991: 9)

Articles like this are an increasingly typical way of representing in the media the 'positions' and 'voices' of the indigene, inscribing them in effect as disputational claimants to a 'territoriality' of the authentic. Whilst it is true that the various Australian Aboriginal peoples may increasingly wish to assert their sense of the local and the specific as a recuperative strategy in the face of the erasure of difference characteristic of colonialist representation, such representations, subsumed by the white media under a mythologized and fetishized sign of the 'authentic', can also be used to create a privileged hierarchy of Australian Aboriginal voice. This voice in practice may serve to represent that community as a divided one as well as to construct a belief in the society at large that issues of recovered 'traditional' rights are of a different order of equity from the right to general social justice and equality. Whilst this may be in part the unintentional product of a worthy liberal desire to recuperate Australian Aboriginal culture, it also frequently results, as in the case I have given, in the media construction of the 'authentic' Australian Aboriginal in opposition to the 'inauthentic' political activists whose claim is undermined (the metaphor is an appropriate one) by a dismissal of their right to represent Australian Aboriginal culture in any meaningful or legitimate way.[1]

In order fully to understand what is involved here, it seems to me that these representations need also to be addressed through their reflection of a larger practice within colonialist discourse, a practice in which the possibilities of subaltern speech are contained by the discourse of the oppressor, and in which the writing of the Australian Aboriginal under the sign of 'authenticity' is an act of 'liberal' discursive violence, parallel in many ways to the inscription of the 'native' (indigene) under the sign of the savage. On the surface the obvious connection is through the reversed sentimental and nostalgic rendering of the Australian Aboriginal under the sign

71

of the primitive (noble savage rather than cannibal savage). But at a deeper level both processes may be about the inscription of ourselves displaced upon the Australian Aboriginal, an inscription which may overwrite and overdetermine the full range of representations through which contemporary Australian Aboriginality might otherwise effectively be represented.

Michael Taussig's powerful study of the massacre and enslavement of the Putumayo Indians in the early years of this century stresses the way in which the silenced subjects of oppression are spoken by the different discourses through which their story is inscribed. For the whites engaged in the activity of 'conquest' the dominant sign for the Indian is that of the cannibal. As Taussig notes it is this signifier which enables the Indian to be characterized as savage:

> The interest the whites display is obsessive; . . . and it is always with what becomes in effect the insufferably comic image of the person-eating Indian that he chooses to represent that fear of being consumed by a wild, unknown, half-sensed uncertainty.
>
> (Taussig 1987: 105)

As Taussig notes, allegations of cannibalism

> [provided] for the colonists the allegory of colonization itself. In condemning cannibalism, the colonists were in deep complicity with it. Otherness was not dealt with here by simple negation . . . . Allegations of cannibalism served not only to justify enslavement of Indians by the Spanish and the Portuguese from the sixteenth century onwards; such allegations also served to flesh out the repertoire of violence in the colonial imagination.
>
> (ibid.)

The narrative of 'savagery' that the colonizer constructs reveals, then, a process of complicity in which the masquerade of terror unveils the mask of the 'savage' as the face of the colonizer.

More immediately for my concerns here, Taussig also records how contemporary Indians, such as the Andoke Yarocamena, subjected to terror by the greed of the rubber companies of our own day, register their perceptions of the powerful ways in which 'narration' functions to control and override their resistance.

Something crucial about such complicity and the magical power of the company employees emerges from what has been said in recent times about Andoke Indians who claim that the rubber company had a stronger story than the Indians' story and this is why, for example, the armed uprising of the Andoke Yarocamena against the company failed and failed so disastrously.

(ibid.: 107)

It is clearly crucial to resistance that the 'story' of the Indians continues to be told. It is only through such counter-narratives that alter/native views can be put. As Taussig notes, however, this contradicts, at a simple level, the Indian assertion that their story is less powerful than the European story. By story here is meant, as Taussig goes on to explain, that narrative (*rafue*) through which a 'necessary mediation between concept and practice that ensures the reproduction of the everyday world' (ibid.) is effected. That is to say, the fundamental systemic discourse through which the world is represented, analogous to other indigenous stories such as that of the various Dreamings of the Australian Aboriginal peoples. The oppressor clearly shows that they are aware that their own narrative of the Indian, what the Andoke called '*Historias para Nosotros* – histories not of, but *for* us' (ibid.) are perceived by the *oppressors* to be successful not because, as the Andoke assert, they possess a greater mystic efficacy but because they override and overdetermine the possibility of the Indians speaking their own position within the alternative discourse of the conqueror. That the conquerors in fact continue to fear the 'story' of the indigene and seek to silence it is graphically and horrifically illustrated by their favoured torture of cutting out the tongues of the Indians and then forcing them to 'speak'. In the light of the concerns raised by such images, the reports on disputes such as the one at Yakabindie may take on new and powerful resonances and the act of constructing the speech of the already silenced may metaphorically, at least, be perceived as an act best characterized, as I have suggested above, by a metaphor of violence, however 'liberal' in intention. In both cases the appropriated features of authentic discourse are installed after the event of silencing by violence.

Strategies of recuperation and texts which insist on the importance of reinstalling the 'story' of the indigenous cultures are, therefore, as many Australian Aboriginal spokespeople have insisted, crucial to their resistance. Such recuperations may be the literal recuperation of the texts of pre-colonial cultures, the narratives of the Dreaming, or the body of pre-colonial oratures, or, as in the case of the work of Mudrooroo such as his recently published novel *Master of the Ghost Dreaming* (1991), attempts to reinscribe the dominant culture of colonial society by retelling the moment of encounter and invasion through indigenous eyes and discourses. In a sense this is part and parcel of Mudrooroo's asserted desire to speak from an 'essential' Aboriginal position (the word is his not mine) and of his belief that Aboriginal texts may be authentic or inauthentic in so far as they cohere within a larger Aboriginal meta-text (which means, I presume, in part at least that alter/native story (*rafue*) of which the Andoke also speak). But Mudrooroo has also argued that 'the Aboriginal writer is a Janus-type figure with one face turned to the past and the other to the future while existing in a postmodern, multicultural Australia in which he or she must fight for cultural space' (Mudrooroo 1990: 24). Thus in a sense he embraces his hybridized position not as a badge of failure or denigration but as part of that contestational weave of cultures which recent critical theory argues is the inescapable condition of all postmodernist experience, though at the same time he asserts in both his critical writing and practice as a novelist the importance of grounding his identity in essentialist difference as a political strategy. In this apparent contradiction he is registering the difficult and ambivalent position which the Aboriginal writer is forced to occupy in the complex task of simultaneously recuperating the traditional and contesting the profile of identity for Aboriginal peoples in contemporary Australian political and cultural space.

As a white critic it is not my task to comment on this strategy, nor to enter the debate as to how Australian Aboriginal peoples might or ought to address their political task. But it is very much my task, perhaps even my moral obligation, to address how the white society constructs its own representations of Aboriginality and the politics of this representation within white-owned media, and it may also be, it seems to me, a legitimate concern as to how the reading of the literary texts of Australian Aboriginal peoples may function in this construction.

With this as my focus, then, it might be argued that many of the problems raised by this issue have also been addressed by those who have sought to theorize the difficulties which arise when we

consider the possibility of a subaltern subject 'speaking' within any
dominant discourse such as colonialism or patriarchy. The questions
these debates have raised include: we know that subaltern people
are oppressed, but how do we know? and how can that oppression
be spoken? Even when the subaltern appears to 'speak' there is a
real concern as to whether what we are listening to is really a
subaltern voice, or whether the subaltern is being spoken by the
subject position they occupy within the larger discursive economy.
Thus, as Jenny Sharpe has argued, the speaker who resists the
colonial necessarily achieves that position within the framework of
the system they oppose – her example is the trial scene from
Forster's *A Passage to India* (Sharpe 1989: 148–50). In inscribing such
acts of resistance the deep fear for the liberal critic is contained in
the worry that in the representation of such moments, what is
inscribed is not the subaltern's voice but the voice of one's own
other. Homi Bhabha has also acknowledged that subaltern speech is
in some sense conditional upon the dominant discourse: 'For it is
between the edict of Englishness and the assault of the dark unruly
spaces of the earth, through an act of repetition, that the colonial
text emerges uncertainly' (1985b: 149).

For Bhabha (1984a; 1985b), if I read him correctly, the possibility
of subaltern speech exists principally and crucially when its
mediation through mimicry and parody of the dominant discourse
subverts and menaces the authority within which it necessarily
comes into being. In these two articles Bhabha offers a convincing
account of how such resistances can be developed and how they
flourish within and through the deployment of mimicry within the
necessarily hybridized condition of the colonized society.

One basis for applying such aspects of colonialist theory to this
topic is that indigenous peoples exist in relation to their own
societies (themselves settler colonies) in ways analogous to the
colonial subject. They have been presented frequently in the
representations of settler societies as subjects who do not possess, to
use Bhabha's phrase, 'a stable unitary assumption of collectivity'
(Bhabha 1985b: 153). This is, in part, the result of the deliberate
suppression of pre-colonial cultures, and the displacement of their
peoples in a policy of assimilation which aimed at the suppression of
difference. The very wiping out of distinctive collectivities under
an undifferentiated term such as 'Aboriginal' is an example of this
process in operation. It is therefore a powerful need of such peoples
to reassert their pre-colonized cultures and to struggle for the

recuperation of their cultural difference and its resilience in and through the local and specific. Let me be quite clear that it is not with *this* process that I am quarrelling, but rather with the uses made of some of the strategies of authenticity associated with this process within white systems of representation which disavow the possibilities for the hybridized subjects of the colonizing process to legitimate themselves or to speak in ways which menace the authority of the dominant culture precisely in so far as it 'mimics' and so subverts it. In such a fetishized use of the inscription of the authentic, a further and subtler example of control emerges, one which in this use may function just as negatively in its impact on the effective empowerment of Australian Aboriginal voices. The danger that I want to draw attention to resides not in the inscription of the alter/native meta-text as such, but in the specific employment of this meta-text under the sign of the authentic to exclude the many and complex voices of the Aboriginal peoples past and present.

The mythologizing of the authentic characterized in the media representation of the Nyoongah in the *West Australian* article I have quoted, is, then, in many ways itself a construction which over-powers one of the most powerful weapons within the arsenal of the subaltern subject: that of displacement, disruption, ambivalence, or mimicry – discursive features founded not in the closed and limited construction of a pure authentic sign but in endless and excessive transformation of the subject positions possible within the hybridized. I want to argue that authentic speech where it is conceived not as a political strategy within a specific political and discursive formation but as a fetishized cultural commodity may be employed within such accounts as that of the *West Australian* to enact a discourse of 'liberal violence', re-enacting its own oppres-sions on the subjects it purports to represent and defend.

Let me repeat again that this is not to deny the vital importance for the various indigenous communities of recovering their own tongues and cultures as vital recuperative strategies. It is rather to indicate that unless this is accompanied by a wider strategy of disruption within the field of the dominant discourse, both in the public arena of the white media and to a lesser but important sense in the literary representation of the Australian Aboriginal peoples the possibilities for winning the larger discursive battle may be lost even as local 'tactical' victories are won. Such a strategy would need to incorporate alongside the assertion of the value of indigenous cultures in and for themselves the simultaneous existence of hybridized texts which replicate the hidden condition of the dominant culture and which undermine and subvert its claims to seamless, discursive unity and dismantle its dominant narrative mastery.

The construction of texts which represent the complex hybridized actuality of recent Australian Aboriginal history and which contain within themselves not only strategies of recuperation towards the distinctive features of difference in the cultures of Australian Aboriginal peoples but which also present the ways in which the subject-positions of Australian Aboriginals within the dominant discourse have been falsely constructed seem to me to be an equally important part of the strategy of resistance to 'those ideological correlatives of the Western sign – empiricism, idealism, mimeticism, monoculturalism . . . that sustain a tradition of English [or in this case Australian] "national" authority' of which Homi Bhabha has written (Bhabha 1985b: 147). Mudrooroo's recently published novel *Master of the Ghost Dreaming* is one such text, reinscribing the colonizer in the alter/native position. This is recuperation in and through an empowering inversion of the master-codes of the dominant narrative and is a powerful strategy. But what I want to address are the texts which disrupt the claim to 'purity' on both sides of the engaged discursive orders, and suggest that a doubling of effect occurs in both dominant and dominated. Such texts reveal through the process of mimicry how the contemporary dominant discourse replicates its own divisions through the construction of myths of purity and authenticity which then enable the continuity of the idea of a stable dominant discourse even at the very moment it appears to 'recognize' the existence of the other as 'authentic'. In fact in practice such recognition frequently disables the 'recognized', limiting their representation to little but a counterpoise within the discursive economy of the speaker.

Sally Morgan's *My Place* (1987) seems to me to be a classic test-case for this kind of presentation of Aboriginality as legitimated by a process of subversive mimicry and displacement rather than as an overdetermined replication of the sign of the authentic. It is, of course, a text which has been vigorously resisted by both Australian Aboriginal and white critics as 'inauthentic' and both have accused it in various ways of falsely conflating a variety of positions of oppression. It is certainly true that Sally Morgan offers no simple model of culture or of the way in which it comes into construction through complex narrative determinations and modalities. In her account of her own spiritual condition, for example, Nyoongah spirituality finds its expression for her through the Christian religion which she simultaneously clearly recognizes was a major factor in the suppression of her people's pre-colonial beliefs. In the same way, when the text shows her grand-uncle Arthur locating himself in the gap between his position and the '"bushie" blackfella', this functions not as a sign of inauthenticity but as a sign of the actual subject position occupied by many Nyoongah people under colonial settler rule in a specific time and place.

The text is explicit, too, about the ambivalent distance which separates Arthur's world from that of the 'bushie' blackfella, and the ways in which he constructs himself in the gap between the two social worlds by which his contradictory and ambivalent subject position is constrained, that of the small farmers of Mucka and that of his 'race'. Talking of the incarceration of Aboriginal peoples during the war he notes that 'I heard a rumour that they were worried the Japanese would get hold of the bushies and the bushies would lead them through the interior. I'd be no good to them. I'd be lost myself, probably' (Morgan 1987: 211).

Such realistic assessment of his own 'impure' condition does not mean that he is other than black, nor that he is unaware of the discrimination against him. The text locates him within the actual subjected position within which he is spoken by the dominant white world, and within which he resists its construction of him by a process of mimicry which dismantles its design. 'I was going by my real name, now. I left Marble behind when I left Davy. Now I was Arthur Corunna, farmer of Mukinbudin' (ibid.: 200); or, 'I was a white man, then, not black. It was a king's life' (ibid.: 204). At such moments Arthur's sense of himself as 'subject' is placed within the conflicting alternative narrative modalities to which the rest of the text gives voice. In a simple sense the result is to ironize the assertion, but the further effect of the process results in the dismantling of the power of the discourse which 'constructs' him as it menaces the authority of that discourse in the act of mimicking it.

The text's sense of marginality also intersects and, in significant respects, is coterminous with the discourse of class. This profoundly hidden and ambivalent discourse in centralist white Australian culture (which is simultaneously denied and employed as a decisive feature of distinction either by embracing it under the sign of egalitarian 'mateship' or by othering it as European and not 'native') is invoked also as a central feature of contemporary Nyoongah experience, where a similar doubling effect occurs in contemporary inscriptions of oppression. White Australian readers who criticize the text for inauthenticity often do so because it offers as evidencing signs of the marginalization of the Nyoongah discriminatory features which, they assert, are shared by all Australians at a certain economic level, irrespective of race. In fact the strength of Morgan's narrative is precisely that it shows how at many points the features of racial and class discrimination in Perth society in the late 1940s and 1950s, as well as in the earlier periods covered by the accounts of Arthur, Daisy and Gladys, overlap, and so positions its subjects not in an ahistorical and timeless warp but in a specific and historically-dense actuality whose features are corrigible and determined by precise and analysable features. Arthur's sense of the timeless concerns of the Nyoongah, for example in his attitudes to land and animals, is located also within an active desire to recuperate the 'history' of his people as it was experienced in his time. In the same way, when the text shows him distinguishing between himself and the mythologized authentic 'bushie' blackfella this functions not as a sign of his inauthenticity but as a sign of the subject position occupied by many Nyoongah people in a specific time and place. Thus, too, for example, in Arthur's account of his problems during the Depression we can see how racism is not just a general condition but is a condition specifically determined through historical preconditions, and we see also how these preconditions can be released into practice by specific and historically determined circumstances. Thus when Arthur begins his farming at Mucka he is not as conscious of opposition to him on the grounds of race as when the Depression begins to bite and his neighbours begin to see him as a rival. As resources shrink, the grounds for discrimination emerge. It is as naive, the narrative suggests, to believe that economic conditions cause racism in any simple way as to believe that their existence is not a powerful determinant in the degree to which its practice surfaces in any society. The first practice erases cultural and racial difference in favour of some generalizing category such as 'class', without recognizing the reciprocity of class and other factors such as race and cultural difference in constructing specific moments of oppression in different times and places. The second ignores the fact that groups oppressed on the grounds of racial or cultural difference are frequently, though not always, also groups oppressed in other ways such as by economic deprivation. Thus when Arthur concludes,

> The Depression didn't do no favours for my neighbour [a man who had been overtly racist towards him] either . . . . He had to sell up, he left the district for good. I had to take my family and start again on new, uncleared land. It's hard for the black man to get ahead.

(Morgan 1987: 209)

it seems to me to be a superficial criticism of the text to accuse it, as white critics have done, of an inappropriate conflation of the injustices of class, race, and gender. Similar intersections occur with the discourse of gender and if I concentrate here on class it is only because space precludes me from unpacking the gender issue, and because it functions structurally in ways within the text which are similar at least at the level of irruption, though in many ways it is perhaps the more crucial discourse which permeates the discourse of race in the bulk of the narratives from which the text is constructed.

It is true of course that some of the discriminations Sally Morgan records would have happened irrespective of her colour. However, what the text demonstrates is how the operation of other oppressions, such as class prejudice, functions as an aspect of the operation of the oppression of race, and, indeed, vice-versa. That the oppression of race may also be modified positively by such intersections when class is a feature functioning to create solidarity between the races at an economic level is demonstrated too when, in the following paragraphs, Arthur discriminates between those who, under the conditions of economic depression, resurrect the racial issue and those who do not. On the one hand there is the neighbour who 'didn't like blacks' and who 'used to shoot my horses and pigs' and on the other there is the neighbour whom Arthur had helped when he was in hospital by '[cutting] his hay and [shearing] his sheep'. Arthur concludes, 'He was my mate' (ibid.: 210). The discourse of class in its resistant aspect as 'mateship' functions here to override race and to create a unity of the oppressed against the oppressor. Thus the text demonstrates the complexities of specific historical moments when many discourses and reading positions register the complex intersections of actual social practice. Through such descriptions it recuperates the voice of Arthur Corunna within a historic subject position, frankly acknowledging the degree to which that position depends upon the appropriation of practices and discourses which are not located within the timeless and the 'authentic'.

The use of a subversive 'mimicry' to reveal the ambivalent reality of the subject position through which Arthur is spoken in his period is revealed, as I noted above, in Arthur's location of himself within the 'pioneer' discourse which is also a historic location of the racist in white Australian colonial texts.

> Mucka was a good place to live in the old days. People were more friendly, they needed each other. The black man was workin' for the farmers, gettin' paid in tea, flour and sugar. Blackfellas cleared the land, put crops in, pulled sandalwood. I remember the lake country used to be full of dingoes, the blackfellas used to track them, hunt them down. Aah yes, no one can say the blackfella didn't do his share of work in Mucka. They helped make it what it is today, I hope they won't be forgotten.

> (Morgan 1987: 211)

The ambivalence of such a passage and the hidden levels of the text which it represents[2] invite the reader to dismantle the racist discourse of the white pioneer whilst simultaneously recognizing how it functions in the construction of Arthur's own possible subject positions.

In everything I have been saying, of course, what is implicit is that any single narrative strand of this complex, multi-narrative, palimpsestic text resists the idea of a unified construction of history or place. At every moment each narrative positions itself against all the others, each one infolded within Morgan's own narrative of her search for her 'place'. This in its turn is displaced by the existence of both the resistant alternative narratives of the text itself, and of the way in which it articulates the alternative modes of construction within the dominant society with which she is forced to negotiate in order to determine who and what she may be as a contemporary Australian of Aboriginal descent.

For example, in its overall narrative strategy, as many people have noted, the text refuses to polarize culturally-defined discourses of time and space, so that it constructs the growing consciousness in historical terms as a literal journey into consciousness and recovery which we also see Daisy, Gladys and the 'author' Sally Morgan undertaking simultaneously. The conscious intersection of the idea of narrative and travel, of history and journey, of time and space encapsulated in the title and its displaced 'other', My Place, My Story, replicates the hybridized culture through which the text must assert its distinctive voice, a voice established in variance to that of the dominant culture's simplified perception of the 'othered' world as that of the mythologized and idealized 'authentic' native.

For Morgan the act of inscribing the complex actualities of Arthur's life, as of Daisy's, Gladys's and finally her own is an act of resistance to the incorporation of the Nyoongah people into the white discourse either simply by assimilation or more complexly by the construction of an equally excluding discourse of the tribal and the authentic. Morgan's place is not only the tribal land and the relatives she discovers on her journey to the north but the restitution of her own actuality that she discovers in her journey within and through her own immediate family and daily surroundings in childhood and adolescence.

Throughout the text it is clear that at the most basic level of structure any simple idea of a unified, pre-social subjectivity is resisted, even though for all the 'personae', including Morgan herself in many places, such a mythic, idealized notion of the subject is the position from which their 'voice' seems to them to be receiving its authority to 'speak'. In fact it is the novel's strength that it dramatizes powerfully this process of the tendency of ideologically-constructed subject positions to be rendered opaque by a process of naturalization. It demonstrates how 'subjects . . . are typically unaware of the ideological dimensions of the subject positions they occupy', and how, as a result, they may as social subjects 'occupy a subject position . . . incompatible with [their] overt political or social beliefs and affiliations, without being aware of any contradiction' or, conversely, how they may 'occupy . . . positions which are ideologically incompatible' (Fairclough 1985: 753).[3] Arthur's perception of himself as a 'farmer of Mukinbudin' or as a 'white man' is a classic illustration of these processes at work.

Texts such as My Place deny the myth of authenticity its authority over the subjected whilst simultaneously recognizing the crucial importance of recovering a sense of difference and identity, and they indicate that the discussion being articulated across the boundaries of the discourses of the dominant and the dominated is not (as colonial texts suggest) between the pure and the tainted, or (as the white myth of the authentic suggests) between the tainted and the recovered pure, but between two orders of the impure. They therefore dismantle the order of the dominant by uncovering its own construction, and refuse to be replicated as an 'other' in a reversed binarism which leaves the dominant intact, or which, indeed, in an important sense, calls it into being.

What I have sought to question in this article is not whether the claim of Aboriginal peoples in Australia and elsewhere to restitution of their traditional lands and sacred places, or to the voices and practices of their traditional cultures, is legitimate. I have no doubt that it is. Nor do I question the importance of locality and specificity in resisting the generalizing tendencies and incorporative strategies of white society. As I have said, it is not my business to comment on this. What I am concerned with is the impact of the representation of that claim when it is mediated through a discourse of the authentic adopted and promulgated by the dominant discourse which 'speaks' the indigene within a construction whose legitimacy is grounded not in *their* practice but in *our* desire. In many ways it is the obsession of the white settler society with the pure and the authentic, that is, with our own crisis of identity, which is spoken in such texts as the *West Australian* article, but spoken through the Aboriginal whose 'authentic' self as idealized 'savage' in truth speaks our own fears about identity and creates for ourselves a useful and self-justificatory Other.

That this has become the dominant practice in the mass media over such major and important issues as Land Rights is especially worrying in its implications. Beyond this specific concern, however, is the wider concern that, as from all subaltern positions, the 'voice' of the indigene may in fact be overdetermined by the voice of the oppressor, and that the speech of the authentic may be inscribed in a space which is dominated by the systemic structures of the oppressor's discourse, whether this is expressed in the form of overt racism or in more liberal forms of discursive 'violence'. I am concerned, too, with the degree to which this is 'inevitable', as is suggested by some aspects of contemporary theorizing of colonialist discourse and colonialist textual practice. I have suggested that resistance may also need to be conducted not only in texts of recuperation but through texts which show that the voice of authority is itself a production of hybridization. The task of maintaining and recuperating the culture of the indigene is not set over in opposition to this. This is a different and distinctive programme with different and distinctive ends. The issue is the degree to which indigenous culture, appropriated by the discursive apparatus of the dominant society as an exclusive legitimating sign for the communities for which this discourse seeks to 'speak', may serve to divide and silence these communities.

Finally, I want to pose two important questions, questions to which I do not have clear answers but which I feel a need to address: first, the degree to which representations in contemporary media discourse override and overdetermine the legitimating of modes of representation employed by the Australian Aboriginal peoples themselves to their detriment, so that, even if the Land Rights issues are won in specific cases using these strategies of the authentic, it is possible that the larger discursive battle for an effective representation of the indigenous voice in, for example, the media may be lost in the very terms of the action of this successful defence. I am concerned, therefore, with the degree to which, in Taussig's terms, the narrative of the indigene is being constructed within the larger disabling narrative of the oppressor, and how in our own times the position of the 'liberal' voice and even, in certain cases, the voice of direct resistance is seduced towards an acceptance of an overdetermined narrative of authenticity and indigeneity which overrides the complex actualities of the social and political condition of the bulk of Aboriginal people. Second, I am concerned with how such constructions can and should be read within the contemporary debates about subaltern speech in colonialist discourse theory. I am therefore also concerned with the degree to which the problems of theorizing inscription within textuality (and specifically within literary texts) may be made to work for or against the possibilities for effective social practice.

These concerns I might represent by two questions to which I have no assured or absolute answers.

We know indigenous people continue to be oppressed within settler societies but how and under what form do we know, and how does this affect their ability to offer resistance and our ability to assist them through our practice?

We may also want to argue as theorists that the silencing of the subaltern subject within colonial discourse permits no speech that is not in some sense constructed within that discourse and its institutions, but how in practice does this affect the development of an anti-humanist, post-structural sociology which can effect action in moments of social crisis? Like most important questions they are ones which I am better able to pose than answer.

NOTES

1 A similar strategy was deployed in the immensely popular South African film, *The Gods Must Be Crazy*, which constructed the unthreatening African from the Kalahari as natural, primitive, peaceable and good, whereas the politically-aware African from the front-line states was constructed as a dangerous and evil, though inept, gangster. The implication is that the indigene sheds authenticity the moment he or she leaves the reserve to claim a position in the wider community.

2 The word 'dingoes', still a common Australian slang term for a treacherous and cowardly person, was frequently applied to Aboriginals during and after the period of European contact. Perhaps the implication was that the Aboriginal attacked in a way perceived by the European as treacherous, analogous to the night-time attacks of dingoes on sheep. Such a racist construction underlies the many nineteenth-century references to the attack of 'treacherous natives' (as in, for example, the inscription on the Brockman monument on the Esplanade at Fremantle, Western Australia). In this passage there is a kind of 'transference' going on in which the widespread practice during pioneer days of hunting 'wild' blacks using 'tamed' blacks as trackers is allegorized. This adds a bitterly ironic level to the passage. A similar use of the 'muchachos' and of imported Barbadian slaves to hunt the Indian is graphically described in Taussig (1987: 47ff.).

3 Fairclough's article is usefully discussed in the Introduction to Orkin (1991) whose very useful analysis of subjectivity and subject construction in South African Theatre draws upon the neglected work of Michel Pêcheux (1982). Such readings offer an important way of breaking down the false categorization of texts in terms of their essential 'authenticity', replacing them with an analysis which seeks to register the political context within which their evaluation as effective inscriptions of actual historical struggles needs to be made. They seek to record their importance within a larger archive of discursive difference and resistance.

6

BREYTEN BREYTENBACH AND THE CENSOR

J.M. Coetzee

ADDRESSING THE STATE

One of the major poems in Breyten Breytenbach's collection *Skryt*[1] (1972) is entitled 'Brief uit die vreemde aan slagter' ('Letter from foreign parts to butcher'), subtitled 'for Balthazar'. Balthazar is clearly Balthazar John Vorster, the Prime Minister of South Africa and formerly, as Minister of Justice, responsible for building up the Security Police and erecting around them a barricade of laws protecting them from legality.

Skryt did not appear in South Africa. Published in the Netherlands in 1972, it was banned for distribution in South Africa, as its author no doubt expected, by the South African censorship board. In banning it, the board singled out 'Letter from foreign parts', interpreting the poem as an unacceptable accusation against white South Africans, against Afrikaners, and particularly against Prime Minister Vorster (Brink 1980: 1–2).

In 1975 Breytenbach paid a visit to South Africa from France, where he was resident. He made his visit in disguise, under a false name and carrying a false passport. The purpose of his visit was to recruit white sympathizers into an underground military organization. He was arrested and tried for treason. At his trial he made a public apology for the poem that had offended Vorster. I quote: 'I would specifically like to apologize to the Prime Minister for a crass and insulting poem addressed to him. There was no justification for it. I am sorry' (Viviers 1978: 59).

The committee of censors almost certainly banned 'Letter from foreign parts' because of unambiguous lines in which the torture and killing of detainees by the Security Police is referred to and Vorster is directly addressed as the butcher/obstetrician presiding over their deaths. There is more to the poem than that, however. It is also one of Breytenbach's most intensely worked out treatments of death and resurrection. Let me therefore say some more about it.

Since his first verse collection, the figure of Lazarus has been part of Breytenbach's poetic mythology.[2] The first half of the *butcher* poem, without naming Lazarus, is spoken in the voice of someone resurrected from the grave/cell. In making this speaker a transworld traveller, Breytenbach seeks to entitle him to the experience of dying (in this case under torture), and so to a right to accuse Vorster in the name of 'the rearisen prisoners of Africa', to speak in the name of the martyred and tortured of John Vorster Square (Security Police headquarters), whose names (some fifteen of them) are given in the appendix to the poem.

The language of the poem progresses from being difficult in a typically modernist manner to being quite plain. This is not only because the poem is designed to grow more and more naked as it builds up towards an historic accusation (the poet in the person of a history yet to be written pointing a finger at the oppressor) but because it takes over the language of the Security Police at its most shameless and cynical when it presents lies *as* lies in the arrogant certainty that, while no one will believe them, no one dares repudiate them. (I refer, of course, to official accounts of detainees jumping out of windows in fits of remorse, slipping on bars of soap and killing themselves, hanging themselves by their own clothing, and so forth.)

> I write slogans in a crimson urine
> over my skin and over the floor
> I stay awake
> suffocating on the ropes of my entrails
> slip on soap and break my skeleton
> murder myself with the evening newspaper
> tumble out of the tenth floor of heaven
>
> (Breytenbach 1972: 27)

When the police explain a prisoner's death by saying that he slipped on a bar of soap, the unstated continuation is: and we defy any court in the land to reject that explanation. It is one of the linguistic practices of totalitarianism to send out coded messages whose meaning is known to all parties, but to enforce (by censorship) a literal interpretation of them, at least in the public arena. Thus 'slipped on a bar of soap' is known by all parties to mean 'died under torture' but its public interpretation is nevertheless forced to remain 'slipped on a bar of soap'. When Breytenbach parodies the codes, as here, his unstated continuation is: here I create an arena in which the codes are unmasked and denounced. His challenge therefore takes place on the grounds of power itself: on the one hand, police power protected from denunciation and reprisal; on the other hand, the power of a rhetoric (a skill with words) employed for the purpose of mockery on a public stage. It goes without saying that the motive for banning the poem was, by denying it a public stage, by reasserting control over public staging, to deny it the power of its superior rhetoric to unmask the codes.

But this is where the position of a speaker speaking 'from foreign parts', 'from abroad' brings in difficulties of a moral as well as of a practical order. Both the speaker and the poem (published abroad) are operating outside the jurisdiction of the rival power (the police, the censors), as they are operating outside the speech community and political community they address. Is the challenge offered by the poem, as an act in the world, therefore not empty? It is not farfetched, in the larger scheme of things, to see Breytenbach's return to South Africa in 1975 as an existential response to this question: the poet placing himself (or being placed) on the same footing as the enemy, acting out the myth of humiliation, incarceration and rebirth into the authority of the reborn – a myth not solely Christian in its currency – on which the poem draws.

The attack on Vorster himself in the poem is twofold. First, Vorster is denounced as the boss of the killers and torturers and therefore as the one who will have to answer to history for their actions. But the second prong of the attack is more interesting and in a way more radical. Picturing the scream of pain issuing from the dying prisoner as a bloody birth in the hands of the butcher-obstetrician, Breytenbach asks:

> does your heart also tighten in the throat
> when you grasp the extinguished limbs
> with the same hands that will stroke your wife's secrets?
>
> (1972: 27)

Secrets: Breytenbach might as well have written *secret parts*. The exposure to public gaze is not just of the forbidden secrets of the torture chamber, not just of the (putative) private revulsions of B.J. Vorster himself (the irony is complex here: Breytenbach asserts that Vorster has a conscience and challenges him to deny it), but of the mysteries (forbidden to the public gaze by decency itself) of the Vorster marriage bed. The poem is a low blow, a dig at the private parts not of the man but of his defenceless wife, an insult to male honour, more rather than less offensive when one considers the age of its targets (Balthazar and Tini were in their mid-fifties in 1972). The excess of the poem is an excess of intimacy.

BREYTENBACH AND THE FORBIDDEN, 1964–75

What does it mean to say that 'Letter from foreign parts' is 'crass and insulting'? Insultingness is not a property internal to a text. An insult is an act, a speech act. After insult, what happens next? What does the transgressive act set in train?

Without implying that one poem by itself gave rise to the animosity against Breytenbach that led to a nine-year (rather than a seven-year or a five-year) sentence, one can say that, as an insult to Vorster, to the Security Police, to the community whose interests they protected, the poem had its consequences. But it was not Breytenbach's first transgression. In writings dating back to 1964, Breytenbach had made one attempt after another, with growing audacity, to turn transgressive speech into transgressive act.

I do not have the space to trace these attempts in detail. Let me therefore simply say that the problem I see Breytenbach confronting again and again is that, while many of the poems he writes are indeed transgressive, all that they transgress in the end is a certain decorum of address. They cannot be said to become *acts* in the sense of completing themselves in the world as the poem on Vorster does. Relying on a rhetoric of abjuration, they remain within the rhetorical realm and so are always vulnerable to being trumped by a yet more violent rhetoric.

The alternative to frontal rhetorical assault is irony. But irony – speaking the enemy's language and seeming to identify with the enemy – particularly when it is sensitively done, raises an unsettling question: is the ironic poem merely a second-best substitute for the private diaries of the tyrant, or does the tyrant truly not know what he intends as well as the poet does? If the latter, whence the secret sympathy of poet for tyrant?

The dilemma can be restated in the form of two questions. If the passion behind my denunciation (I take the liberty of speaking in the person of Breytenbach) is not the passion of an idealistic moralism whose target might as well be universal as South African tyranny, what does it stem from? And if there is any risk I take in denouncing tyranny, what is it? The answer to the first question seems to be: my passion stems from the fact that I am implicated (historically, emotionally) in the tyranny of South Africa and cannot disown that implication. The answer to the second question seems to be: I risk the European (French) identity I have half-adopted by resuming a white South African identity I detest. Thus the paradox clarifies itself: to repudiate white South Africa I have to be a white South African; or: to repudiate evil I have first to embody evil.

The paradox is lived out by Breytenbach in writing in Afrikaans, what he calls 'a bastard language', the language of a split self, the language of the community at whose head stands Balthazar Vorster, spoken nowhere but in the land of Vorster, but also the language of his own cradle:

> I write poetry in afrikaans . . . brew-smell
> of my first milk, grain of my father's fingertips
> (1964: 20–1)

There is no doubt that the paradox of being and not being an Afrikaner has been lived out personally by Breytenbach in the most intense terms.

THE PRISON WRITINGS

'Imagine a dialogue of two persons', writes Mikhail Bakhtin,

> in which the statements of the second speaker are omitted, but in such a way that the general sense is not at all violated. The second speaker is present invisibly, his words are not there, but deep traces left by these words have a determining influence on all the present and visible words of the first speaker. . . . Each present, uttered word responds and reacts with its every fibre to the invisible speaker, points to something outside itself, . . . to the unspoken words of another person. . . . The other's discourse . . . is merely implied, but the entire structure of speech would be completely different if there were not this reaction to another person's implied words.
>
> (Bakhtin 1984: 197, 195)

Such *hidden polemic* and *hidden dialogue* Bakhtin identifies in all Dostoevsky's mature novels. He goes on:

By no means all historical situations permit the ultimate semantic authority of the creator to be expressed without mediation in direct, unrefracted, unconditional authorial discourse. When there is no access to one's own personal 'ultimate' word, then every thought, feeling, experience must be refracted through the medium of someone else's discourse, someone else's style.

(ibid.: 202)

It would be as naive in Dostoevsky's case as in Breytenbach's to argue that a change in 'historical situation', specifically the removal of external censorship, would have resulted in 'direct, unrefracted, unconditional authorial discourse' from which hidden dialogue would have been absent. Censorship, or at least the office of the censor, is not the sole 'semantic authority' at which Bakhtin hints. But the work Breytenbach did in the period 1975–82 was written under extraordinarily restricted circumstances, and, even though there was opportunity afterwards for revision, it bears traces, not always in the most obvious way, of a censored origin. As the concept of hidden contestatory dialogue opens up hidden areas of Dostoevskian discourse, it also alerts us to the possibility of a hidden contestation in Breytenbach. I will make no attempt to survey the whole body of Breytenbach's prison poetry, but quote from one remarkable poem in an effort to bring out these hidden voices *against* which he speaks.

Even in detention, before his trial, Breytenbach was allowed to write. The poems that emerged were published as *Voetskrif (Footwriting)*, dedicated to his principal interrogator, at the latter's insistence: 'You dedicate this to me and I allow you to have it published', as Breytenbach reported it.

In prison, writing was permitted on four conditions: (1) that it would be shown to no other prisoner or warder, (2) that it would not be smuggled out, (3) that each piece would be handed in for safekeeping when completed, and (4) that all notes would be destroyed (Breytenbach 1985a: 156–7, 159). Four volumes of poetry from the prison period were eventually published.[3]

Breytenbach describes his position as a prisoner *vis-à-vis* the censor:

A bizarre situation . . . when you write knowing that the enemy is reading over your shoulder . . ., knowing also that you are laying bare the most intimate and the most personal

nerves and pulsebeats in yourself to the barbarians, to the
cynical ones who will gloat over this.

(ibid.: 159).

Here is the poem I referred to: '— 'n Spieëlvars —':

> you! you! you!
> it's you I want to talk to cunt
> you ride around without saddle or driver's licence
> in the gutters and yards of my verses
> my death
> you dig around with your lance in the white acres
> where I wanted to multiply
> for nation and fatherland
> (but soon there will be nothing left of either)
> my death . . .
>
> you with your yellow eyes you with the left hand
> you with the missing beard you with the sand
> over the tongue
> with your nine-year sentence like a pregnancy
> I'll make you a widower chop-chop
>
> for you make me shiver
> you make plaints
> of pleasure
> you lay the cold caress of your lips
> here upon my life
> and *here* and *here*
> come kiss me in my mouth
> you hand-picked dog
> come and draw lines through my young thoughts
> and pack stones over my slack wings
>
> must I wait still longer?
> o my snow-white shadow Death
> o my own secret police
> I will be yours forever
> and you are
> mine mine mine

(1984: 41–2)

The imprint of Sylvia Plath lies heavily on this poem in its jagged
rhythms and wild swings of mood. But, from Plath, Breytenbach

has learned something deeper too: that I and You need not stand for fixed positions. The I here is the vindictive, death-ridden gaoler and killer, but he is also the self that longs for liberation despite seeing no other form of liberation looming but death. *You* is clearly Breytenbach the prisoner, in comic form; but he is also the persecuting figure of the oppressed slave, as well as the lover death whose perverse embrace ('*here*' and '*here*') he craves, the ever-watchful other in the mirror, and, finally, a figure with wings that answer to his own (unused?) wings. In fact, many of the avatars of the I – censor, secret policeman, winged guardian-persecutor – are shared by the You. What we have is a true mirror-poem, *spieëlvers*, in which it is not clear what is self, what image. It is a poem of accelerating dialogical frenzy in which it is no longer possible to say what the *position* of the self is: the interchange between self and other is, in effect, continuous.

THE MIRROR PHASE

The figure of a man looking into a mirror dominates Breytenbach's retrospective post-prison writings, *True Confessions of an Albino Terrorist* and *Mouroir*. The surface of the mirror and the surface of the blank page touched by the pen become indistinguishable: moving the pen, the self both creates and calls up on that surface a sardonic counter-self mocking his effort to see himself transparently, telling him to try again. The figure in the mirror behaves, in fact, just like the security policemen who, at the time of Breytenbach's first interrogation, put two blank pages in front of him and told him to write down the story of his life; then, when he was finished, read them, tore them up, and told him to try again (Breytenbach 1985a: 28–9).

Breytenbach drafted *True Confessions* by talking into a microphone, a process he calls 'this jumbletalk, this trial'. What truth will emerge from the trial? Whatever it is, it cannot be foretold: only in the process of dialogue between self and mirror/page will it reveal itself. If there were to be a new interrogation, a new trial, the truth would come out differently: 'I'd be somebody else – as sincere, as keen to help, as obsessed by the necessity to confess', he confesses (ibid.: 13–14). Thus the posture of the writer before the mirror/page is assimilated with the attitude of the co-operative prisoner under interrogation. And who is the interrogator? In a sense, the reader who wants to read what Breytenbach has to say; but also the self that writes itself. 'Mr Investigator: *you* know that we're always inventing our lives. . . . You and I entwined and related, parasite and prey, image and image-mirror' (ibid.: 17, 56).

Thus far we have only another ingenious post-structuralist figure of textual self-production, 'writing as a looking in a mirror and construction of the self' (ibid.: 155). But the African connection has not been elided. Coming to the end of his long confession, Breytenbach can write:

> Mr Investigator . . . I see you now as my dark mirror-brother. We need to talk, brother I. I must tell you what it was like to be an albino in a white land. We are forever united by the intimate knowledge of the depravity man will stoop to.
>
> (ibid.: 260)

Who is the interrogator here? Not (or not only) the persecuting white brother who polices the psyche but a black mirror-brother, just as haunting and persecutory, an accomplice in a crime (an historical crime?) in which there have been two parties, not one. Simone Weil is helpful. In every act of destruction, she writes, the I leaves behind its trace. 'A hurtful act is the transference to others of the degradation which we bear in ourselves' (Weil 1952: 65). Since the victim loses his integrity in the process of suffering, taking into himself the degradation of the oppressor, the I becomes double, multiply double: interrogator and revolutionary, criminal and victim, colonizer and colonized, even censor and writer. The black in the mirror is not Other but other/self, 'brother I'.

The long talking in the empty room with which *True Confessions* began thus culminates not in dialogue with the dark brother but in the discovery that for true knowledge to come about, or at least before true knowledge can come about, dialogue must take place with the mirror. So when Breytenbach writes, in retrospect, that he does not regret having gone through the 'underground' experience, the word is rich in significance, referring not only to his history as a secret agent and a prisoner but to a history of blind burrowing that has led not into the light of liberation but instead to the illumination, the insight that light-seeking is a process of blind burrowing. 'What one has gone through becomes a new corridor outlining the innards of the labyrinth; it is a continuation of the looking for the Minotaur, that dark centre which is the I (eye), that Mister I [mystery]' (1985a: 87).

The white policeman, the black revolutionary, enemies brought together in the mirror. Is the mirror the place, then, where history is transcended? Does the dialogue with the mirror-self shade into dialogue between the selves in the mirror? And can the dialogue with the mirror be trusted to proceed peaceably, or will it degenerate into hysterical confrontation and self-accusation? These are the questions Breytenbach addresses in *Mouroir*. I will not say much about *Mouroir*. I regard it as, in a specific sense of the word, an inconsequential work, a doodling with Ariadne's thread rather than a search for the Minotaur. Breytenbach is not without moments of clarity about how essentially fragile and intermittent his mastery is over the voice of the censor, the voice of the Father, and every voice that says No. Prison-writing is a way of survival, he writes; 'but . . . at the same time it is the exteriorization of my imprisonment, . . . the walls of my confinement' (1985a: 155).

The hysteria of a consciousness that encounters wherever it looks nothing but reflections of itself had already received extreme embodiment in Dostoevsky's *Notes from Underground* (1864). One of the fates of confession since Rousseau – of secular confession at least – has been to spin itself out endlessly in an effort to reach beyond self-reflection and the sterile multiplication of selves to truth. In both Breytenbach and Dostoevsky the task of taking charge of the process of self-reflexion at first seems to the narrating self no more than a preliminary task to be performed (a sentry to be passed) before the real work, the real story-telling, can begin. Only later does the realization dawn that getting to the real self (finding the Mystery I) is a life's task, like cleaning the Augean stables.

THE CENSOR

In his public, political person, Breytenbach expresses attitudes towards censorship typical of the cosmopolitan, progressive intellectual. 'Censorship is an act of shame. . . . It has to do with manipulation, with power, with . . . repression.' For the writer to consent to being censored is fatal. 'It takes root inside you as a kind of interiorized paternalism. . . . You become your own castrator.' 'Once you submit to the thought restrictions of the power managers, enter their game, . . . they have already won the day' (1986: 111, 133–4, 109).

There is no hint in these post-1982 utterances that the policeman/censor of the imagination is already in place in Breytenbach as his mirror-self, or that for him writing has become, if not playing at the censor's game, at least playing a game with the censor. For public occasions (I do not count the books as public occasions) something is therefore censored out. What we have from Breytenbach is a split account of censorship, split between what I will call the exoteric and esoteric. The exoteric account is constituted by public utterances of the kind I have just quoted: in this account there is an unambiguous contest between a voice struggling to utter itself and a gag that stifles it; the censor is demonized. The esoteric account, the doctrine to be teased out of the books, is that the writer writes *against* and cannot write *without* a manifold of internalized resistances that are in essence no different from an internalized censor-twin, cherished and hated.

In some of its most intense forms – and here I speak in a general way – writing throws up evidences of bloody or asphyxiating struggles against blockages and resistances: gagged words gagged out. The voice struggles to breathe in, to breathe out, against intimate persecutory figures. Breytenbach's poetry, and particularly his poetry of the prison and post-prison period, is writing of this kind. He may choose to – indeed, for the continuation of his life's enterprise he may have to – denounce his heritage, linguistic and historical, for the impurity of his voice, call himself a bastard neither European nor African afflicted with the schizophrenic consciousness (whatever that means) of the bastard. But the very gesture of blaming, so widespread in his writing (not necessarily in the best of it), mirroring the blaming of him by censor and judge (for softening the moral fibre of the nation, for treason against the state), belongs to a futile strategy of demonization, or mutual expulsion. The poems that emerged with Breytenbach into the fresh air from prison have at the very least the power to point him toward ways of living with the demons and the daimon that possess him.

NOTES

1 The neologism *Skryt* is a composite of *skryf* (write) and *skyt* (shit). It also recalls *stryd* (struggle). Breytenbach's Afrikaans, which is full of word-play and neologism, presents sometimes insuperable problems to the translator. Breytenbach himself prepared the English texts of *True Confessions of an Albino Terrorist* (1985a), *Mouroir* (1985c), *End Papers* (1986) and *Judas Eye* (1988). Other translations in this essay are my own.

2 See 'Death begins at the feet', in Breytenbach (1964).
3 *Eklips* (1983), (*'Yk'*) 1983, *Buffalo Bill* (1984) and *Lewendood* (1985b), all published by Taurus of Johannesburg. *Yk*: to give the stamp of approval to; there is a further play on *ek* (I) and English *ache*.

7

DE-SCRIBING ORALITY
Performance and the recuperation of voice

Helen Gilbert

In writing on orality and performance in contemporary Aboriginal drama, I am immediately faced with at least two limitations. First, through my privileged position as a white literary critic, the task partially re-inscribes indigenous voices at the same time as it attempts to mobilize the oral text as a mode of decolonization. Second, since this drama has proliferated within a context of commercial theatre, literacy, and access to a print culture, it is always already marked with the traces of writing and European theatrical conventions. Furthermore, my examination of specific plays frequently relies on a text which is not the oral performance but a written transcription of what it might be (or, in some cases, an approximation of what it was in the first production). In a sense, then, I am always dealing with simulacra, and the difficulty of delineating a moment of enunciation for the text increases when you consider that many of the plays to be examined were developed through workshopping processes involving non-Aboriginal actors, directors, writers, technicians. The notion of authorship thus becomes even more complex than in other narrative genres, as does the concept of text, especially given the potential variance of each enactment of a play. That the performance text is difficult to define and radically unstable, however, need not be as problematic as it appears. Within a post-colonial framework that promotes 'hybridization' and 'literary contamination'[1] as weapons of cultural transformation, delimiting notions of an authentic indigenous voice becomes a far less useful task than examining how the multiplicity of Aboriginal voices might be deployed. This essay, then, is not so much concerned with developing an oral poetics/aesthetics as with outlining the strategic possibilities of performance for the textual production and consumption of oral discourse as cultural expression.

A further problem arises in attempting to define or even name this discourse, without subscribing to the limiting binaries that justify the representation of oral cultures as socially and intellectually inferior to literate ones. Walter Ong, among others, decries terms like 'oral literature' which stress the pre-emptive nature of writing by implying that oral narratives are merely variants of written ones (1982: 11). Such theorists favour the terms 'orature', 'verbal art', and 'oral cultural production', which I support in principle for their attempts to avoid hierarchies of value that privilege the literate. This terminology, however, does not completely evacuate itself of prejudice, nor does it account for the frequent interplay of oral and written forms. Ruth Finnegan makes the important point that the 'supposed cleavage' between the two has blinded theorists to their possibilities as complementary rather than contestatory modes of communication (1976: 17). I cannot suggest a better name for the specific cultural productions we are talking about, but I would argue that drama has long enacted the intertextuality of oral and written forms, and that well before Barthes announced the 'death of the author', drama praxis clearly recognized the de-authorizing function of performance. Because each performance text defers and deflects the authority of any written version, drama offers the most enabling context for the recuperation of orality in forging post-colonial voices. Performance further provides a space in which naming the specificity of oral discourse becomes less important than vocalizing it. This de-scripted (performative) model of orality is by no means new, but it does seem to have been largely overlooked in the growing body of criticism on indigenous texts. Such a model refers not to a text which has never been written, but to one which is *unwritable* at its moment of enunciation.[2]

Post-colonial critics have speculated much about the ways in which orality informs the narrative structures and discourses of texts written by literate members of Aboriginal cultures. Kateryna Arthur (1989) and Craig Tapping (1989a, 1990), for example, focus on narratives which, through linguistic innovation and structural repetition, evoke notions of performed speech or story-telling. In a related endeavour, Stephen Muecke and others have been intent on finding an appropriate medium for the packaging of oral texts for consumption in book form. Muecke wisely locates his interest in the 'relation between [the] epistemology and conditions of production' of such books (1988: 48), and makes no claim to reproduce a verbal text with 'authenticity'. While these theorists are careful to acknowledge the mediating function of the written word, they tend to shy away from closely examining the ephemeral and problematic oral. Most critics writing on Aboriginal drama, on the other hand, seem to take the oral so much for granted that they deem it scarcely worth noting other than to advocate a performative context for its fullest expression, without considering the political effects of this enactment.[3] However, when we listen to what Aborigines them-selves say about orality, performance emerges as fundamental to the on-going process of de-scribing empire. Jack Davis, for example, points to theatre's facility for verbal improvization, humour, and irony, along with non-verbal narrative techniques such as mime and dancing, all of which have traditionally been part of his culture (Chesson 1988: 190–211). Mudrooroo Narogin stresses as well the social manifestations of theatre for the representation of Aboriginal identities (1990: 117–29), and both Davis and Mudrooroo share a concern with the spatial locations of oral enunciation, and the dislocation of voice that has resulted from European imperialism. To discuss the political effects of the oral in drama, I want to turn to some of these factors in examining who speaks, for whom, and under what socio-cultural conditions.

Language itself is obviously paramount in the articulation of hitherto muted[4] indigenous voices, and it is widely accepted that the appropriation and abrogation of the colonizers' linguistic codes are essential to post-colonial writing. Like their literary counterparts, Aboriginal performance texts have incorporated these processes in varying degrees by using words (indigenous and creolized), syntax and grammar that differ from those of standard English. Kevin Gilbert's *The Cherry Pickers* (1988), initially performed in 1971 and regarded as the 'first Aboriginal play' in the European sense, makes a point of 'bastardizing' (Gilbert's own term) conventional English beyond the limits of the purely colloquial by using words like 'tremendaciously' and 'rememberising', as well as neologisms such as 'kunstidonus' or 'amphiskkulus', to satirize the pretentiousness of white speech and signal its inappropriateness to an Aboriginal context. This strategy is not specific to drama; what is specific, and particularly empowering, are the possibilities for enunciating such discourses orally and with recognizably Aboriginal inflections. Aspects of speech like tonality, diction, rhythm, and accent are clearly important performative tools here, as are associated meta-linguistic features. Jimmy Chi's *Bran Nue Dae* (1991), for example, makes abundant use of such devices to produce a distinctive performance which, while conforming structurally and thematically to the popular musical genre, simultaneously subverts and extends its conventions. Opportunities for individual characters to articulate multiple identities abound in this text, which uses different *voices* for dialogue, story-telling and singing. Some of the most politically humorous moments in the play also arise from the deployment of voice. Willie's aping of Father Benedictus as the mission boys raid the school tuck-shop is a case in point: 'Yah it is gut to eat at der Lord's table. First ve haff made un inwentory of der spoils. Den ve haff to partake of der fruits ov our labours. Thankyou Lord!' (Chi 1991: 7). Although I can't recreate the specificity of the performance I attended, this quotation perhaps gives some idea of how accent might be used subversively to produce colonial mimicry which, as Homi Bhabha has shown, 'is at once a mode of appropriation and resistance' that reveals the ambivalence of colonial discourse and turns the 'insignia of its authority [into] a mask, a mockery' (1985c: 103).

Plays by Jack Davis, Bob Maza and others introduce substantial dialogues in Nyoongah and Boandik with minimal or no glossing, in attempts to recuperate Aboriginal languages as viable codes of communication. Because these languages are performed rather than inscribed, they proclaim radical alterity in a context where non-Aboriginal audience members can neither 'look up' the meaning, nor quite imagine how such words might be scripted. If, as Ong suggests, the literate mind's 'sense of control over language is closely tied to the visual transformations of language' (1982: 14), this alterity, which prevents the seamless application of writing to the oral, enacts an important mode of resistance for oral cultures against the hegemony of literate ones. Bill Ashcroft's discussion of unglossed foreign languages in the written text illuminates this point:

> Signifiers of alterity are not necessarily inaccessible; rather they explicitly establish a distance between the writer and reader functions in the text as a cultural gap. The gap of silence reaffirms the parameters of meanability as cultural parameters, and the language use offers its own hybridity as the sign of an absence which cannot be simply traversed by an interpretation. It directly intercepts notions of 'infinite transmissibility' to protect its difference from the incorporating universalism of the centre.
>
> (1989: 72)

The oral text, I would argue, politicizes the signs of absence enacted through indigenous language usage even further by intensifying the ambivalent 'fear and desire' responses which codes of difference evoke in a majority audience. Whereas a reader will rarely read or sound out each word of an unglossed text, preferring simply to skip over to the familiar, an audience member experiences difference in complicated ways. On the one hand, aural signifiers, along with gesture and facial expression, make meaning more tantalizingly accessible and thus attach a promise of some understanding, and hence control, to the effort required to decipher the foreign. Nevertheless, at the same time, the verbal mode of communication conjures an 'other' that occupies theatrical time and space through a series of implosive sounds which cannot be ignored or fully appropriated.

The articulation of oppositional voices also raises the problem of translation, which is further complicated when one attempts to describe and/or enact a performative mode in a written text. Louis Nowra's *Capricornia*[5] (1988) invalidates this activity by illustrating the comic effect of the reverse when Tocky, his part-Aboriginal protagonist, 'translates' the Bible into an oral performance in pidgin for her classmates while her teacher reads in a flat voice:

> MRS HOLLOWER: 'And the Philistine said unto David," Am I a dog and thou comest to me with staves?"'
>
> TOCKY: The Philistine was a mongrel.
>
> MRS HOLLOWER: 'And the Philistine cursed David by his gods.'
>
> TOCKY: He told him to fuck off.
>
> MRS HOLLOWER: 'Then said David to the Philistine, "Thou comest to me with a sword, and with a spear, and with a shield . . ."'
>
> TOCKY: He had sword, nulla nulla and woomera.

This passage only begins to suggest the subversive possibilities in such a scene; more striking in dramatization are the particular inflections of a pidgin dialect and the rigidity of Mrs Hollower's voice and stance as opposed to the fluidity of Tocky's. As she translates, Tocky incorporates more and more gestures into her narrative until finally it becomes a full-blown carnivalesque performance when she '*mimes cutting off [Goliath's] head and shows it to the crowd, strutting as would David*' (Nowra 1988: 31). Mrs Hollower intervenes at this point and her comment that Tocky's translation is 'more than sufficient' (ibid.) is an uncomfortable recognition of the subversive power of the mode of excess created in the performance.

What she objects to most is Tocky's over-literal enactment of a text which largely derives its authority and 'truth value' (in the Foucauldian sense) from the historical contingency of its closure in written form. For Tocky, however, translating involves more than simply substituting one linguistic code for another. The differences between the two narratives can be discussed according to Emile Benveniste's notions of *histoire* and *discours*,[6] though these terms should not be set up as absolute binaries. Mrs Hollower's reading, which avoids interpretive nuances, attempts to abstract the narrative from any enunciative context and to suggest that meaning is fixed in the priority of language. Tocky's performance, on the other hand, foregrounds the role of the interlocutor and the specific context of utterance in the creation of meanings unfixed in *discours*. Aware of her audience (both onstage and in the auditorium) and her own position as entertainer, she undermines the agency of Mrs Hollower's *histoire* by refusing to represent the story symbolically or take its supposed message seriously. While Mrs Hollower insists that 'the word of God requires no translation' (ibid.), Nowra's text makes a quite different point: that translation is never a neutral act but a political one which involves operations of power, usually of the translator over the translated.

The proselytizing activities of missionaries are represented in many indigenous plays as similar confrontations between *histoire* and *discours*, the former usually claiming authority through writing, the latter most often pertaining to speech events. Though less overtly theatrically, Ruby in Robert Merritt's *The Cake Man* (1978) also 'translates' the Bible's content and reworks its forms so that the word of God is transmitted through oral story-tellings rather than liturgical readings. This process establishes what Bhabha calls 'partial knowledges' through a kind of splitting and doubling that undermines the authority of colonialist discourse (1985c: 102). While preserving the priority of writing in the Bible's 'par-adigmatic presence' as truth, Ruby's appropriation of 'the word' 'empties [that] "presence" of its syntagmatic supports', in Bhabha's terms, by replacing the codes, conventions and cultural associations of a particular written event with those of a distinctively different oral one. The resultant hybrid text, when scrutinized by Ruby's husband, Sweet William, reveals its problematic relationships with the truth value of both 'blackfella yarns' and 'gubba [white] books'. Informed by both modes of communication, it resists claiming 'authenticity' or unproblematic 'origin' for either narrative.

In performance contexts, the truth, if any, is in the telling. By offering a wide range of potential articulations, dramatic texts amplify the splitting and hybridization of dominant discourses. The acoustic variability of actors' voices and the specific spaces they resonate in become significant sites of meaning. In particular, irony, mimicry and ambivalence, key linguistic strategies in post-colonial texts, can be inflected in diverse ways in performance. Discord, harmony, synchronicity, simultaneity and other auditory signifiers also offer possible ways of creating a performative heteroglossia that demonstrates the dialogic interactions between voices which Bakhtin outlines. Hence, whereas indigenous *writing* has been termed necessarily 'double-voiced since it must partake of the colonizing discourses in the process of literary decolonization' (Arthur 1990: 24), Aboriginal *drama* could be more appropriately called voluntarily 'multi-voiced'.

In its multiple dissembling of axiomatic meanings, performance also opens up the possibility of enacting silence as a viable vocal mode of expression. As one of the framing devices for *The Cake Man's* mission narrative, silence is the Aborigines' audible response to the colonizing moment when three white men attempt to 'civilize' a tribal family by proffering the Bible. The Aborigines' mute rejection of the 'gift' can be interpreted as an active protest against imposed languages, as can the increasingly frequent Pinter-esque pauses in Sweet William's epilogue to the play. In performative contexts, silence enacts more than a problematic absence of voice which marks an untraversable gap between Aboriginal and white discourses. Unlike readers who must imagine silence through the words which evoke it, and who then fill this potential gap with plenitude as they read on, an audience experiences silence as a code of speech with its own illocutionary and perlocutionary effects. These emerge through the length and depth of the silence in the specific spaces of its enunciation, through its tenor in relation to the volume, tone and intent of the speech which circumscribes or interrupts it, and through the gestures and postures of the silent. And since an audience will normally respond to silence with more of the same, amplifying the initial presence/absence with multiple echoes, this collective silence marks an unusual chiasmus, a moment of discursive conjunction of Aboriginal and non-Aboriginal voices that is both democratic and anarchic.

In apposition to the silent voices in the initial scene, Merritt reintroduces the father of the tribal family as Sweet William, a particularly loquacious contemporary Aborigine who, in a long monologue or, more accurately, series of dialogues, alternately adopts the guises of story-teller, singer, biblical interpreter, drunken yarn-spinner, amateur philosopher and cultural mediator. The effectiveness of these voices, which articulate the rhetoric of a paradigmatic trickster figure, clearly relies on performative contexts and the vocal virtuosity of the actor to convey diverse subjectivities. Hence, although Sweet William sets himself up as a kind of souvenir, 'the Australian Aborigine . . . made in England' (Merritt 1978: 12), this identity is a 'rort' in more ways than one. As trickster, his adoption of different voices can be seen as a series of verbal rorts which are particularly theatrical in the sense that acting always implies deception in the notion of role. Continually shifting subjectivities are important here because they forestall attempts to fix the actor/character as the reified object of the viewer's gaze.

As well as facilitating multiple enunciations of silence and voice as complementary rather than oppositional modes, the theatre offers a particular space to the disembodied voice. Voice-overs, radio voices, offstage voices, and voices of the dead have been used effectively to indicate the linguistic disjunction between Aboriginal reality and the means available for its expression in white cultural contexts. Writing, itself a form of disembodiment that separates the speaker from his/her discursive context, translates its own absences into a series of visible signs – the script. In performance, however, the disembodied voice is indexical rather than symbolic, and it is fully present at the same time as it points to its speaker's absence. This situation might be seen as metonymic of many Aborigines' experiences in the sense that indigeneity is the marginalized aural sign in European history, the voice whose absence is inscribed by the colonizers as a lack of subjectivity at the same time as its presence insistently demands recognition.

I have outlined the specifically linguistic functions of a performative orality as the endless deferral of the authority of writing, the political intervention in translating processes, and the deployment of culturally inflected voices with which Aborigines can truly speak their differences, their partialities and their silences. The results are a Brechtian defamiliarization of language as a transparent signifier and a focus on 'voice' itself as a site of contestation. Also important in the performance of oral discourses are the specificities of their enunciative occasions, which will vary according to the actors involved, the spaces they perform in, and the audiences with whom they interact. Ong argues that orality relegates meaning largely to context whereas writing concentrates meaning in language itself (1982: 106). Current reader-response theories and studies in communication clearly show that writing as a signifier is not so unproblematic; however performance does utilize a wider range of semiotic systems in the production of meaning. Many of these systems, clearly influenced by culturally specific artistic conventions, are far too complex to be discussed in this paper except in so far as they evoke the oral in ways that an unperformed text cannot approximate.

The opportunity to build on speech with movement further revivifies oral traditions and aids the production of Aboriginal subjectivities. Terry Goldie has argued that since 'history awarded semiotic control to the invaders . . . the image of native peoples has functioned as a constant source of semiotic reproduction, in which each textual image refers back to those offered before' (1988: 60). Performance intervenes in this object-signifying process through what Isidore Okpewho calls an 'expansion and ventilation of the body' (1979: 181). In performance, the Aboriginal body has three functions. First, as a physical body, it is a sign of otherness that resists appropriation through the metaphysics of its insistent presence on stage. As a social body, however, it becomes a site of contestation showing the historical inscriptions of indigenous and colonizer cultures and their competing ideologies. Finally, as an artistic body, it bridges the gap between physical and social, grounding Aboriginal voices in speaking, moving subjects. Dancing, in particular, features in many plays as a contextual adjunct to voice in the production of orality through rhythms, repetitions, and conscious postponements of telos, all of which parallel conventions of traditional oral narratives.[7] But, like music, dance is not necessarily the signifier of a static pre-colonized identity. Oodgeroo Noonuccal's *Why the Corroborees*, workshopped at the 1989 National Black Playwright's Conference in Sydney, illustrates this point by creating a corroboree and then paralleling it with a rap dance.

Theatre offers a variety of other resources to augment the enactment of voice and create an appropriate mood for story-telling. Finnegan stresses the setting and the function of the actual occasion of enunciation in the detailed content and form of oral narratives (1976: 11–12). And since site has long been a key aspect of narration in Aboriginal cultures (Muecke 1983a: 94), the proxemics of theatres, or spaces co-opted as theatres, significantly affect oral discourses, just as relationships between listeners and speakers vary according to spatial evocations of distance, intimacy and the like. Contemporary theatre, however commercial, establishes particular spaces and occasions for the production and reception of oral discourse as cultural expression. Jack Davis's *Barungin* (1989), developed specifically for production in 1988 as part of a trilogy including *No Sugar* (1986) and *The Dreamers* (1982), incorporated the occasion of its utterance as a protest against the official Bicentennial celebrations of European invasion. Along with actors' T-shirts bearing the Aboriginal counter-bicentennial slogan, 'Don't celebrate '88', the choice of the Fitzroy Town Hall in Melbourne as venue added a sharp political edge: the performance was at once valorized by its enactment in a public edifice to white history, at the same time as that edifice became a site of symbolic reclamation of Aboriginal land when truckloads of sand were poured over large parts of the interior to create a suitable set. The production also explored the proxemic possibilities of that particular building by compelling audience members to move as different sections of the theatrical space were annexed by the actors, forming a metaphorical parallel to the forced dislocation of Aborigines in the play.[8]

Theatre is not only occasional but temporal. Unlike writing, which remains as residue between readings, thus announcing its own historicity, performance is characteristically ephemeral, latent, potential.[9] This forces a recognition of the role of the present in constructions of the past, which sets up the dialogic processes that post-colonial representations of history must engage in if they are to operate counter-discursively. Aboriginal performance has long recognized that the past is remade in every telling. Concepts of non-linear time are important to these tellings. Even though a performance is a linear event in real time, a movement no matter how circular from beginning to end, it allows for the representation of different temporal moments simultaneously, thus questioning the 'narratability' of the world, or at least opening up the possibility of synchronic histories that are not necessarily bound to any notion of telos. Many Aboriginal plays use this framework to enact ritual reappropriations of history, especially through Dreamtime stories and corroborees that stress the contemporaneity of past, present, and future (see H. Gilbert 1990; Tompkins 1993). Davis's Dancer in *The Dreamers*, for example, establishes points of contact and overlap between time frames. These ritualized moments tend to represent timelessness, or the state of being outside the time of every day life, so that a ceremonial catharsis of oppression is possible. Other plays, like Davis's *Kullark* (1982), use notions of synchronicity to speak their incompleteness by presenting in juxtaposition, many different voice fragments from history. This kind of narrative depends on what Robert Kroetsch calls an archaeological sense of history in that 'every unearthing is problematic, tentative, subject to a story-making act that is itself subject to further change as the "dig" goes on' (1989: 24).

Performance techniques such as improvization aid the production of oral discourse that avoids fixing its trajectory in time and/or space. Different versions of the Koolbardi and Wahrdung (magpie and crow) story in Davis's plays also illustrate the importance of extemporization and elaboration in oral narrative. Along with verbal variability, new twists to the story's delivery stress guardianship rather than ownership of oral material and problematize ideas of authenticity and original composition. Hence, as Finnegan argues, performance lessens the split, characteristic in writing, between composition and transmission of narrative forms (1976: 7–9).

Self-referentially, story-telling in theatrical contexts foregrounds the role of the viewer/listener functions in de-scribing orality as it frequently situates an audience onstage as well as in the auditorium. The onstage audience often consists of children and usually shares the culture of the story-teller, emphasizing the alienation of the 'real' (mostly non-Aboriginal) viewers. Members of fictional audiences in Aboriginal drama are never passive listeners; they interject, ask questions, and make corrections to performers' versions of stories, further de-authorizing the text. Meta-dramatic emphasis on audience also occurs when characters deliberately position themselves as speakers to the larger audience. Jack Davis and Bob Maza use white speakers ironically to give historical addresses, implying audience collusion in colonization. Black speech-givers, on the other hand, tend to have a more antagonistic relationship with the audience which is in keeping with certain kinds of traditional oral expression such as fliting (the ceremonial exchange of insults) in which speech is a conspicuously aggressive weapon. In such practices, Ong (following Malinowski) argues, language is more obviously a 'mode of action' than a 'countersign of thought' (1982: 32).

If 'rhetoric . . . is essentially antithetical [because] the orator speaks in the face of at least implied adversaries' (Ong 1982: 111), Merritt's Sweet William is perhaps the paradigmatic Aboriginal orator. His rhetoric is designed to unsettle audience members, to make them aware of their prejudices, and to intervene in the illusionistic signifying processes of realist theatre. To a certain extent, his oratory 'alienates' Aboriginality, thus exposing it as an ideology that is mapped across the body as a system of beliefs and behaviours. This ideology reflects the dominant group's expectations and status quo as much as any essential identity. Sweet William's disingenuous pose as an 'authentic' boomerang-throwing Aborigine, for example, explicitly makes the audience complicit in the discourses of tourism, at the same time as it *im*plicitly subverts the voyeuristic conventions of both tourism and theatre.

I have thus far frequently referred to 'audience' as if it is comprised of a homogeneous group, which is a gross simplification. Responses to oral discourses are likely to differ greatly between Aborigines and whites as well as among class, age, and gender groups. I can't speak for the Aboriginal audience, but I will discuss briefly some important issues that arise *apropos* of the white viewer and the institutional structures affecting the production and consumption of Aboriginal performances as commercial theatre. If the process of 'linguistic capture' has limited what can be said by indigenous peoples since Prospero first taught Caliban 'how to curse', the agency of a majority audience has also limited what can be heard, where, and within what contexts. Although I have postulated that the temporality of oral performance resists the priority of writing, there are, however, many other written texts – programme notes, reviews, photographs, advertisements – that act as authoritative mediating devices in the reception of minority group performances. Following Penny Van Toorn's arguments, these texts could be categorized as 'patron discourses', 'metalanguages' that add value to minority texts by referring them to other sign systems operating in the dominant culture (1990: 109–11), in this case those relating to the conventions of commercial theatre. Van Toorn's concern about these patron discourses focuses on their tendency to situate alterity within dominant 'interpretive codes and evaluative criteria' (ibid.: 108). But, as she also points out, such discourses occupy a politically ambiguous position since they also function as possible modes of empowerment if appropriated by the minority to valorize their own texts (ibid.: 112).

The problem of how orality is articulated and received in the nexus of power through which colonial theatre operates can be partly understood in terms of the carnivalesque. Carnival rejoices in the hybridization of forms and languages that I have talked about, the bricolage, the fragmentation, the trickery, the collapsing of boundaries which occurs when spaces designated as stage and auditorium become interchangeable. But, the freedom which carnival implies is by no means complete or permanent. As Stephen Slemon has pointed out, 'the practice of Carnival articulates a double movement of obeisance and transgression' (1988: 68) in that the purchase it seeks to obtain against hegemony also reveals the limits of its possibility. In the context of Aboriginal theatre, this double movement is indicative not only of how orality resists inscription but also of how it is inevitably circumscribed by the superstructures of our society. The political effects of orality will be located in the interrelationships between these two movements until Aborigines have control over their own means of production of such discourses. Within this system, orality should not be relegated to the realm of the archaized pre-literate or seen as a defining Aboriginal characteristic, for that naturalizes the dominance of literacy and keeps the grounds for racism intact. Rather, orality is a practice and a knowledge, a strategic device potentially present in recuperating indigenous voices, potentially effective in de-scribing empire.[10]

NOTES

1 For a more comprehensive discussion of these concepts see Ashcroft *et al.*, (1989: 33–7), and Brydon (1991: 191–6).
2 I am grateful to Brian Edwards for provoking me to consider the idea of orality and the 'unwritable' in terms of Derrida's work. Although Derrida makes an important point in arguing that language 'implies an originary writing' (1976: 52) in the sense that signification is inscribed through the senses in a space that is exterior to thought, his valorization of the idea of writing does not take into account the differences between visual and aural signs, nor does it consider the political and cultural effects of writing on the oral. In claiming that 'oral language already belongs' to writing (ibid.: 53), Derrida is surely speaking from the perspective of the literate for whom speech is irrevocably linked to its hypothetical visual transformations in writing.
3 Shoemaker (1989: 132–3), Goldie (1988: 72), Scott (1990: 127), and

Nelson (1990: 33), for example, all argue for the mobilization of drama as enabling an authentic Aboriginal voice, but they do not deal substantially with the theoretical aspects of the oral or of performance.

4 I use 'muted' in Showalter's terms to suggest mediation rather than full silencing. Working through Ardener's concepts, Showalter explains that the term 'muted' suggests 'problems both of language and of power' because 'dominant groups control the forms or structures in which consciousness can be articulated' (1981: 200).

5 Although Nowra is not Aboriginal, he collaborated with Justine Saunders and other Aborigines in the adaptation of the novel *Capricornia* to develop a text which uses orality as a political strategy. I therefore regard his play as providing sites of resistance for Aboriginal voices.

6 See Elam for a discussion of these distinctions in dramatic discourse (1980: 144–8), and Muecke (1983b: 72–3) who applies Benveniste's theories to Aboriginal oral narrative.

7 As I have written elsewhere on the dance in Aboriginal drama (Gilbert 1992) my discussion here is cursory.

8 I am grateful to Leigh Dale for alerting me to the use of this innovative technique. The formal venue (the proscenium-arched Playhouse) of the 1990 Perth production situated performance within more conventionally delineated actor/audience spaces.

9 George (1989) discusses theatre in relation to the liminal realm posited by quantum physics and thus argues potentiality as one of performance's most striking characteristics.

10 This description of orality relates to Muecke's arguments on nomadology as a practice (Benterrak *et al*. 1984: 217) and to Arthur's idea of nomadic reading which 'roam[s] randomly *between* positions, . . . causing multiple fractures and disruptions' to existing orders (1989: 39).

Part III

READING EMPIRE

8

INSCRIBING THE EMPTINESS
Cartography, exploration and the construction of Australia

Simon Ryan

Although maps offer themselves as primarily mimetic, functional tools, the inevitable selectivity of what they record and their normal reference to that most vital of individual and national empowerments, land, make them a crucial and fascinating element in the project of Empire. The process of colonial inscription begins even before the arrival of the explorers who prepare maps of the country for subsequent settlement. For their practices, their ways of seeing – and hence selecting – detail to be recorded, are predefined not just by the centuries-old traditions of European map-making but also by the ideology of the expansionist colonialism which they serve.

Despite this inherent relativity, however, conventions concerning the production and interpretation of maps evaluate them almost exclusively in terms of 'accuracy' – a concept fraught with problems. Traditionally, historians of cartography have castigated certain categories of maps as compilations of hypotheses and suppositions rather than as veracious representations (Beazley 3: 528). This argument implies a progressivist, teleological view of mapping, that is, that cartography is working towards perfectly accurate representation, and establishes a valorized hierarchy which privileges one mode of representation (European, mimeticist and realist) over alternate modes. Thus, not only are non-European cartographies such as those used by Polynesians and Aborigines ignored, but those elements within the Western cartographical tradition which can be labelled 'inaccurate' are assigned to marginal areas of 'myth', 'imaginary geography' or simply 'obsolescence'. This critical stance insists on the anteriority of the 'real' while reducing the map to a purely transparent or mimetic re-present-ation of this reality. Constructing maps as innocently mimetic

115

ignores the fact that maps are productions of complex social forces; they create and manipulate reality as much as they record it.

My central point in this paper is that the cartographic practice of representing the unknown as a blank does not simply or innocently reflect gaps in European knowledge but actively erases (and legitimizes the erasure of) existing social and geo-cultural formations in preparation for the projection and subsequent emplacement of a new order. The antipodality of Australia joins with its construction as a *tabula rasa* to produce the continent as an inverted, empty space desperately requiring rectification and occupation.

J.B. Harley (1988: 278) points out that there are advantages to be gained when 'maps cease to be understood primarily as inert records of morphological landscapes or passive reflections of the world of objects, but are regarded as refracted images contributing to dialogue in a socially constructed world'. The rejection of the reflectionist or mimetic model of cartography renders irrelevant the question of whether certain maps are accurate. Instead of reinscribing the old dialectic of subject/object in empiricist terms it is more useful to see mapping as temporally embedded and transformative of previous discourses, rather than as an innocent inscription started afresh on blank paper. A critical move of this nature avoids comparing maps to a pre-existing normative 'real', but instead interrogates the mimetic assumptions they embody. The crucial step in deconstructing mimeticist claims is the realization that the given 'reality' is as socially-constructed as the representation, and operates in a way which not only legitimizes the representation but also enables the self-privileging of Western modes of knowledge.

Historically, maps and other cartographic representations have served as symbolic icons of power – the Holy Roman Emperor Charles IV is depicted holding a tripartite globe signifying political dominance (Harley and Woodward 1987: plate 10) – the thirteenth-century Ebstorf *mappamundi* is structured by the body of Christ, whose left hand reaches to embrace even the twenty-four monstrous races of the antipodes (ibid.: 291, 310). The proprietorial relationship that the Emperor has with the globe suggests the picture acts as a projection of imperial power and offers an implicit argument that Charles IV is the rightful ruler of the globe he holds; the body of Christ in the Ebstorf map creates a world structurally dependent on Christ, and by extension on his earthly institution, the Church. The map projects the inevitability of the institution's homogenizing rule – Christ's reaching left hand is perhaps a sinister prefiguration of the missionary project. Maps also became directly involved in political rivalries. The most obvious example of this is Pope Alexander's division of the New World in two, an operation which was entirely cartographic, ignoring geographical and indigenous differences in favour of a solution which reflected the European balance of power. The reaching hand of Christ and the apparent inconsequentiality of indigenous and geographic differences to the division of the New World are evidence of the powerful homogenizing effect of maps. The 'universal' applicability of one cartographic practice allows the transportation of power to a world-wide empire where maps perform the function of allowing power to be 'gained, administered, given legitimacy, and codified' (Harley and Woodward 1987: 506).

The implicit claims of maps to accuracy are undercut by the fact that they are embedded in a continually transformative discourse, and thus they tend to utilize obsolete forms. A network of classical and medieval myths are found in explorer's constructions of Australia, and especially in the metaphoric references to mapping within the text. The pre-discovery European mythic construction of Australia needs to be examined in terms of Europe's 'othering' the rest of the world. The imaginative construction of a *terra australis*, an antipodean continent which served to balance the Eurasian landmass, was not simply the result of an aesthetic or pseudo-scientific desire for symmetry. Nor was it some charming but errant myth, whimsically utilized in the early European responses to Australia, but soon discarded for more realistic appraisals. Brian Elliott (1966: 51) has recognized that the word 'antipodes' still carries 'hints of oddity, of perverse variations from the civilized norm'. The 'antipodality' of the Australian continent should be seen as part of the impulse of 'othering', the simultaneous recognition and disavowal of difference that characterizes imperial/colonial relations. The cartographic discourse that gives rise to the notion of the antipodes begins long before the expansion of European empires, but is both part of the imaginative preparation for Empire and an aspect of its administration.

Macrobian zonal maps provide a useful introduction to the ways in which cosmological formulations create imaginary geographies. Ambrosius Theodosius Macrobius (or Macrobes) (AD 399–422) revived Crates' notions of an equatorial ocean dividing the earth's north and south land masses (see Figure 8.1). In his *Commentary on the*

Figure 8.1 Macrobius's mappamundi with equatorial ocean. From Macrobius's *In somnium Scipionis exposito*, 1485. Reproduced by permission of the Huntington Library, San Marino, California.

Dream of Scipio, Macrobius (1952) presents the southern hemisphere as basically isomorphic of the northern. The difficulty faced by Macrobius' proposal was, of course, that which faced all pre-Newtonian theories propounding the sphericity of the earth – why the people on the other side did not fall off. Macrobius neatly combats this by sidestepping the question of gravity and instead repeating his geographic isomorphism in terms of the thoughts of the antipodal inhabitants.

> I can assure you that the uninformed among them think the same thing about us and believe that it is impossible for us to be where we are; they too, feel that anyone who tried to stand in the region beneath them would fall.
>
> (1952: 204)

This is a successful rhetorical defence against the doubters, but it is also a very early example of the European assumption of homogeneous ways of thinking that forms one of the structures of othering. Richard Brome's play, *Antipodes*, written in 1636, similarly constructs the southern hemisphere as isomorphic of the northern:

> They walk upon firm earth, as we do here,
> And have the firmament over their heads,
> As we have here . . .
>
> (1967: I.vi.90–2)

The idea of the existence of an antipodal region was sometimes rejected as perverse or irrational. Lucretius characterized the theory of the antipodes as the result of 'twisted reason' (1947: ll. 1072–3), while Cosmas Indicopleustes, an Egyptian monk writing in the sixth century, asserted:

> But should one wish to examine more elaborately the question of the Antipodes, he would easily find them to be old wives' fables. For if two men on opposite sides placed the soles of their feet each against each, whether they chose to stand on earth, or water, or air, or fire, or any other kind of body, how could both be found in the natural upright position, and the other, contrary to nature head downward. Such notions are opposed to reason, and alien to our nature and condition.
>
> (1967: 17)

The pervertedness of the idea of the antipodes translated easily into the idea that the antipodes, if they existed, were a place of perversion. Even the common argument for rejecting the existence of antipodes – that its inhabitants would have their feet where their heads should naturally be – becomes a sign of moral perversion. Tommaso Campanella's socialist utopian story, *The City of the Sun* (1623), includes a list of penalties the imaginary antipodean society imposes on aberrant behaviour. Those who are homosexuals are 'made to walk about for two days with a shoe tied to their necks as a sign that they perverted natural order, putting their feet where the head belongs' (Foss 1986: 85). Published long after many voyages south of the equator, the story can still utilize the easy transference from antipodes as opposite to antipodes as perverse.

Such projections of antipodal reversal and perversion abound. For Brome, at the antipodes the natural order is reversed so that women overrule the men, parents and masters obey the child and servant (1967: I.vi.127), and, in a reflection of Campanella's alignment of

119

antipodality with sexual irregularity, the 'wives lie uppermost' (I.vi.142).

Australia's natural perversity was, of course, one of the central tropes of early European landscape description. The animals were seen as bizarre, the trees peculiar and even monstrous, the vegetation continually green; indeed the country in its entirety seemed to be the product of whimsy and an affront to good taste. The French explorer, M.F. Péron, evinced considerable dismay at the failure of the Blue Mountains to cool the wind which passed over them. That mountains cool air was

> so natural and so conformable to all the principles of natural philosophy, that it would seem not to admit of any kind of modification; and, nevertheless, it receives, in the case in question, the most decided and absolute exception; as if the atmosphere of New Holland, as well as the animals and vegetables of this singular continent, has its peculiar laws . . .
>
> (1809: 291)

The antipodal positioning of Australia had set up a number of paradigms into which the land, the animals and the inhabitants could be placed. Tropes of oddity characterized nineteenth-century writing about Australia – trees shed their bark instead of their leaves, the bees were stingless, mammals had pouches. (Sometimes the fauna fell neatly into the constructions that had been made for them – a character in Brome's 1636 play, *Antipodes*, had asked 'are not their swans all black' (I.vi.157), a prediction that was to be confirmed empirically.) Yet the very 'perversity' of the land and the animals posed a challenge to the geography and the Linnaean biology of the time. Péron notes that the continent's peculiar laws 'differ from all the principles of our sciences and all the laws of our systems' (1809: 291) and that 'experience of every kind is always to be overturned in this singular part of the world' (ibid.: 307–8). Likewise, Oxley remarks that

> the whole form, character, and composition of this part of the country is so extremely singular, that a conjecture on the subject is hardly hazarded before it is overturned; everything seems to run counter to the ordinary course of nature in other countries.
>
> (1820: 81)

For biologists, however, Australian fauna and flora's stubborn refusal to fit into existing Linnaean categories meant the necessity for a paradigm shift in their discipline. White (1981: 9) and Serle (1973: 5) have both noted that the scientists who contributed to the obsolescence of the 'great chain of being' biology – Darwin, T.H. Huxley and J.D. Hooker – all visited Australia.

The increasing trend towards the consideration of the relationship between animals and their environment was, in part, a result of the novel flora and fauna of the southern continent. But the construction of the land, and particularly its inhabitants, as perverse, demonstrates the ease with which biological theories could be transformed for political use. As late as 1927 the anthropologist Baldwin Spencer could argue that the Aboriginal race was as perverse and outmoded as Australian fauna.

> Australia is the present home and refuge of creatures, often crude and quaint, that have elsewhere passed away and given place to higher forms. This applies equally to the aboriginal as to the platypus and kangaroo.
>
> (Markus 1990: 38)

In Spencer's formulation, the Aborigines have survived only because they have been sheltered from the progressive outside world, and their 'extinction' is naturalized through an implicit mobilization of the inevitability of evolution. George Grey, musing on the future of Australia, establishes the Aborigine as just as perverse as any other fauna.

> I sat in the fading light, looking at the beautiful scenery around me, which now for the first time gladdened the eyes of Europeans; and I wondered that so fair a land should only be the abode of savage men; and then I thought . . . of their *anomalous* position in so fertile a country, – and wondered how long these things were to be.
>
> (Grey 1841: 1, 207; my emphasis)

The perversity or anomalousness of the antipodean Aborigine stands in the way of the inevitable progress of white civilization. The lack of a recognizable agriculture, an obvious exploitation of the land, is constructed as a perversity associated with the Aborigines, and this perversity justifies the 'corrective' imperial enterprise. It is not surprising that the colonization process should activate the discourse of antipodeanism that works in its favour nor that from the earliest age of imperial expansion the antipodes has been seen as a legitimate field for ambition. Marlowe's Tamburlaine swears that

> . . . when holy Fates
> Shall stablish me in strong Egyptia,
> We mean to travel to th' Antarctic pole,
> Conquering the people underneath our feet . . .
>
> (1981: IV.iv.143–6)

The cartographic construction of the southern continent is bound up with questions of method, and what these methods of mapping claim to be able to represent. The concept, *terra australis*, must negotiate changing paradigms in map-making and the power structures which enable and licence these methods. The map in Figure 8.2 is an example of the tripartite T-O or *orbis terrarum mappamundi*, which shows the world divided into the three parts appropriated and occupied by the sons of Noah. The map is oriented towards the east, so Europe is on the bottom left.

There is a hybrid type of *mappamundi* which conflates the Macrobian zonal map and the tripartite T-O map which may be categorized as quadripartite. This type of world map retains the tripartite division of the northern hemisphere and adds a southern hemispheric continent. The so-called Beatus maps, the characteristics of which can be traced back to the *Commentary on the Apocalypse of Saint John,* are often of this type. In them a fourth continent is placed on the far right (south) of the map. Woodward translates the inscription on the otherwise blank antipodal continent on a Turin copy of the map thus:

> outside the three parts of the world there is a fourth part, the farthest from the world, beyond the ocean, which is unknown to us on account of the heat of the sun. We are told that the Antipodeans, around whom revolve many fables, live within its confines.
>
> (Harley and Woodward 1987: 304)

Increasing merchant activity created demand for new, accurate maps, but the old structures remained surprisingly resilient. The mercatorial revolution in cartography offered a system for representing relative distance more accurately, but retained the notion of an antipodal balancing landmass. Mercator's 'World Chart' of 1569 declares that 'under the Antarctic Pole [lay] a continent so great that, with the southern parts of Asia, and the new

Figure 8.2 Isidorian T-O map. From Isadore of Seville, *Etymologiarum Sive Originum, Libri XX*, Augsburg, 1472. By courtesy of the John M. Wing Foundation, The Newberry Library, Chicago (Inc. 1532).

India or America, it should be a weight equal to other lands' (Skelton 1958: 193–4). The tenacity of this idea can be seen when Alexander Dalrymple combines it two centuries later with Newtonian astronomy. He argued that the southern landmass must exist to 'counterpoise the land on the North, and to maintain the equilibrium necessary for the earth's motion' (ibid.: 229). One reason for the imperiousness of the idea of the great southern land was that it provided a site of European fantasy and desire. Mercator's 1569 map had a legend describing one area of the southern landmass, 'Beach', as a land of gold, and the neighbouring 'Maletur' as a land of spices (ibid.: 14).

Mercator's formalization of the cartographic paradigm in which European discovery was enacted, did not, then, destroy the impulse to imagine and fantasize. The south land was thus at once unknown and known, a contradiction which evoked this complaint from one of Mercator's contemporaries:

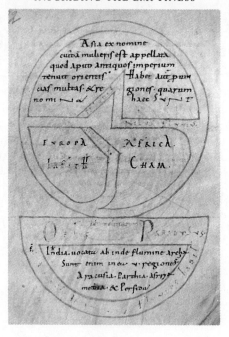

Figure 8.3 Isidorian T-O map with antipodal continent. By courtesy of the Stiftsbibliothek, Einsiedeln, Switzerland (Cod. Eins. 263(973)).

It hath ever offended mee to look upon the Geographicall mapps, and find this: Terra Australis, nondum Cognita. The unknowne Southerne Continent. What good spirit would but greeve at this? If they know it for a Continent, and for a Southerne Continent, why doe they call it Unknowne? But if it bee unknowne; doe all the Geographers describe it after one form and site?

(Hall 1605: 12)

This cartographic double movement, of erasure and projection, creating a blank, and filling that blank with a legend (both in the sense of a myth and a cartographical inscription) continued into the eighteenth century. The map-maker Emmanuel Bowen produced in 1744 a map of Australia which shows the collision between the evolving claims for accuracy and the use of new discoveries as sites for mythic projections. There are two legends spread across the otherwise blank outline of what was known of the continent. The first emphasizes the accuracy of the cartographic reproduction:

This map is very exactly copied from the original and therefore the Dutch names have been preserved . . . the reader is desired to observe that nothing is marked here but what has has [sic] been actually discovered.

(Tooley 1979: plate 12)

The second and rather longer legend creates the southern continent as a place of great and readily accessible riches. It provides a patina of scientific justification by pointing to the equally rich countries sharing the same latitude. Swift had satirized this practice of using the blank areas on maps as an area for fantasy.

> So Geographers in *Afric* – Maps
> With Savage – Pictures fill their Gaps;
> And o'er uninhabitable Downs
> Place elephants for want of towns
>
> (1983: 526)

Bowen had not used the blank spaces on the Australian map for simple pachydermal fancies, however, but rather to project the possibility of profit from, and control of, the new land.

It is impossible to conceive a country that promises fairer its situation, than this of Terra Australis; no longer incognita, as this map demonstrates, but the Southern Continent discovered . . . whoever perfectly discovers & settles it will become infalliably [sic] possessed of territories as rich, as fruitful, & as capable of improvement, as any that have been hitherto found out . . .

(Tooley 1979: plate 12)

To realize the possible profits it was necessary, as Bowen notes, to discover the continent. The complex arguments about which Europeans first visited Australia are too well known to be repeated here. What is of more interest is how the outline of Australia, once formed in maps by a thin line and a halo of names, is filled in by the terrestrial explorers.

As the discipline of surveying leads the explorers to valorize verticality over horizontality of landscape, so too does it encourage them to see the land as a system of signs, or as a language. This might initially seem an innocent activity, and certainly one of immediate practical benefit. If signs such as a line of gum trees, a bird flying in a particular direction, or the presence of a certain formation of land can be interpreted correctly then it is possible to determine the probability, existence, or location of water. The explorers' production of the land as a system of signs provides a method for determining the nature and geological history of the land as well as what their next advance should be. Trees become a sign of water, hot winds the sign of a desert, sand hills the signs of an inland sea.

The exploration journals often favour more specifically linguistic notions of earth as a text, similar to those of the immaterialist philosopher Bishop Berkeley who argued that objects of vision 'constitute a universal language of the Author of nature' (1948: 1, 231). Ernest Giles proposes that explorers must be expert in reading 'characters in the book of Nature' (1889: 2, 200), while Charles Sturt reiterates that God is the author of nature in Australia, despite its apparent peculiarities (1849: 2, 21).

To posit the land as a text is to claim its readability, and thence to arrogate power over it. Gayatri Spivak observes that the assumption of an uninscribed earth enables the 'worlding a world' (1985b: 133). The textualization of the landscape by the explorers reifies space as a blank text, ready to be inscribed by the impending colonial process. Maps themselves have played a significant role in the visual production of the continent as a *tabula rasa*, for cartographical emptiness is not simply a display of geographical ignorance but a statement of economic and demographic availability.

The blanks in the maps included in the journals reveal the constant selection of knowledges considered appropriate for display. They consistently efface the Aboriginal groups whom the explorers have contacted and about whom some knowledge is possessed, while carefully including locations of any white settlement. In this sense the maps produced by the explorers can be criticized as failing to reflect the land, but also failing to reflect the empirical knowledge produced by exploration. This is partially the fault of the map genre itself, as there was no readily available iconography which could indicate nomadic inhabitancy.[2] Politically, though, the map acts as an incitement to the alteration of ownership. Sturt rightly links the appropriation of knowledge with the appropriation of land:

> An ample field is open to enterprise and to ambition, and it is to be hoped that some more decisive measures will be carried into effect, both for the sake of the colony and of geography,

to fill up the blank upon the face of the chart of Australia, and remove from us the reproach of indifference and inaction.

(1833: 1, 160)

Ostensibly, the filling up of the blank will be a matter of exploration and discovery, but there is the intimation that the 'enterprise and ambition' may take the course of an energetic emplacement of civilization and the blank will be filled up this way. In their roles as surveyors, of course, the explorers did not just record the expansion but enabled it. The land's existence as *tabula rasa* for Mitchell is both cartographic and real – in fact there is little difference.

This territory, still for the most part in a state of nature, presents a fair blank sheet, for any geographical arrangement, whether of county divisions – lines of communication – or sites of towns.

(1839: 2, 333)

For surveying purposes the construction of the land as a blank sheet is necessary. In the erasure of the land not only is previous Aboriginal occupation and ownership ignored, but the land itself is inserted into a particular narrativization of history. A blank sheet, of course, intimates that there has been no previous history, but also teleologically constructs the future as a place/time for writing. These new inscriptions are firstly cartographical but also metaphorical of the transformation of the land by colonization – as I have shown, the cartographic inscriptions are not simply reflections of reality but organize and license the appropriation and exploitation of land.

The particular narrative of history the explorers construct positions them at the beginning of a long and glorious history. This is seen in a fetish for possession ceremonies as when Stuart hopes that the raising of the flag 'may be the first sign of the dawn of approaching civilization' (1865: 410). In following the course of the Peel River, Mitchell describes how he

advanced with feelings of intense interest into the country before us, and impressed with the responsibility of commencing the first chapter of its history. All was still new and nameless, but by this beginning, we were to open a way for the many other beginnings of civilized man, and thus extend his dominion over some of the last holds of barbarism.

(1839: 1, 36)

The privileging of written over oral history is here so strong that the existence of a history previous to white incursion is utterly effaced. Mitchell's emphasis on the 'nameless' nature of the *tabula rasa* he constructs is that of the map-maker. Naming is, of course, one of the prime aspects of cartography, and Paul Carter (1987), amongst others, has had much to say of interest on this topic. But cartography is especially important because it connects textual and material vectors of colonialism in a unique way. An inscription on a map is in some senses performative. As a plan it licenses material construction, and also monumentalizes that same construction. Mitchell boasts that he has 'written the name of Britain deeply in the rocks and mountains of Australia by the roads and passes already made' (Foster 1985: 170). On another occasion, however, he writes that 'I have written *my* name on the rocks and on the mountains of the country, so that they will be monuments of my labour' (ibid.: 151). Assuming that he is referring to his cartographic achievements rather than to graffiti, this is a revealing conflation of the imperial project with its textual agency. The explorer/surveyor in both recording and imposing reality, is not merely *reflecting* a material arrangement, but *enabling* it.

The idea of Australia as a *tabula rasa*, and the historicizing of this notion are by no means the province of explorers alone but were bequeathed to later generations. The idea can be found in fiction – in Catherine Martin's *An Australian Girl* (1890), for example, the narrator combines some of the commonplace descriptions of the country as a melancholy, monotonous waste with constructions of it as a *tabula rasa* awaiting future inscription:

> These great unpeopled spaces . . . call up thoughts of the early dawn of creation. Under some aspects, they are sombre in their monotony, melancholy in their primeval solitude; their strange silence weighs on the heart at times with a sense of indefinite anguish. It is as though one had come upon a waste world sealed against the traditions and presence of the human race. There is no trace of the immemorial past – no buried record of the ages that have gone. But the unstoried blank stirs the imagination curiously with dim guesses at the chronicles which may be written of this land in days to come.
>
> (1890: 2, 269)

The Aborigines and the signs of their existence are excluded from the construction of the land as text; thus when this text is read they are absent. The French-Australian writer Paul Wenz also activated the trope of a storyless Australia. History for Wenz is necessarily productive of myths and permanent structures. Australia is deficient in this regard as its

> forests are generally not dense enough to shelter elves or ghosts; no Red Ridinghood could gather strawberries in them, or meet a wolf or a doe in them, for the shade of the tall eucalyptuses is too scanty for strawberries; wolves and does have never existed in Australia. . . . There is no history; the childish primitive legends that peopled the great deserts died with the tribes. . . . In Australia there is a total lack of the ruins that are the tangible past, of the old castles and the old temples that form part of the history of a people.
>
> (cited in Friederich 1967: 202)

The land has not been written about, but it has also not been written *on* by its inhabitants. Wenz's description begs for deconstruction – how are the Aboriginal legends more 'childish' than Red Riding Hood? – but the denigration of aboriginal legends and the assumption of their disappearance with the presumed (and unexplained) extinction of their creators is simply another way of creating a *tabula rasa* from the land. The trope of Australia as a blank slate is also used by D.H. Lawrence to combine landscape, history and possibility in fine ambivalence:

> The soft, blue, humanless sky of Australia, the pale, white unwritten atmosphere of Australia. *Tabula rasa.* The world a new leaf. And on the new leaf, nothing. The white clarity of the Australian, fragile atmosphere. Without a mark, without a record.
>
> (1950: 365)

That Australia possesses the 'white clarity' of the empty page repeats exactly the explorers' descriptions of the land, but does so with far less confidence that a glorious destiny will be inscribed on it. The trope, then, has outlived its genesis and has even been deployed in a reverse way to assign the historied landscape to Aboriginal culture and the featureless tenure to European settlement. In 'Ordering the Landscape' Rhys Jones describes the reactions of a northern Australian Aborigine on seeing a large city (Canberra) for the first time.

> The idea of buying and selling land like any other commodity and of attachment to the land only as a matter of transient convenience was totally alien to Gurrmanamana, and he regarded it with a mixture of suspended belief and with some mild revulsion, as if there was something deeply wrong in this state of affairs. Here was a land empty of religious affiliation; there were no wells, no names of the totemic ancestors, no immutable links between land, people and the rest of the natural and supernatural worlds. Here was just a vast *tabula rasa*, cauterised of meaning.
>
> (Jones 1985: 207)

This is the kind of sentimentalist or nostalgic inversion of imperial crimes through which imaginary rectification of historic wrongs and therefore forgiveness are sought. In seeking some recuperation via inversion Rhys Jones' eurocentric construction of Gurrmanamana's response displays the depth of guilt associated with cartographic erasure that still exists within Australia.

NOTES

1 Excellent general accounts are found in: Skelton (1958), and Williams and Frost (1988). Wood (1922) sets out the traditional view of Dutch priority in discovery, and has been joined by Sigmond and Zunderbaan (1979) in arguing the Dutch claim. The case for Portuguese priority has been argued by Collingridge (1983) and by McIntyre (1977).
2 There had been some attempts at the cartographical representation of spatially stable populations in the early nineteenth century. Robinson (1982: 113) notes while the concept of population had been understood for a long time, no population map of any sophistication had appeared before 1828. These maps in any case could record only non-nomadic populations.

9

THE UNFINISHED COMMONWEALTH

Boundaries of civility in popular Australian fiction of the first Commonwealth decade

Robert Dixon

In his book, *Culture and Truth: The Remaking of Social Analysis* (1989), the anthropologist Renato Rosaldo calls for a new ethnography of the borderlands between cultures. Under classic norms, 'the borders between nations, classes, and cultures were endowed with a curious kind of hybrid invisibility'. Ethnographers now look 'less for homogeneous communities than for the border zones within and between them' (1989: 217). These cultural border zones, Rosaldo argues, are always in motion.

In this paper I want to use the thematics of travel and border zones to frame a reading of three early twentieth-century 'ripping yarns' of Empire: Alexander MacDonald's *The Island Traders* (1909), Ambrose Pratt's *The Big Five* (1911) and Louis Becke's *The Pearl Divers of Roncador Reef* (1908). These texts inhabit a number of border zones. They were written by travellers who often lived on the margins of respectability. Their characters are also on the move: on horseback, under sail, under steam, and even in the new motor cars and airships. They travel in the borderlands of the new Australian nation: in the Northern Territory, Far North Queensland and Melanesia. In developing notions of the frontier, adventure stories tend to follow classic norms, mythologizing what Peter Hulme has called 'the boundaries of civility' (1985: 26): they make visible the maintenance of discursive boundaries concerned with race, nation and gender.

Yet the frontier is not simply the site of national differentiation – it is also a site of border crossings. At a time when definitions of Australia' were in the process of formation, immigration and increasing fears of invasion threatened to blur and even rupture accepted definitions of race. The boundaries of Australian civility were permeable – to Aborigines, the French, the Germans and Melanesians. 'Ripping yarns' centre the nation by narrating it from the limits of its territory and civility. Yet these limits, as Homi Bhabha argues, are a difficult and 'heterogeneous' site inscribed by many voices (Bhabha 1990b: 301).

In September 1901, the Prime Minister of the new Commonwealth of Australia, Edmund Barton, sought from the British Government a political map of the South Pacific showing the existing claims of European powers. In a report to his West Maitland electors later that year, Barton expressed concern that the New Hebrides were still in dispute between Britain and France. 'Situated at no great distance from our coast, they are', he explained, 'a sort of no man's land' (cited in Meaney 1976: 95).

Barton's reading of the map from the Colonial Office is a synecdoche of Australian imperialism in the South Pacific: it constructs the nation by inscribing a frontier, beyond which it projects its own codes of representation onto the places and peoples there depicted. Gayatri Spivak has termed this process 'othering'. Spivak argues that Europe 'consolidated itself as sovereign subject by defining its colonies as "Others", even as it constituted them, for purposes of administration and the expansion of markets, into programmed near-images of that very sovereign self' (1985b: 128). Such acts of discursive projection are inherently unstable since they require as their impossible precondition the assumption of an 'uninscribed earth', the assumption that territory to be colonized is, in Barton's words, 'a sort of no man's land'.

Alexander MacDonald was one of the many Anglo-Australian writers who travelled in this 'no man's land'. His novel, *The Island Traders* (1909), draws upon the New Hebrides crisis of 1901–5. Australia resented French ambitions in the South Pacific, seeing French ports as bases from which attacks could be launched against the mainland. Commonwealth policy was to prevent the New Hebrides coming under exclusive French control; if needs be, it favoured annexation. *The Island Traders* deals with this threat to the nation's borders by rendering the islands 'uninscribed earth'.

MacDonald's young Australian hero, Raymond Fairfax, has just completed a degree at Sydney University majoring in the

Melanesian language Mota when he is recruited by Captain Murchison of the steamship *Mota* into an affair of espionage and military intrigue. The British Government will create a diversion by disavowing all interest in the New Scotias, a group of islands in the Western Pacific transparently based on the New Hebrides; meanwhile, Captain Murchison, disguised as a trader, will claim the group for Australia: 'Unlimited wealth . . . is placed at my disposal by a firm . . . [which] is the acting agent for the government, but it also really possesses great interests in the islands . . . and this trade it will lose should any foreign power annex [them]' (MacDonald 1909: 65). These details suggest the role of Burns, Philp and Company, which monopolized shipping to the New Hebrides. Wilson Le Couteur, Australia's first spy, travelled around the New Hebrides for several months posing as a Burns Philp agent and reporting on the French (Thompson 1980: 168). What is interesting here is the unquestioned conjunction of Commonwealth authority and private business interests.

On the New Scotias, Raymond uses his knowledge of Mota to impersonate the Melanesian chief Kalii, who lies bound and gagged aboard the Australian ship for collaborating with the Germans. Gail Ching-Liang Low argues that enactments of the fantasy of cross-cultural dressing are bound up with the libidinal economy of adventure stories (1990: 108). Paradoxically, young Raymond gets his manhood by consuming the status of the cannibal chief. But his cross-dressing is also an enactment of 'othering' in Spivak's sense. When German troops move to annex the New Scotias, Raymond, as Kalii, speaks for 'his people'. Dressed in Melanesian costume, his skin darkened with dye, and using the language he learned at Sydney University, Raymond pledges his people's loyalty to Australia, 'the young nation whose glorious destiny it is to rule the great south' (MacDonald 1909: 283), the land that freed them from slave labour and gave them 'all the good things the white man makes' (ibid.: 245). At the conclusion of Raymond's speech, the Melanesians cheer their chief, assuring him of their willingness 'to sweep the foreigner from existence' (ibid.: 246). This act of discursive projection involves a massive repression, since 'their chief' *is* the foreigner, an Australian filibuster come to annex the islands.

As 'Kalii' negotiates with the Germans, a company of French marines arrives with a machine gun (ibid.: 262). The three powers enact the conflict for Western control in the Pacific but the text must accept its own fiction, so the Australians' presence is concealed: the 'New Scotians' in the crowd are actually the crew of the *Mota* in disguise. The narrative turns at this point on the suspenseful 'absence' of the Australians. But they are already there – they are the 'natives'.

Just as the French and Germans are about to open fire, the army of another Melanesian chief, Tamii, rushes out of the forest to drive them away. Tamii is the supreme chief of the islands and the success of the Australian annexation depends on his approval. But the closing pages of the novel disclose another impersonation: Tamii is Captain Murchison's long-lost Scottish friend, Mac, a trader and adventurer with whom he first explored the islands years before. Believed missing in action against cannibals, Mac took on the White Man's Burden by impersonating a dead chief:

> as I hadna the heart to leave the puir ignorant and innocent folk without a chief, I had to tak' his job on myself . . . an' wi' ma friend Kalii an' me askin' for Australian protection, Australia shouldna hae much troubling o' conscience at annexing the islands.
>
> (ibid.: 289–90)

While acknowledging that it would be uncivilized of Australia simply to annex the New Scotias, the text seeks to justify that very act by having a Melanesian chief ask for Australian protection.

This sequence of impersonations is a striking enactment of 'othering': the definition of colonies as 'others', even as they are constituted, 'for the purposes of administration and the expansion of markets, into programmed near-images' of the self. In this way the text discloses the motive force of colonialism – free trade – which is embedded in its ambiguous title, *The Island Traders*. The traders of the title are not simply men who trade *among* the islands, but powerful political agents who literally trade *in* island nations. In the future, the New Scotias will become a private-enterprise colony protected by Commonwealth naval power (ibid.: 290). But the Melanesians, whom the text tells us were present at these events and invited this conclusion, were a significant absence in this act of colonial representation.

The map Edmund Barton obtained from the Colonial Office in 1901 empowered Australia as a sovereign nation by inscribing its boundaries and by rendering the New Hebrides beyond them 'uninscribed earth'. On 1 February 1909, the Sydney magazine *The*

Lone Hand published another map that was its negative or mirror image. With that issue there began a series of articles under the title, 'Our Unfinished Commonwealth'. On the cover was a map of Australia on which the Northern Territory was left blank. The article warned that the 'huge mass' of the Northern Territory is 'driven right into the heart of this our Australian Commonwealth', yet 'is no more a part of [it] than the New Hebrides' (*Lone Hand*, 1 February 1909: 374). Here, then, was another 'no man's land' that made the boundaries of the new nation porous. It was not, in fact, a blank space, but a difficult site of other inscriptions: it was 'an open portal, through which may sweep at any hour a tidal wave of coloured conquest, which, even if it receded, would leave our race so tainted that a thousand years would not remove the stain' (*Lone Hand*, 1 March 1909: 503).

These confused images of rape and emasculation remind us that borderlands not only surface *between* nations, but also *within* nations at the intersection of genders. The Asian menace was associated with another, domestic threat: the New Woman. Noting the connection between ideologies of race and gender, Chandra Mohanty (1988: 81) observes,

> It is only in so far as 'Woman' . . . and 'the East' are defined as *Others*, or as peripheral, that (western) Man/Humanism can represent him/itself as the centre. It is not the centre that determines the periphery, but the periphery that, in its boundedness, determines the centre.

In my second 'ripping yarn', those 'Others' – 'Woman' and 'the East' – contest the centre by breaching their proper boundaries.

Ambrose Pratt's novel, *The Big Five* (1911), was one of several 'invasion' narratives written by contributors to *The Lone Hand*.[1] It begins at the 'centre' of Australian civility by invoking the discourse of mateship. Having fallen on hard times, a gang of mates known as the Big Five come together for a last drink at the Australia Hotel in Sydney when Sir Philip Trevor invites them to form an expedition to Arnhem Land. This trope is conventional in imperialist romance, recalling the meeting of Allan Quartermain, Sir Henry Curtis and Captain Good in *King Solomon's Mines* (1886). The expedition will rejuvenate a threatened masculinity, saving the Big Five from the unmanly fate of 'stewing in a city office' (Pratt 1911: 15).

The Big Five are also drawn together by their opinions about men and women. Sir Philip Trevor is an English dandy whom McLean, the leader of the group, dismisses as 'a little begloved and dolled-up dude' (ibid.: 14). Like many Australian romances of this period, *The Big Five* feminizes the British gentleman, reflecting new imperialist assumptions about the declining moral fibre of the British and the vigour of the 'Coming Man'. Lady Trevor, on the other hand, who is to accompany the expedition, 'is an Amazon'. According to her husband, 'She has yet to learn the meaning of fear. She is an expert markswoman, and she can shoot her man without the least compunction' (ibid.: 27). This is why Sir Philip asks McLean to act as leader of the party. Twelve months earlier, on an expedition in Africa, Sir Philip lost the lives of ten men, including his best friend, because he allowed his wife to make the decisions. McLean is put in command of the present expedition to prevent this happening again. Lady Trevor is a problem the narrative must work to resolve. Like the recent film, *Crocodile Dundee* (1986), *The Big Five* must restore the conventional boundaries of male and female civility. This is best done on the borders of the nation's territory – the sort of country that is 'no place for a woman'.

At Port Darwin, McLean responds ambivalently to the north, sensing its otherness: 'It was hard to realise this wondrous place an undivided part of my native land' (ibid.: 86). He attributes this otherness to the 'inertia and ineptitude' of the people, qualities that properly belong to those beyond the bounds of Australian civility: women, British dandies and 'the Asiatic hordes so perilously near' (ibid.). In fact, the north has already been inscribed by those others.

McLean's discovery of an Asian colony in the middle of the Northern Territory confirms that boundaries have indeed been breached. Pratt here adapts to new use the conventions of the lost-race romance. Several hints earlier in the novel anticipate the discovery of a lost race (ibid.: 196). To readers of Haggard's *She* (1887) and *Allan Quartermain* (1887), or their numerous Australian imitations, these create expectations of a lost race living in the interior of Australia (Dixon 1993). But in Pratt's novel, they introduce a hidden settlement of Asian invaders.

No sooner does the party enter the settlement than Sir Philip Trevor is killed, and McLean and Molly, whom the Asians assume to be married, are captured. The captivity narrative is another convention of imperialist romance, and Pratt uses it for two of its usual purposes: to affirm the baseness and inferiority of the coloured races, and to bring about the moral reformation of the nonconforming white woman (Dixon 1986). Peter Hulme argues that repetition of such tropes in colonial discourse confirms, intertextually, readers' 'knowledge' of the 'other' (1985: 28). Racial stereotypes play a crucial role in maintaining discursive boundaries (Bhabha 1983), and the captivity trope is ideal for rehearsing stereotypical notions of both women and orientals. Tied to a post and drugged with opium, McLean observes his Malay and Chinese captors. The Malays are stereotypically short and savage, while the cowardly Chinaman is 'a large stout person, with a long pigtail, an immense stomach, and a round smooth oily face beaming with smiles' (Pratt 1911: 211). The object of their attentions, Lady Trevor, is bound and dishevelled, an icon of outraged Anglo-Saxon womanhood. The threat of miscegenation – essential to a captivity narrative – eats at McLean's mind as he views this scene and he vows, if needs be, to kill the woman he has come to love (ibid.: 217).

The tale closes with the rescue of McLean and Molly by the crew of Sir Philip's yacht. Molly Trevor has been punished sufficiently for her independence, and in response to torture and threats of rape has become more 'womanly'. As they leave Arnhem Land, McLean generously admits that he began to care for her even before she changed: 'The true woman in you must have spoken to my heart without my knowledge, perhaps without your own' (ibid.: 289). On their return to Sydney, a Commonwealth ship is sent north to destroy the Japanese consortium that has taken over from the Malays and Chinese. The bounds of Australian civility have now been repaired by the death of the English dandy, the expulsion of the Asians, the repentance of the new woman, and her marriage to the coming man.

The anxieties about race and gender manifest in *The Big Five* hollow out the colonial discourse evident in *The Island Traders* by disallowing the construction of a 'no man's land' that is truly blank or uninscribed. Yet both narratives eventually work to reinscribe the boundaries of nation, race and gender. This is not the case with my third 'ripping yarn', Louis Becke's *The Pearl Divers of Roncador Reef and Other Stories* (1908), which, for that reason, invites rereading as a post-colonial text. Becke's own relation to the metropolitan culture was notoriously ambivalent and several of his stories turn on a recognition that the boundaries of civility are, as Bhabha argues, a difficult and 'heterogeneous' site inscribed by other voices.

The short story 'For the Benefit of Sailors' Kids' is set in far north Queensland. Sailing north between Port Douglas and Cooktown, Tom Drake and his crew spend a day fishing and hunting on a river near Cape Tribulation where they discover the bodies of two diggers in a camp site littered with gold nuggets and Chinese artefacts. They conclude that these were the murderers of some missing Chinese, now murdered themselves by myall blacks.

Tom Drake is at first distanced from the chaos of the frontier by his association with government. His ship has been 'chartered by the naval authorities at Sydney to take a cargo of coal to Cooktown . . . for the use of one of Her Majesty's ships then engaged on the New Guinea survey' (Becke 1908: 141). The New Guinea survey inscribes the metropolitan culture upon the blank sheet of colonial territory. Sydney and New Guinea delineate the centre and margin of the text's discursive space. Far north Queensland, 'a sort of no man's land' between them, is a border zone where the boundaries of civility cannot be maintained.

Metropolitan categories begin to haemorrhage when Drake runs into an officer of the Native Police. The officer's task of patrolling boundaries in the new territory is another synecdoche of the colonial economy. His instructions are to patrol only along the northern bank of the river, since 'the other side and all the coast southward is in charge of another sub-inspector, who patrols the Cardwell . . . District' (ibid.: 145). Yet for all this precision of inscription, the boundaries are fluid. As the narrator acknowledges, 'Great confusion existed as to the names of these rivers. . . . Some of them had half a dozen names, each party of cedar-getters who entered a river giving it a name of their own choosing' (ibid.: 142).

The officer also deconstructs the opposition between white and black. He not only lives with Aborigines, but is coming to look like one: 'the swarthy-faced sub-inspector trotted off, followed by his sooty-faced blue-uniformed Danites [the black native police]' (ibid.: 146). Racial categories are deconstructed with stunning clarity when he explains, 'It is not always the niggers who murder these gold-carrying Chows – take away the "n" from niggers, and substitute a "d," and you'll get at the truth' (ibid.: 147).

Drake and his mates enter this chaos the moment they discover the bodies of the white diggers. The camp site is a scene of confusion, 'the bodies, or rather skeletons, of two human beings, lying amongst a heap of articles – broken spears, torn clothing, saddles, boots, and battered prospecting dishes' (ibid.: 150). Drake's problem is to separate the gold which lies scattered about the camp site mixed with dirt. His solution is to carry a boat-load of earth back to the ship and pan it out on deck, but as they return to the ship the lust for gold once more turns 'diggers' into 'niggers': 'the crew took to the paddles, and sent the deeply-laden boat down the river, Drake and the officer, too excited to talk, paddling with their brown-skinned shipmates' (ibid.: 154).

Despite this final attempt to separate categories, the story ends with their collapse, as the authority of government invoked at the beginning is comprehensively debunked at the end. When the mates discuss whether to turn the gold over to the Curator of Intestate Estates, they realize that only the Government coffers will be enriched (ibid.: 156). Rather than surrender the gold, they keep it for themselves and, as a concession to their consciences, give a small percentage to a home for sailors' children. In keeping for himself a share of the gold, which is 'damning proof of the guilt of the prospectors' (ibid.: 155), Tom Drake enters the border zone where 'diggers' become 'niggers'. As Becke notes in another story, all money circulating in the colonies 'bore upon it, metaphorically if not literally, the stain of blood' (ibid.: 162). The figure of circulation is indeed an apt one for Becke's frontier. His text offers several figures for colonial inscription: the New Guinea Survey, the naming of rivers, the patrolling of territorial limits. But in the end they are all undone by the promiscuous circulation of gold, which acknowledges no boundaries.

These three 'ripping yarns' of the first Commonwealth decade confirm the importance of uncanonical texts to historians of colonial discourse. As Gayatri Spivak argues, colonial inscription takes place throughout the entire archive of the imperial power: its 'agents . . . are not only great names . . ., but small unimportant folk [as well]' (1985b: 133). The copy of *The Island Traders* in the James Cook University Library was originally owned by one of these small, unimportant folk – it was presented to a teenage boy in 1910 by his priest at Christian Brother's College, Melbourne, on the occasion of his going abroad. This ship-board reading formed a discursive space in which ideas about his nation, his gender, his 'race' and the people he would encounter abroad could be actively defined through fantasy.

Yet in allowing the enactment of such fantasies, 'ripping yarns' help us both to understand and undermine the boundaries of civility. They confirm Renato Rosaldo's arguments that 'the fiction of the uniformly shared culture' seems increasingly tenuous; that 'more often than we . . . care to think, our everyday lives are crisscrossed by border zones . . . and eruptions of all kinds' (1989: 207). Such border zones, as Bhabha observes, are a difficult site from which to narrate the nation: constructed as a 'no man's land', they are already inscribed by other voices. As a consequence, these texts are impossible to read without displacements and disavowals: 'diggers' become 'niggers', white men become effeminate, orientals make successful colonists, and women behave like 'Amazons'. It is these moments of uncertainty that make 'ripping yarns' worth re-reading today as, in the Middle East, the Pacific and elsewhere, the West continues to narrate its identity through adventures conducted abroad.

NOTES

1 *The Big Five* was serialized in *The Lone Hand* in 1907 and published in book form in 1911. Other 'invasion narratives' include 'The Commonwealth crisis', by C.H. Kirmess, serialized in 1908 and published as *The Australian Crisis* in 1909; and Randolph Bedford's melodrama *White Australia*, first performed in Melbourne on 27 February 1909.

10

'THE SOFTEST DISORDER'
Representing cultural indeterminacy

Fiona Giles

This essay addresses the entangled relations of post-colonial female subjectivity by considering an Australian nineteenth-century text (Tasma's *The Penance of Portia James*, 1891) which has been excluded from the discourse of cultural difference and post-colonialism. The central argument is that the heroine is situated obliquely between the positions of colonial Anglo-Australian, nationalist Australian and colonizing Anglo-Saxon, without unequivocally occupying any position, thus suggesting that each of these positions is historically determined, conditional and changing. In an earlier paper (Giles 1989) the term enjambement was used to describe the subject-position between these categories which are themselves in movement, resulting in the quest to occupy a transcendent or culturally neutral space. In her quest for this space, the heroine of Tasma's romance is engaged in a series of sacrifices – of romantic love, cultural affiliation and discourse itself. The key words to describe the condition of the enjambed heroine are movement, silence, and indeterminacy.

Two questions raised by Homi Bhabha in a recent paper are useful in reading a text which has been excluded from the Australian canon on the grounds that it is insufficiently nationalist and from the English canon since it is insufficiently located within an Anglo-Celtic tradition. The first question, 'How do we begin to historicize the dehistoricized?' may be approached by returning to the text via a reading of the author's representation of herself as an enjambed heroine. Her persona may be regarded as a composite of her narrative voice and her public writing persona. Keeping an open mind on intentionality, it is possible to see that the author, Tasma, is presented in an image of non-compliance with any straightforward definition of nationality. Not unlike the heroine of her novel, The *Penance of Portia James*, Tasma as author-narrator presents an identity as it is caught in the act of resisting nationalist closure. Tasma thus becomes a heroine-as-narrator engaged in a romance quest not dissimilar to Portia's: both women grapple with the obstacles towards self-definition set up by an inadequate array of subject categories; and both resist a simple allegiance to any nation-state while also claiming recognition as civil subjects.

This leads to Bhabha's second question which may be useful in this context: 'What is the relation of the self to the otherness of the self's own history?' That is, where does Tasma as a woman and an author situate herself in relation to the two cultural options of Englishness and Australianness, where both of these are an inadequate representation of her cultural and political allegiance? The self that is assembled through the course of the romance is at odds with its cultural archive. As a result, the discourses available for its interpretation will also be inadequate. In this case, Tasma's disruption of nationalist expectations reveals that she is represent-ing herself both as a romance heroine who transcends culture, and as a historically contingent and multi-dimensional subject. Just as her fiction invites comparison with her personal experience, so her 'real' image as captured by photography or biography is presented as a fictional construct, an elaborate cultural joke.

Of the Australian women writers of the second half of the nineteenth century, Tasma represents the most personal and domestic edge of the feminine romance genre. As a genre, the romance is customarily seen to concern itself with the private realm, dramatizing an individualist quest for self-definition. It is typical of the reception of this body of literature, however, that its evident social dimension was overlooked. While romantic love may itself be interpreted as historically contingent, it is also clear that writers such as Catherine Helen Spence, Catherine Martin, and Rosa Praed, were politically aware if not actively engaged in politics, and included political issues within their novels. Many of the novels included direct reference to colonial politics, and introduced political conflict into the central relationship; others referred to politics abroad – for example, Martin's *An Australian Girl* (1890) – and many to black–white relations in the colonies. Nevertheless, they have been read by critics as dramas of a private, ahistorical realm.

In Tasma's case, critics seemed more determined than usual to deny her work any relevance to the public sphere and, by extension, any contribution to the development of national culture. The tendency was to favour texts which overtly endorsed an anti-British nationalism, particularly realist short stories about masculine rural life. Tasma wrote one or two short stories about mates in the bush, one of which was anthologized in the 1950s; but, together with many other novelists of the period, her work was dismissed in Australia as colonial by virtue of its female readership and ostensibly Anglo-Celtic generic traditions. In a climate promoting working-class, masculine, rural values, Tasma's fiction was not only regarded as middle-class, feminine and urban; it was also relegated to the non-literary realm of autobiography:

> In these novels the husband is invariably at fault for one reason or another – and for a different reason in each novel. Methinks the lady doth protest too much – it is some such reaction that a reader experiences. The parallel with her own unhappy first marriage is so close, almost so obsessive, that the novels give off a perceptible whiff of self-exculpation.
>
> (Beilby and Hadgraft 1979: 41–2)

H.M. Green expressed a similar objection, implying Tasma's need to draw from personal experience: 'she had not so fertile an invention, so that she soon ran out of material' (Green 1961: 253–4).

It was not just that the feminine romances (broadly defined, these include the work of Spence, Martin, Cambridge, and Praed) failed to conform to national-realism; they also failed to declare a cultural allegiance of *any* kind in an unqualified or unequivocal way. A reading which steps outside the critical standards of the 1890s can show how these writers nevertheless dealt with cultural difference. While they are distinct from the national-realist anti-British stance, their heroines are continually required to affirm or reject their nascent Australianness, most usually represented by the nationality of the man they choose to marry.

The quest structure of the romance is represented by movement and travel (analogous to personal progress) and accommodates each heroine's indecision, experimentation, and ambivalence. The heroine is often allowed experimental and *risqué* adventures, remaining virtuous as long as she is chaste and determined upon marriage in the end. The advantage of this often circuitous route towards closure is that it offers the heroine a 'metatemporal' quality, to use Paul Ricoeur's terminology, so that she endorses the position (or non-position) outside the available categories for identification.

143

Unlike the contemporary pattern of Mills and Boon romance, the marriage itself is rarely without serious qualification and usually at the cost of personal sacrifice so that even this category is only reluctantly occupied. Not unlike Said's figure in exile, the heroine is always in danger of being pulled back into a state of endless, contrapuntal mobility. Her refusal to settle (indeed, her reluctance to be a settler) exemplifies the cultural indeterminacy of these texts.

The historian Beverley Kingston has written that the history of Australian culture has largely been confused with a history of Australian nationalism (Kingston 1977: 157). Reception of Tasma's work is symptomatic of this tendency, leading to her expulsion from the canon on grounds which are collusively gendered and nationalist.[1] While it made the novels unappealing to critics and historians with a nationalist agenda, it is this instability which may now make them interesting to a post-colonial reader.

Rather than instability or indecisiveness, the refusal of strident nationalism may also be seen as an attempt to maintain a complexity of affiliation. In his Introduction to *Nation and Narration*, Homi Bhabha quotes Frantz Fanon's statement that 'National consciousness, which is not nationalism, is the only thing that will give us an international dimension' (Bhabha 1990a: 4). It is exactly this project – to describe a national consciousness which is not nationalism – which characterizes Tasma's fiction, and which is most particularly visible in her novel, *The Penance of Portia James* (1891). Other novels by Tasma, especially *Not Counting the Cost* (1895), also address this issue of finding a level of national consciousness which enables a sense of Australian nationality without sacrificing a connection to the international context.

As noted above, the photograph of Tasma (Figure 10.1) makes an autobiographical link between her life and her fiction (as have done earlier critics), but reveals Tasma's self-conscious play with cultural difference and ambiguity in the construction of her public image. The photograph accompanies an essay in a sesquicentennial volume celebrating Australian women pioneers (Eldershaw 1938). As a self-consciously nationalist publication, the layers of multi-cultural symbolism in this image may be read in a way which foregrounds the indeterminacy of images of the feminine in Australia.

A brief outline of Tasma's life shows that geographical place – and migration between places – was significant to both her personal life and career. Tasma's name (originally Jessie Huybers) refers to

Mme. Couvreur 'Tasma'

Figure 10.1 'Tasma'. By courtesy of the Fryer Memorial Library, University of Queensland (PIC 120).

the island of Tasmania where she lived with her family as a child after migrating from London, and she retained this name for authorship. She left her first husband (an Australian) after they lived together in the Victorian rural area of Kyneton. She then travelled to Europe (where she had already spent some time) and married the Belgian journalist and politician Couvreur. They lived in Belgium (another marginalized culture, relative to France) and she took on his job as correspondent to *The Times* after his death, having previously worked as a freelance journalist. She died in Europe in 1897 and was buried in France. Indicative of her travels, Tasma's fiction was set in Victoria and Tasmania, London and Paris.

The photograph complicates her cultural affiliations by reference to Oriental culture and includes an allusion to the underworld activity of opium smoking that is also self-consciously literary. The photograph is captioned with both of her names (neither of which is her family name) further destabilizing her basis for identification, and insisting on its plurality. Her almost masculine pose, in which she gazes steadily at the camera rather than being passively displayed before it, also destabilizes gender expectations in an interesting way. This is perhaps a reference to Manet's painting *Olympia* in which the subject is seductively aware and willing to confront the voyeuristic gaze, so that the questioning witness who seeks a statement of gender or nationalism is being challenged. Renoir's *Odalisque*, in which the recumbent female figure returns the viewing gaze and is unapologetically sexual, is perhaps another visual reference.

Presumably the separate names also refer to the division between Tasma's married and professional life, a common strategy for nineteenth-century women writers and often the reason for their use of a pseudonym. This is not simplistically to insist on an autobiographical reading: the issue of whether Tasma's fiction is drawn from her life is of less interest here than the choices she made in writing given that she was freed by her disguise. Subject and object are equally constructed by history and by the position of the viewer. Undercutting the image of a Caucasian woman in Oriental costume are also the posture and setting which recall the French Empire painting tradition, *Madame Recumbier*. The photograph is thus a European framing of a colonial Tasmanian woman with a Belgian name (from her second marriage) cavorting with images of an underworld which are neither antipodean nor colonial but those of oriental otherness existing within European traditions of literary and visual representation.

It should also be noted that the ahistorical, essentialist image of the Oriental is emphasized by its deployment, in an anthology of women writers which is very much a political, historically-grounded account: a collection of essays by contemporary women writers about pioneer women writers, in an effort to contribute to 1930s nationalism, specifically in the sesquicentenary of the European 'settlement' of Australia. Yet the photograph draws attention not only to spatial ambivalence – which category? which country? – but to temporal ambivalence: the idea that a culture is fixed and unchanging, having emerged in a natural or organic fashion from an acknowledged moment of origin, is also being questioned.

Without reading too much into this image, it is possible to see that Tasma drew on a multitude of cultural backgrounds in the construction of her persona as a public figure. The publication in which this photograph was published appeared in 1938 when the dominant Australian nationalist discourse emphasized a reductionist authenticity based on the topographical and botanical specificities of the Australian landscape and its emerging rural culture, privileging the working-class, male subject. Although we don't know the circumstances of this photograph's origin or the reason for its inclusion in the volume, it is clear that Tasma had at some point excluded herself from the Australian national-realist culture by her overt display of sexuality, urbanity, aesthetic decadence, and the orient.

Many feminist critics have pointed out the conjunction of nationalism and masculinity in the development of Australian cultural difference in the 1890s;[2] and recent work on 'settler' cultures following from Benita Parry's essay in *Oxford Literary Review* (1987) also draws attention to the unstable relationship between female subjectivity and nationalism. In addition to the problematics of 'half-colonization' (Visel 1988) for white women in settler cultures, Jane Mackay and Pat Thane point out that this instability is also experienced by women in colonizing or imperial cultures. Referring specifically to the invention of Englishness in the nineteenth century, they write that:

> the Englishwoman remains a more shadowy figure than the Englishman, because women were believed to possess trans-national qualities. Nationality, we suggest, played a more significant role in the redefinition of masculinity as it emerged in the later nineteenth century than in that of femininity; one of the distinctions between male and female was that the concept of nationality was almost always on the male side of the divide. Women, indeed, *had* no fixed nationality . . . they were identified not with nation but with *race*.
>
> (Mackay and Thane 1986: 191–2)

Given the correspondence between universalism and the identity of woman, at least at the level of race as it was then understood, it is not surprising that most women writers chose the romance genre with its narrative of quest for transcendent sources of subject-unification such as love and duty. In contrast, masculine national-realism emphasized locality and distinctiveness, stressing severance from the metropolitan centre and the literary ideal of 'mimetic adequacy'. This was matched by a form of criticism concerned with 'authenticity' and 'image analysis' which was 'largely content oriented' (Bhabha 1984b: 100, 104).

The heroine of Tasma's novel, Portia James (whose name

147

suggests a portion and also portal, and hence liminality) is asked to confront the given opposition between Australia (insofar as these are stable terms), and then rejects the limits of her choice. Specifically, she is required to choose between an English and Australian suitor (as is the pattern in most of these novels), but instead she points to Europe, to other cultures, and to the construction of nature – whether the Victorian bush, the native Australian flowers in a London drawing room, or the stars she sleeps under on her way across the English Channel to Paris. Despite her indecision, the point is that she cannot say 'no'. Choice is unavailable, and it is in this that she most resembles Shakespeare's Portia from *The Merchant of Venice* who says, 'Is it not hard, Nerissa, that I cannot choose one, nor refuse none?' (*The Merchant of Venice* I.ii.25). Perhaps it is also for this reason that Jessie Couvreur chose to play a game when being photographed for a biographical profile. Again the question is raised: 'what is the relation of the self to the otherness of the self's own history?'

In *The Penance of Portia James* the standard nineteenth-century Australian heroine's dilemma is more than usually acute since the narrative also explores the issue of subject appropriation by the various competing interests. Whether she is to be an Australian or English wife is only one of several possibilities: she might also become a French model, a bohemian lesbian's lover in Paris, or regress to become her father's rural daughter.

The narrator is also conscious of the dangers of appropriating her fictional subject when the point is to highlight her desire for freedom from any categorizing constraints, including those imposed by the techniques of narration. Portia is hard to describe, continually escapes definition, and is likened to an impressionist painting, hazy, out of focus, and in 'the softest disorder'. Her transience is also noted by a character who regretfully comments that she is 'not a permanent; she is only some beautiful bird of passage. With us, and not of us' (Tasma 1891: 217). It is at this point that Portia is seen to be tracing with her parasol in the gravel, and the narrator remarks parenthetically, '(many a hieroglyph drawn by the point of a woman's parasol is the unenduring record of some paramount passage in her life's history)' (ibid.: 266). The problematics of discourse, both written and spoken, are continually posed.

A resolution of the crisis seems to be provided through a call to womanhood in its most essentialist and sacrificial guise. It transpires that Portia's Australian fiancé has made another woman pregnant while Portia has been agonizing over her desire to break her engagement due to her love for an English painter. She runs away upon hearing this news, as it is just the excuse she has been waiting for, but is recalled not by her betrothed, but by the wronged woman, now on her death-bed and beseeching Portia to look after her illegitimate child. It is clear that nothing less could possibly have persuaded Portia to give in to the arranged marriage, and she is reluctantly reconciled with her Australian fiancé. Images of Madonna figures abound, the archetypal Western figure of woman-as-sacrifice which enables Portia to escape more pressing and complex questions of cultural allegiance.

Portia does not fully return to Australia but is left at the moment of her departure, as the boat waits to embark from the London port. The irresolution is explicit, indicating the heroine's continuing ambivalence to the conflated sexual–national relationship. Portia has failed to discover a new cultural basis for identification through her relationship to individuals, institutions or ideologies. Her only recourse is to Heaven (in a text which is not overtly religious) and it is in this transcendent realm that her forsaken lover (the painter) hopes she will find her reward.

Fixed awkwardly between the various options, just as the ship steams forever between continents, *The Penance of Portia James* resists any unquestioning endorsement of identificatory categories. This suggests that a sense of loss is felt to be necessary to the development of fixed nationality, particularly where this is linked to the exclusion of the feminine, as it was in the Australian context. The contemporary reader, however, can now make a positive interpretation of this atopic state, particularly in view of recent work on the multicultural voice and the 'privileges' of marginalization. Nevertheless, it is important to stress that this position was not celebrated by the nineteenth-century women writers: it was merely described. Caught between cultures, one of which was still undefined, and seeking to accommodate a sense of continuity which acknowledged the advantages of both, they had their heroines resort to the platonic never-never lands of whatever transcendent option they could devise. (For Portia this is the quasi-religious gesture of virgin birth and the taking on of the husband's sin.) Since the development of post-colonial studies, however, and what Stuart Hall has referred to as 'the romance of the margins', being in a Platonic never-never land is to have an idealized if not privileged literary voice.

Given the difficulties of defining the Anglo-Australian female subject simply in terms of coloniality, with its connotations of invasion and appropriation, the terms of migration used in the discussion of contemporary post-colonial writing may also be useful in this context. Since migration often entails the disenfranchising and alienation of the immigrant party, this term allows for the complex relationship of nineteenth-century women to colonial structures of power; and it acknowledges that many of the white women were reluctant settlers accompanying their husbands or seeking employment. The politics of migration may be particularly suited to analysis of the female subject in transit between states for, as Visel has noted, she is only half-colonized, negotiating an identity in a cultural environment that is itself in formation. At the same time, it cannot be denied that the texts emerge from a problematic of colonization, cultural differentiation, and nationalist formation, and that the authors represent, however involuntarily, a white colonizing force. Clearly, both theoretical contexts may be helpful in reading these novels.

In her analysis of contemporary migrant women writers in Australia, Sneja Gunew discusses the issue of the migrating subject, suggesting that 'it is possible that it is not so much a question of *being* a migrant but of writing from a migrant position'. If theirs is to be regarded as an 'authentic' voice, then it is necessarily 'a problematic category, which can only ever be partially defined':

> Indeed, it is a necessary condition that it should escape complete definition since otherwise it could not extend the theory: this is its rationale for existence, that the personal history should shift our ways of conceptualizing systems of representation in general.
>
> (Gunew 1985: 168–9)

This point could be applied equally to Tasma the novelist and to Portia the romance heroine. Allowing for an autobiographical reading which need not reduce the novel's value as a literary text, Gunew's observation allows for ways of reading which incorporate the history of the writing subject in a positive and legitimizing manner. By writing from a migrant position, Tasma at once disrupts myths of purity and authenticity in relation to nationality, while invoking the myth of essential, sacrificial womanhood, which itself is never permitted to become convincing within the narrative. The strategies of displacement, ambivalence, and mimicry found

150

in the photograph supplied Tasma with a playful disguise which was also 'artistic' within a bohemian tradition, just as the indeterminacy of her fictional heroine facilitates a virtuous narrative resolution. Such a writing strategy allows for the portrayal of a heroine who speaks from a shifting and contested position, and draws from impressionist theories of perception to highlight the importance of the position of the reader in locating the writer and in constructing the figure of the heroine, not to mention the author. As Gunew suggests, it is by drawing attention to the position from which the subject can speak that the writer calls critical categories and generic expectations into doubt, shifting 'our ways of conceptualising systems' (ibid.: 169).

NOTES

1 Although I acknowledge Simon During's point that nationalism can be a positive form of resistance to imperialism (During 1990), this can overlook minority group interests, and the differences *within* nations that can be elided in the process of post-colonial resistance. As Barbara Johnson (1987) has argued, it is the differences within, as much as those between, categories which deserve acknowledgement.
2 See, for instance, Sheridan (1985), Lake (1986), Giles (1988), Schaffer (1988).

11

'THE ONLY FREE PEOPLE IN THE EMPIRE'

Gender difference in colonial discourse

Bridget Orr

Late in 1916 Lady Ottoline Morrell wrote to Katherine Mansfield to ask for her account of a recent incident in the Café Royal. Mansfield had been irritated by what she regarded as the pretentious conversation of some 'University Blacks' sharing her table and, encouraged by her companions, she appropriated the copy of Lawrence's poems they were discussing (Alpers 1982: 216–17). In her written response to Morrell's inquiries she was notably evasive:

> Dearest Ottoline
> What am I to make of this? Of course *if* the coloured gentleman with the young party with the pink hair *was* Suhrawadi – then indeed I do know the 'reverse of the story'. . . . At any rate, Huxley's languid letter doesn't tempt me dreadfully to tell him – to satisfy even his 'very idlest curiosity' and 'merest inquisitiveness'. I am afraid I am not young enough to dance to such small piping. Heavens! his letter makes me feel so old – and inclined to dress up, alone in the studio here – Tie up my head in a turban, make myself fat, don a fur coat with lace frills slightly spotted with tea, and act Lady Mary Wortley Montagu receiving a morning leg from – Swift perhaps.
>
> (Mansfield 1984: 280)

Mansfield does not attempt to explain or justify herself directly: but expresses a desire to assume the identity of an eighteenth-century bluestocking famous for her travels in the East. As I have argued elsewhere, this passage suggests that Mansfield could account for her imperious assertion of cultural (and racial) authority only through an implicit acknowledgement of her own imbrication in

152

the highly mobile and fractured structure of colonial subjectivity; like the 'coloured gentleman' she has abused, she is herself a kind of colonial mimic whose participation in advanced metropolitan culture is both ambivalent and constantly under threat (Orr 1989).

Mansfield's invocation of Mary Wortley Montagu in this passage reflects the period's fashionable interest in the Orient; but I am primarily concerned with another issue suggested by the identificatory gesture. To what extent can one argue that Wortley Montagu's and Mansfield's shared gender, their position as internal others within a metropolitan imperial or a settler society which is profoundly patriarchal, inflects their representations of exotic or native others? Does being female make a difference to their production of colonial discourse? If so, how can we characterize that difference and on what basis? Robert Young has argued recently that both feminist and colonial discourse analysis participate in an attempt to disrupt or rework the

> phenomenological account of the constitution of knowledge that works according to the structure of a subject perceiving an object, a same/other dialectic in which the other is first constituted by the same through its negation as other before being incorporated within it.
>
> (Young 1990: 6)

However there is 'no possibility of exchange or dialogue' (ibid.) in this schema – and the alternatives for those defined as other (women, non-Europeans) are intolerable, in that women for instance can either conform to the stereotypical patriarchal female roles or, by refusing their position as other, identify with men in a denial of our difference. As Young points out, this theoretical double bind recurs in theorization of racial differences (ibid.).

Young is a defender of various post-structuralist projects which he sees as crucially concerned with revealing not just the Eurocentrism of the Western philosophical tradition but the complicity of the knowledge produced under its aegis with the violence of imperialism. Apart from defending Derrida's deconstructive project, which provides a critique of the process by which European knowledge is constituted through a comprehension and incorporation of the other, he cites the work of Emmanuel Levinas as an instance of a theorization of a non-violent relation to the other. In Levinas' schema 'a respect for the other [stands for] the grasping of it, and a theory of desire' as infinitely separate substitutes for desire

153

as negation and assimilation (Young 1990: 12). Levinas champions dialogism, arguing that the sociality of linguistic exchange allows the self to open up to the other without assimilating the other: parties in the dialogue establish a relation to each other but neither is subsumed – the radical difference of each interlocutor can remain intact.

Levinas' emphasis on dialogism as a way out of our entrapment in a dialectic of same and other intersects suggestively with Arun Mukherjee's emphasis on the utility of Bakhtin's dialogical model of the relations between literary and social discourses in the analysis of Third World writing. In an article generally critical of what is seen as a post-modernist insistence on reading 'post-colonial' texts only in terms of their relation to an absent centre (as parody or mimicry of metropolitan writing), Mukherjee (1990) emphasizes the heteroglossial complexity of Third World writing, arguing that the primary cultural work of such texts is done on its home ground, outside that dialectical relation with the metropolitan centre.

Young's and Mukherjee's positions are widely different but they share an interest in the possibility that various forms of dialogism may get us out of the Hegelian double bind. I want to bear these dialogic models in mind when pursuing my primary concern, the question of whether one can argue that gender inflects the production of colonial discourse. On the one hand, it is clear that a series of ancient identifications between women and land, earth or territory, and women and the mother-tongue or orality, as well as recurrent tropes, such as the predication of the founding of empires on the rape of women, are constantly recirculated in imperialist texts; on the other, the most powerful theoretical analyses of colonialism and its representational strategies, such as those provided by Manoni, Fanon and Bhabha, draw on psychoanalytic models in which sexual difference is crucial. And yet Bhabha's powerful series of readings of colonialist tropes, as Young points out, simply bracket questions of gender: he 'seems to regard the troubled structures of sexuality as a metaphor for colonial ambivalence' (Young 1990: 119) but his discussions of the 'desire of hybridity' or the desire of colonial difference 'invoke the structures of desire without addressing structures of sexuality' (ibid.).

The irresolution of this issue has not impeded the production of readings in which gender and race function in tandem as analytic categories. Recurring strategies in colonial discourse which have been located and discussed include the displacement of anxiety about the colonizers' possible degeneration into the savage being figured by the madness of settler women; the violent appropriation of the other's territory being naturalized through the feminization of the native or exotic culture, often narrativized in love and conversion plots; the citation of the enslavement of women as an index of a society's barbarity, thus justifying intervention and regulation, and so on. All these accounts share the assumption that there is a peculiarity in the position of women within the imperialist culture, that she already figures an alterity which can be mobilized in diverse ways. Feminist analysis suggests that the original binary division which organizes Western thought and reaches its apotheosis in the Hegelian dialectic is a gendered one: Cixous, Clément and Irigaray have extended Derrida's critique of logocentrism to point up the inevitable identity of the negative terms of a structuring opposition with the feminine.

Said has suggested, citing Sophocles' *Persians* as an example, that the dialectical structure of Western thought is also imbricated from the beginning in processes of producing external others, as barbarians (1979: 21). What I want to speculate about, in relation to Wortley Montagu and Mansfield, is the extent to which the gendered nature of the position of enunciation in colonial discourse affects its functioning. Are women, the internal other, who produce travel writing about the external other, male mimics – or subversive female hysterics? It is demonstrable that much women's travel writing does subvert the dominant terms of its discourse, but beyond locating such deconstructive manoeuvres (which are historically specific) the question remains of the extent to which another relation – a dialogic relation with the other – may be identified. And here perhaps one might invoke a third dialogical or non-violent theorization of the relation to the other such as Irigaray's attempt to appropriate Levinas' work to develop an ethics of sexual difference. Elizabeth Grosz (1989: 176–8) argues that in order to produce such an ethics, governed by a recognition and acceptance of the irreducible alterity of each to the other, Irigaray turns to Descartes' text 'The Passion of the Soul' in order to use his notion of wonder. Grosz suggests that for Irigaray, 'wonder' is a non-oppositional term, always singular in that it refers to the surprise of the first encounter. Thus, instead of the hostility and contempt held for women's alterity in a particular culture, Irigaray invokes the primary passion of awestruck surprise at the new and unfamiliar as a model for the way in which the two sexes could meet and marvel at each other's difference. In such an encounter there would be no identities, opposites or complements but instead two irreducibly different beings.

This construction of encounters with the other as productive meetings in which the autonomy and difference of each partner is left intact is clearly utopian but I have found it suggestive in relation to Wortley Montagu's if not Mansfield's accounts of her relation to the exotic. Despite the contemptuous dismissal by Rousseau and Porter (1990: 12) of Wortley Montagu as a woman who saw in Turkey only what she wished to see, Wortley Montagu's texts reveal an overt attempt to revise earlier travel accounts which she saw as primarily motivated by the instrumental purposes of commerce. There is also a conscious tendency to identify with the Turks, especially the women. While the figure of the renegado, the European who goes 'native' in the Ottoman Empire is uniformly excoriated by other voyage writers, Wortley Montagu's cultural mimicry, her adoption of Turkish dress, her acquisition of the language, her friendship with various individuals and her 'admiration' for their 'right notion of life' suggest she becomes a kind of 'renegada'. This identification with and desire for the other may appear to keep her locked within the non-dialogic logic of the same but certain moments in her texts suggest the breakdown of that incorporative drive in a moment of wonder, or admiration. Mansfield's texts, however, written at a time when imperialist ideology saturated both the colonies and the metropolitan centre, seem to be caught entirely within a dialectical structure in which a dialogic encounter is impossible.

MONTAGU IN TURKEY, 1716–18

Mary Wortley Montagu's 'Embassy Letters' from Turkey were written between 1716 and 1718 during her husband's posting as ambassador, but were published only posthumously, in 1763. They achieved an immediate Europe-wide success and remained influential in the nineteenth century: Ingres, for instance, used Montagu's description of the women's bagnio – or the bathhouse – as the basis for that archetypal orientalist representation, 'Le Bain Turc'. This kind of appropriation suggests that the letters participate in an emergent orientalist discourse, whose construction of the Levantine and East Indian societies as stagnant, despotic, luxurious, corrupt, effeminized and brutalizing has been cogently analysed by

Said. And indeed, precisely this kind of interpretation of Wortley Montagu's text has been made recently by Cynthia Lowenthal (1990) who reads Montagu's reframing of the Turkish scenes in terms of heroic romance as an appropriative eradication of their difference.

In contrast, I want to stress the extent to which the 'Embassy Letters' not only consciously take issue with the conventional wisdom of authoritative accounts of the Turks but reveal a desire for and identification with Turkish women in particular which destabilizes the kind of position established by writers such as Rycaut, de Thévenot, Hill, Tavernier, Dumont and Withers. Using the privileged access provided by her gender and her status she is constantly aware of presenting scenes which are entirely novel, of filling in the tantalizing gaps in the extant literature; and in so doing, as she unveils the female bagnio, and the harem, her writing repeatedly reveals both a dependence on and a difference from conventional modes of representation. While accounts such as Dumont's (1696) strive for ease and familiarity, they nevertheless follow a fairly rigid generic pattern, moving from accounts of the Turkish polity through religion and only latterly turning to 'manners and customs'. Their claims for authority stem from the completeness of their survey and the accumulation of empirical observation; Wortley Montagu's letters, however, are thoroughly 'occasional', produced in the context of a series of often intimate epistolary exchanges, and they reflect her increasing involvement and interaction *with*, rather than distanced observation *of*, a variety of Turkish individuals. She is much closer both to her audience (friends and relations in England) and to her subjects (Turks with whom she engages in sociable commerce) than male writers such as Dumont or Hill, a double proximity which at points suggests some collapsing of the distance from one's object which guarantees knowledge.

This collapsing of distance is most apparent in relation to her representation of women. This is a topic she takes up in her first intimate encounter with a Turk, the learned Achmet-Beg, with whom she stays in Belgrade:

> I have frequent disputes with him concerning the difference of our Customs, particularly the confinements of Women. He assures me there is nothing at all in it; only, says he, we have the advantage that when our Wives cheat us, no body knows

157

it. He has wit and is more polite than many Christian men of Quality.

(Wortley Montagu 1965: 307)

The enclosure of women is a staple in the voyage writing Wortley Montagu perused before her visit: Rycaut, de Thévenot and Tavernier all devote chapters to the subject – for Dumont, writing in the 1690s, it is already a cliché:

I need not tell you with what severity they are guarded by the white and black Eunuchs, who never permit them to enjoy the least shadow of Liberty. All the relations of Travellers are full of stories and reflections on this Subject and therefore instead of repeating the Observations of others, I shall only add, that 'tis a Capital crime to look upon one of these Women.

(Dumont 1696: 167–8)

And later he adds: 'There is no slavery equal to that of the Turkish women' (ibid.: 268–9).

Rycaut's remarks in *The Present State of the Ottoman Empire* are typical of those relations Dumont alludes to:

And since I have brought my reader into the quarter of these Eunuchs, which are the Black guard of the sequestred Ladies of the *Seraglio*, he may chance to take it unkindly, should I leave him at the door, and not introduce him into those apartments, where the Grand Signiors Mistresses are lodged! And though I ingenuously confess my Acquaintance there (as all other my conversation with Women in *Turkey*) is but strange and unfamiliar; yet not to be guilty of this discourtesie I shall to the best of my information write a short account of these Captivated Ladies, how they are treated, immured, educated and prepared for the great achievements of the *Sultans* affection; and as in other stories the Knight consumes himself with combats, watching and penance to acquire the love of one fair Damsel; here an army of Virgins make it the only study and business of their life to obtain the single nod of invitation to the Bed of their great Master.

(1668: 38)

The tone here of jocular insinuation, explicitly addressed to a male reader, is quite different to the impersonal narrative voice used elsewhere in Rycaut's account; but it renders peculiarly transparent the occidental fascination with such Turkish institutions as the harem and polygamy. That fascination with the strange and unfamiliar practices which organized sexual relations so differently from European custom was doubtless inflamed by the complete inaccessibility of Turkish women; and Wortley Montagu's penetration of that previously unknown female space, the harem and the bagnio, doubtless accounted for much of the contemporary interest in her writing.

Wortley Montagu's sense of her position – as one who is 'got into a New world' (1965: 312) and can provide 'an Account of such a sight as you never saw in your Life and what no book of travells could inform you of' (ibid.: 315) – is complex. At first glance, her account of the bagnio does function as a classic instance of orientalist description, unveiling and reframing a scene of extraordinary and sensuous beauty, as a multitude of undifferentiated female bodies are displayed before the viewer in elaborate nakedness.

The first sofas were cover'd with cushions and rich Carpets, on which sat the Ladys, and on the 2nd their slaves behind 'em, but without any distinction of rank by their dress, all being in the state of nature, that is, in plain English, stark naked, without any Beauty or defect conceal'd, yet there was not the least wanton smile or immodest Gesture amongst 'em. They Walk'd and mov'd with the same majestic Grace which Milton describes of our General Mother. There were many amongst them as exactly proportion'd as ever any Goddess was drawn by the pencil of Guido or Titian, and most of their skins shineingly white, only adorn'd by their Beautifull Hair divided into many tresses hanging on their shoulders, braided either with pearl or riband, perfectly representing the figures of the Graces.

I was here convinc'd of the Truth of a Reflexion that I had often made, that if twas the fashion to go naked, the face would be hardly observ'd. I perceiv'd the Ladys with the finest skins and most delicate shapes had the greatest share of my admiration, thô their faces were sometimes less beautifull than those of their companions. To tell you the truth, I had wickedness enough to wish secretly that Mr. Gervase could have been there invisible. I fancy it would have very much improv'd his art to see so many fine Women naked in different

> postures, some in conversation, some working, others drinking Coffee or sherbet, and many negligently lying on their Cushions while their slaves (generally pritty girls of 17 or 18) were employ'd in braiding their hair in several pritty manners. In short, tis the Women's coffee-house, where all the news of the Town is told, Scandal invented, etc.
>
> (Wortley Montagu 1965: 313–14)

Here, as in a later account of a visit to a harem, the entry into female space and its subsequent representation seem to press Wortley Montagu into assuming a male spectatorial position, as she invokes the sublime descriptive powers of Milton, Guido Reni and Titian in order to render something of the 'agreeable prospect' available to her correspondent. And yet, there is a slight slippage between the kind of masculine eye – and hand, or pen – which she continuously alludes to as necessary for representing the scene, and her own position, both within the bagnio and as its recorder. Lady Mary wishes Charles Jervas could be there improving his art: for the male viewer, it seems, these women would function as objects demanding an aesthetic response. For Wortley Montagu, however, they are in the first instance individuals with whom she must negotiate a social exchange. When she thinks of trying to represent them, she underlines her own need to borrow the terms of a masculine tradition: but when she interacts, she must improvise and meet the other women to some extent on their own terms.

And here an interesting reversal occurs. It is Lady Mary's insistence on keeping her clothes which differentiates her from the other women, her sisters under the skin. The Turkish women interpret Lady Mary's stays rather literally, as a material sign of her husband's dominion over her body:

> I was at last forc'd to open my skirt and shew them my stays, which satisfy'd 'em very well, for I saw they believed I was so lock'd up in that machine that it was not in my own power to open it, which contrivance they attributed to my Husband.
>
> (1965: 314)

She regards this view as a misreading because it implies the Turkish women have identified a slavish relation to her husband which she implicitly rejects: the physical constriction of the stays is one she has control over. But it is Lady Mary who is here an overly literal reader, mistaking her manual freedom to unlace herself (if in fact she could do so without a servant's help) for a more significant mental liberty. Psychologically, she was completely unable to remove herself from the machine which kept her trussed up and sweating among the naked women of the bathhouse: even more impermeable than the bonds of bone and metal are the mental contrivances by which she is bound.

The rest of the 'Embassy Letters' suggest a progressive revision of the simple certainty of superiority revealed in the conversation with Achmet-Beg and a shift from a dependence on a tradition of sublime description in the accounts of her visits to the women's quarters. In a letter on 17 June 1717, she writes:

> Your whole letter is full of mistakes from one end to t'other. I see you have taken your Ideas of Turkey from that worthy author Dumont, who has writ with equal ignorance and confidence. 'Tis a particular pleasure to me here to read the voyages to the Levant, which are generally so far remov'd from Truth and so full of Absurditys that I am very well diverted with 'em. They never fail giving you an Account of the Women, which 'tis certain they never saw, and talking very wisely of the Genius of the Men, into whose Company they are never admitted.
>
> (ibid.: 368)

For in fact, she has already argued:

> Now I am a little acquainted with their ways, I cannot forbear admiring either the exemplary discretion or extreme Stupidity of all the writers that have given accounts of 'em. 'Tis very easy to see they have more Liberty than we have, no Women of what rank so ever being permitted to go in the streets without 2 muslins, one that covers her face all but her Eyes . . . . You may guess how effectually this disguises them. . . .
>
>   This perpetual Masquerade gives them entire Liberty of following their Inclinations without danger of Discovery. . . . Upon the Whole, I look upon the Turkish Women as the only free people in the Empire.
>
> (ibid.: 327–9)

This kind of overt revision of conventional wisdom about the East in order to reflect critically on the practices of European societies is a strategy employed by a variety of radical writers and not just feminists, for example Voltaire's *Zadig* (1747) and *L'Ingénue* (1756). However, Wortley Montagu's texts reveal more covertly those processes by which European identity is open to subversion. On 10 March 1718 she wrote to Lady Mary:

> I am allmost falln into the misfortune so common to the Ambitious: while they are employ'd on distant, insignificant Conquests abroad, a rebellion starts up at home. I am in great danger of loseing my English. I find it is not halfe so easy for me to write in it as it was a twelve-month ago. I am forc'd to study for expressions, and must leave off all other Languages and try to learn my mother tongue.
>
> (ibid.: 390)

She continues with the martial metaphor: "'Tis as impossible for one Humane Creature to be perfect master of ten different Languages as to have in perfect subjection ten different Kingdoms' (ibid.). Wortley Montagu's immersion in a new world involves the danger that she may lose both linguistic and national identity. The ambitious project of taking possession of the other's tongue, figured as an imperial conquest, destabilizes the 'native' self.

The other threat to the colonial subject is not that expressed in the martial metaphors of mastery and conquest, power through knowledge, but that defined in the language of desire. As we saw in the scene in the bagnio, Wortley Montagu describes its delights by invoking that tradition of refined and sensual description which takes female beauty as a privileged object. But Wortley Montagu is implicated as both subject and object of the gaze: she is forced to undress herself by the Turkish women whose naked beauty she represents so seductively, in a context already inscribed in the European imagination by transgressive forms of female desire. Joseph Withers puts this in its baldest form:

> Now it is not lawfull for anyone to bring ought in unto them, with which they may commit the deeds of beastly, and unnatural uncleanesse: so that if they have a will to eat, radishes, cucumbers, gourds, or such like meats; they are sent in unto them sliced, to deprive them of the means of playing the wantons; for they being all young, lusty and lascivious wenches, and wanting the society of men (which would better instruct them and questionless far better employ them) are

doubtless of themselves inclined to that which is naught, and will often be possest with unchast thoughts.

(Withers 1650: 59)

In her intimate intercourse with Turkish women, Wortley Montagu is drawn into an economy of female desire which modifies her position as Western observer. This is most striking in her accounts of friendship with Fatima, wife of the Khaya of the Emperor. The conclusion of the first letter on the subject, which describes the initial meeting, encapsulates something of this ambiguity.

I retir'd through the same Ceremonys as before, and could not help fancying I had been some time in Mahomet's Paradise, so much was I charm'd with what I had seen. I know not how the relation of it appears to you. I wish it may give you part of my pleasure, for I would have my dear Sister share in all the Diversions of, etc.

(Wortley Montagu 1965: 352)

The pleasure produced by 'Mohamet's Paradise' was, notoriously, intended for men only – women were its instruments; here Lady Mary casts herself as a kind of honorary man by virtue of her role as the recipient of such enjoyment. And yet, in desiring to share such pleasure with her sister, she underlines its specifically feminine quality: it is enjoyment which can be produced and circulated among women alone.

This kind of ambiguity runs through the whole letter. In reflecting on her own ecstatic evocation of Fatima's beauty Wortley Montagu comments:

I am afraid you will accuse me of extravagance in this description. I think I have read somewhere that Women always speak in rapture when they speak of Beauty, but I can't imagine why they should not be allow'd to do so. I rather think it Virtue to be able to admire without any Mixture of desire or Envy. The Gravest Writers have spoken with great warmth of some celebrated Pictures and Statues. The Workmanship of Heaven certainly excells all our weak Imitations, and I think has a much better claim to our Praise. For me, I am not asham'd to own I took more pleasure in looking on the beauteous Fatima than the finest piece of Sculpture could have given me.

(ibid.: 350–1)

On the one hand, the passage objectifies Fatima in a familiar (masculinist) manner by both aestheticizing her and emphasizing her utterly 'natural' status, but on the other, Wortley Montagu is palpably struggling to find a speaking position and lexicon to express her female 'admiration'. Fearing the description will be found extravagant, she invokes the two negative poles of predictable enthusiasm or envious detraction by which women's praise of other women is always judged, expressing anxiety and pleasure in equal parts – or rather, anxiety over pleasure. Clearly part of the defensiveness and 'shame' of the passage is produced by the sheer difficulty of finding a way of expressing a desiring rather than an envious admiration: trying to find a language of female admiration for femininity. On the one hand, these passages suggest Wortley Montagu's inevitable dependence on – her literal entrapment within – Western terms of representation even as she revolted against them. But as well as the uneasy oscillation between the assumption of a masculine position – as voyeur in the bagnio – and identification with the other – speaking Turkish in her ferignée – there is her 'admiration', her sheer wonder at the beauty and grace of the Turkish women. Her problems in finding language to describe the pleasure produced by her encounter with Fatima is not only an index of the difficulties inherent in representing a feminocentric female desire, albeit one licensed by its imbrication in the exotic – it may also perhaps be read in the terms Irigaray has suggested, as an encounter marked primarily by 'admiration' or wonder at the other.

MANSFIELD IN THE UREWERAS 1907

Mansfield's trip to the Ureweras consisted of a three-week trek organized by her father late in 1907. She travelled with four companions from Hawke's Bay through the Ureweras to Rotorua and Taupo. Carefully framing the somewhat fragmentary primary material from the rough notebook which forms the text's source, with biographical and historical materials, Ian Gordon reconstructs the piece as evidence of a process of self-consolidation, in which Mansfield emerges, as a 'vigorous, independent-minded' and 'confident' young woman (Mansfield 1978: 20).

Recent accounts of Mansfield's writing which attend to the specifically colonial dimension of her texts have tended to emphasize her rejection of settler values and her revision of dominant forms of colonial literature. W.H. New (1987: 129), for instance, argues that when she returned to New Zealand, 'She rejected her father's control over her, rejected the male networks that controlled power in his society, and sought out the Maori on a 1907 camping trip', also suggesting that her stories reveal a 'widespread colonial impulse: the need to rebel against the biases of gender, race, place, and romantic speech' (ibid, 114.). This assessment coincides to a large extent with Lydia Wevers' (1988) view that Mansfield's New Zealand stories consistently subvert the conventions, structures and discourse of colonial romance as she rewrites the preoccupations of colonial self-representation.

Such efforts to reveal Mansfield's work in a colonial context seem to me laudable, but I am less happy with the implication that Mansfield rebelled against racial bias. In the *Urewera Notebook*, Ian Gordon's inserts, describing the recent history of the Tuhoe resistance to European penetration, highlight the conventionality of Mansfield's representation of the Maori in terms of sentimentalized pathos or antique nobility. In the entry of 18 November, for example, Mansfield describes her responses on an evening spent at Petane, near the site of an 1866 engagement between British and Maori in which most of the Maori were killed.

> Round us in the darkness the horses were moving softly with a most eerie sound – visions of long dead Maoris – of forgotten battles and vanished feuds – stirred in me – till I ran through the dark glade on to a bare hill – the track was very narrow and steep – and at the summit a little Maori whare was painted black against a wide sky – Before it – two cabbage trees stretched out phantom fingers – and a dog, watching me coming up the hill, barked madly – Then I saw the first star – very sweet and faint – in the yellow sky – and then another and another like little holes – like pinholes. And all round me in the gathering gloom the wood hens called to each other with monotonous persistence – they seemed to be lost and suffering – I reached the whare and a little Maori girl and three boys – sprang from nowhere – and waved and beckoned – at the door a beautiful old Maori woman sat cuddling a cat – She wore a white handkerchief round her black hair and wore a green and black cheque rug wrapped round her body – Under the rug I caught a glimpse

of a very . . . pale blue print dress – worn native fashion the skirt over the bodice.

(Mansfield 1978: 37–8)

Far from representing a revision of current modes of colonial discourse, this account mobilizes a commonly-made analogy between Highlanders and the Maori, one which identifies the Maori with the archetypal archaic, bloodthirsty and defeated colonial people. This trope figures the Maori as a group whose independent political history is definitively closed although their potential as an aesthetic resource (for novels, sketches, short stories or painting for the colonizer who lacks a local history) is enthusiastically exploited. The passage then moves from elegiac projection to a sentimental tableau (of children, an old woman and a cat) set in a gloomy landscape of loss and suffering, figuring the current vulnerability of the Maori, reduced to the picturesque aged and infantile.

At the same time that the *Urewera Notebook* reveals Mansfield attempting to differentiate herself from the 'ultra-colonials' with whom she is travelling – 'give me the Maori and the tourist but nothing in between' – identifying herself with the 'real English' or the native – it also shows her uncritically deploying the familiar tropes of that in-between settler culture (Mansfield 1978: 61). The 'Vignette' she writes at Taupo, the one fairly finished piece of writing the *Notebook* contains, positions a 'young Maori girl' on a little knoll overlooking the lake and hills under the observant eye of the writer. Marked emphatically as Maori, the girl sits down native fashion, wears greenstone and bone earrings – but she is also the 'very incarnation of evening', the literal embodiment of her environment. Mansfield's preceding reverie, which also seems to draw her into a relation of romantic isomorphism with the landscape, is halted by the entrance of the Maori girl, who displaces and objectifies the process by which the narrator is becoming engulfed by the landscape (ibid.: 83–5). The narrator's unseen gaze serves here to secure her own identity: as a hidden witness she observes the other's complete immersion within the fairy scene.

Mansfield's revision of the material contained in the *Urewera Notebook* in various stories suggests a more complex relation to modes of colonial self-representation, produced in large part, I am sure, by the anxieties attendant on her recognition in London that she was precisely one of those 'colonials' she had so despised in New Zealand. It is in that context that I would agree with Witi Ihimaera

(1989: 45–6), whose novella 'Maata' retells the story of Mansfield's complex relation of desire and identification with Maata Mahupuku, that the heroine of the fragmentary eponymous novel is precisely a character who represents both women. Rather than evoking the immutable alienation of the modern subject (as Vincent O'Sullivan suggests), Maata's possession of Maori ancestry and Parisian sophistication seems to figure Mansfield's often painful sense of herself as expatriate New Zealander, *déclassé* colonial hybrid, in an idealized form (O'Sullivan 1989). As in the vignette, the anxieties attendant on colonial subjectivity may be displaced on to a 'Maori girl' – but in Maata's case, a Maori recognized and rewritten as an exotic aristocrat.

Mansfield's attempts to negotiate the insecurities of colonial subjectivity through the construction of an identification with Maata suggest that whatever modifications of the dominant terms of colonial self-representation her stories may show, she remained locked within the dialectical structures of negation and assimilation. This seems hardly surprising, given the point at which she wrote: Wortley Montagu produced her text at a point when the first British Empire was emergent, Mansfield when it had reached its maximum extent. By 1907, imperialist ideology had saturated both colonial and metropolitan territories: whereas in 1717 the Ottoman Empire was still a powerful threat to all of Middle Europe, and Occidental superiority could by no means be assumed. For Wortley Montagu, the whole Turkish 'notion of life' offered an alternative to her own which she found seductive, and to some extent adopted. For Mansfield, engagement with Maori culture focused primarily on an erotic and psychic involvement with one exceptional individual. (My remarks here are indebted to discussion with Linda Hardy.) For both, however, the encounter with an exotic culture seems to have focused and negotiated dissatisfactions with their own in a process which included the eruption of feminocentric female desire.

I am not sure how much these texts can tell first (or second) world feminist critics about how to read 'Third World' women now: it seems to me that by and large we are still, like Lady Mary, trussed up in cognitive machines invented by (European) men. Gender offers us no privilege. On the other hand, if we take seriously demands by writers like Arun Mukherjee that Third World texts be read on their own terms, in ways which recognize the 'epistemological privilege' (Mukherjee 1990: 5) of their primary, local audience, a laborious (though pleasurable) task lies ahead of the Western critic. To acquire any understanding of the local heteroglossia of a post-colonial text will involve displacing interpretative strategies which privilege metropolitan-marginal dichotomies and learning about other ways of reading. Perhaps in the course of this engagement, a different kind of dialogue may begin.

Part IV

RE-WRITING AND
RE-READING EMPIRE

12

DE-SCRIBING
THE WATER-BABIES
'The child' in post-colonial theory

Jo-Ann Wallace

> I can see the great danger in what I am – a defenseless and
> pitiful child . . . . It is possible that like an ancient piece of
> history my presence will leave room for theories.
> Jamaica Kincaid, 'Wingless' (1983: 23–4)[1]

If we accept Craig Tapping's argument that 'Practice, the self-
representations of formerly silenced, marginalized or negated
subjects, is always already a *theory* of the other' (1989b: 52, my
emphasis), what is the theory suggested by the presence of Jamaica
Kincaid's 'defenseless and pitiful child' narrator in this extract?
Who is the 'formerly silenced, marginalized or negated subject' of
this story? What does it mean to speak for the child, through the
voice of the child, as the child? How does the figure of the child
circulate in colonialist texts and post-colonial theory?

In its attempt to address these questions, I take 'de-scribing
Empire' to mean the writing, unwriting, and rewriting of imperial-
ist texts – in this case, texts for children. The 'ur-text' of this
discussion is the original edition of Charles Kingsley's *The Water-
Babies* (1863), a novel which was 'unwritten' in the 1984 abridged
Puffin Classics edition and 're-written' by Jamaica Kincaid in
'Wingless', a short story from her 1983 collection, *At the Bottom of
the River*. I will argue that 'the child' who, in Kingsley's *The Water-
Babies*, is the focus of mid-nineteenth-century educational, social
reform, and imperialist debate, is subsequently *de*politicized in the
abridged Puffin Classics edition and *re*politicized in 'Wingless'. I
argue further that what these various circulations and recirculations
have in common is an investment in the figure of 'the child', and
that it is an idea of 'the child' which makes thinkable both
nineteenth-century English colonialist imperialism and many
twentieth-century forms of resistance to imperialism.

171

1

Ashcroft *et al.* point out that 'the historical moment which saw the emergence of "English" as an academic discipline also produced the nineteenth-century colonial form of imperialism' (1989: 3). Furthermore,

> It can be argued that the study of English and the growth of Empire proceeded from a single ideological climate and that the development of one is intrinsically bound up with the development of the other, both at the level of simple utility . . . and at the unconscious level.
>
> (ibid.)

English Studies was, of course, established as a discipline in England first in the mechanics' institutes, working men's colleges, and women's colleges of the early to middle nineteenth century, and substantially later in the universities of Oxbridge, and only then, as Chris Baldick (1983) has pointed out, in response to changes to the foreign civil service examinations prompted by the 1853 India Act and the 1855 East India Company report.[2] Gauri Viswanathan (1987), on the other hand, cites the Charter Act of 1813 as a paradigmatic moment in the establishment of English Studies in *India*. What is significant about both arguments is that they describe an increasingly and peculiarly literary education directed to the marginalized, those outside the centres of political power or cultural production by reason of class, gender, or race.

However, also coincident with the establishment of English Studies and the rise of nineteenth-century colonial imperialism was the emergence of what has since been called a 'golden age' of English children's literature. The 'golden age' is typically regarded as beginning in the 1860s with the almost simultaneous publication of Kingsley's *The Water-Babies* (1863) and Lewis Carroll's *Alice's Adventures in Wonderland* (1865), and drawing to a close in the late 1920s with the publication of A.A. Milne's *Winnie-the-Pooh* (1926) and *The House at Pooh Corner* (1928) (see Carpenter 1985). Children's literature of the 'golden age' is primarily a fantasy literature and, in its appeal to the child's imagination, critics have traditionally described it as representing an enormous advance upon the more obviously didactic Sunday School literature which preceded it. It is a literature which has been described as having 'the sole aim of giving pleasure' (Townsend 1974: 100), and its appearance has been heralded as the culmination of more than a century's work in rethinking the nature of 'the child' and of childhood.[3]

I should emphasize here that I use the terms 'the child' and 'childhood' in quotation marks and I do not mean to suggest any easy identification with historical children. Rather, I distinguish between 'the child' or 'childhood' and *children* much as feminism has taught us to distinguish between 'woman' or 'femininity' as discursive constructs, and *women* as what Teresa de Lauretis has called 'real historical beings who cannot as yet be defined outside of those discursive formations' (1984: 5). The construct I am calling 'the child', however, has a much more recent discursive history than does 'woman'. Philippe Ariès (1962) traces the *idea* of 'childhood' – as a separate stage in life characterized by the need for protection and education – to the middle to late seventeenth century. Born of the early Renaissance and the humanist revival of interest in theories of education and in vernacular languages, the idea of childhood is firmly consolidated by the time of the Enlightenment as is evident in such texts as John Locke's *Some Thoughts Concerning Education* (1693) and Jean-Jacques Rousseau's *Emile* (1762).[4] As Foucault (1979) reminds us, this was the period which saw the birth of the school *and* of the prison and, indeed, 'childhood' is a discourse marked by this contradiction: 'the child' represents potential or futurity, both of which need protected spaces in which to flourish, *and* a subjectivity and corporeality in need of discipline.

2

Jamaica Kincaid's child narrator says of herself, 'I am primitive and wingless' (1983: 24), and this description captures perfectly the ways in which 'the child' is constructed both as the 'subject-to-be-educated', the 'subject-in-formation' (the term 'wingless' implying the pupal stage of insect and 'pupil' stage of human evolution) and (as the term 'primitive' implies) as the subject in need of discipline. The term 'primitive' has, of course, only a relative meaning; the *Oxford English Dictionary* (*OED*) defines it in terms of its Latin roots – *primitivus*, the first or earliest of its kind, *primus*, first – thus stressing an evolutionary or narrative progression: after all, one can only have a 'first' if more come after. Marianna Torgovnick traces the evolution of the word 'primitive' in English, pointing out that 'its references to "aboriginals", "inhabitants of prehistoric times", "natives" in non-European lands date from the end of the eighteenth century' (1990: 19), the period I am describing as that in which a discourse of childhood is firmly consolidated. The child is thus 'primitive' in the sense that the child predates and will evolve into the adult; to quote Wordsworth, a famous apologist of childhood, 'the Child is Father of the Man'. We are even more likely to think of 'primitive', however, in terms of its binary opposites, 'advanced', 'civilized', and it is no accident that the first non-literary books written for children were books of civility or manners. Erasmus's *Manners for Children* (1530) is a case in point, and I want to quote at some length from its opening which signals perfectly the discursive contradiction between 'the child's' innate goodness and his need of strict training in self-discipline.

> If a child's natural goodness is to reveal itself everywhere (and it glows especially in the face), his gaze should be gentle, respectful, and decent. Wild eyes are a sign of violence; a fixed stare is a sign of effrontery; wandering, distracted eyes are a sign of madness. The glance should not be sidelong, which is a sign of cunning, of a person contemplating a wicked deed. The eyes must not be opened too wide, for this is the mark of an imbecile. To lower and blink the eyelids is a sign of frivolousness. To hold the eyes steady is the stamp of a lazy mind, and Socrates was reproached for it. Piercing eyes signify irascibility. Too keen and eloquent eyes denote a lascivious temperament. It is important that the eyes signify a calm and respectfully affectionate spirit.
>
> (Revel 1989: 169–70)

To civilize: 'To make civil; to bring out of a state of barbarism, to instruct in the arts of life and thus elevate in the scale of humanity' (*OED*). The child as primitive must learn to control his body as well as his spirit; he is in need of physical, moral, and intellectual discipline or training. As the famous opening sentence to John Locke's *Some Thoughts Concerning Education* indicates, 'A Sound Mind in a sound Body, is a short, but full Description of a happy State in this World', and subsequent theorists of education followed Locke in emphasizing physical as well as intellectual conditioning. The body of 'the child' – like that of the 'savage' or 'primitive' – is ambivalently invested with fear and desire.

The term 'primitive' also signifies the pre-literate: that is, the pre-writing, pre-historic. It is well known that in *Emile* Rousseau valorized the child as a kind of noble savage (because closer than the adult to a state of nature) who was to be protected from writing, from all books save one: *Robinson Crusoe* (1719–20), empirical man's guide to the book of nature. However, as Peter Hulme has pointed out, *Robinson Crusoe* also thematizes the paradigmatic moment of European colonial encounter, and it is significant that – as the following passage from *Emile* indicates – Rousseau's choice of book *naturalizes* the relationship between childhood, education, and colonialism.

> I hate books; they only teach us to talk about things we know nothing about. . . . [However,] since we must have books, there is one book which, to my thinking, supplies the best treatise on an education according to nature. This is the first book Emile will read; for a long time it will form his whole library, and it will always retain an honoured place. It will be the text to which all our talks about natural science are but the commentary. It will serve to test our progress towards a right judgement, and it will always be read with delight, so long as our taste is unspoilt. What is this wonderful book? Is it Aristotle? Pliny? Buffon? No; it is *Robinson Crusoe*.
>
> (1984: 147)

The child, like the savage or the primitive, is pre-literate (the word 'infant', from the Latin *infans*, meaning literally 'without speech') and, as Craig Tapping has pointed out, a European, print-based culture has assumed that 'Groups of humans who do not use script are – by definition – inferior, and often less than human' (1989b: 89).[5] It is as 'primitive', then, that 'the child' represents to the West our racial as well as our individual past: the child is that 'ancient piece of history', to quote again from Kincaid, whose presence has left room, if not for theories, then for the parent–child logic of imperialist expansion.

There is obviously considerable slippage between constructions of 'the child' and of the native Other under imperialism, and I am certainly not the first to gesture to these similarities. Ashcroft *et al.* have pointed out that parent–child metaphors underwrite nineteenth-century colonialist imperialism (1989: 16), and Homi Bhabha has commented on the ambivalence of a colonial discourse which, in Macaulay's words, directs the colonizer to 'Be the father and the oppressor' (1985a: 74). Erasmus's 'wild-eyed' child shares in

175

the discursive space of the wild-eyed savages of such obviously imperialist writers for children as H. Rider Haggard, R.M. Ballantyne, and G.A. Henty, and these kinds of linkages have been widely commented upon. I am interested here, however, in taking this work in a slightly different direction to argue that an idea of 'the child' is a *necessary precondition* of imperialism – that is, that the West had to invent for itself 'the child' before it could think a specifically colonialist imperialism – and, further, that while this ideological complex is overtly coded in such children's books of the period as the boys' adventure novel, it also underlies the more critically respected fantasy literature of the mid- to late-nineteenth century. It is no accident that the 'golden age' of English children's literature peaked – to borrow a metaphor from Patrick Brantlinger – during the high noon and faded with the dusk of Empire. That is, an idea of childhood, together with a mercantile imperialism, began to emerge in the early Renaissance, the 'Age of Discoveries'; it was honed by the Enlightenment emphasis on individual development through empiricism, reason, and training; it reached its apogee by the middle of the nineteenth century with the consolidation of an enormously contradictory discourse surrounding 'the child' as, on the one hand, a sentimentalized wisdom figure and, on the other, national human capital, responsive to careful husbanding and investment. This construction of 'the child' coincides with the apogee of English colonial imperialism; indeed, it was an idea of 'the child' – of the not yet fully evolved or consequential subject – which made thinkable a colonial apparatus officially dedicated to, in Macaulay's words, 'the improvement of' colonized peoples (1972: 240). The contradictions of this discourse are evident not only in the original publication but also in contemporary recirculations of children's literature of the 'golden age'.

3

Helen Tiffin (1991) has written about the interpellating apparatus of address in imperial and post-colonial literatures, and Homi Bhabha has discussed the presence or appearance of the English book 'as a signifier of authority' (1985b: 149). What, then, can we make of Jamaica Kincaid's 'Wingless', which opens with a scene of Antiguan schoolchildren reading Charles Kingsley's *The Water-Babies* and with a series of direct quotations from that novel?

'Once upon a time there was a little chimney-sweep, whose name was Tom.'

'He cried half his time, and laughed the other half.'

'You would have been giddy, perhaps, at looking down: but Tom was not.'

'You, of course, would have been very cold sitting there on a September night, without the least bit of clothes on your wet back; but Tom was a water-baby, and therefore felt cold no more than a fish.'

(1983: 20)

Who is the 'you' interpellated by this embedded text? The nineteenth-century, middle-class, male child reader suggested by Kingsley's many direct addresses to 'my dear little man'? The mid-twentieth-century Antiguan schoolgirl? Or the later-twentieth-century adult – Caribbean, Euroamerican or Australasian – reader of 'Wingless'? Significantly, the complicated interpellation with which Kincaid's story opens also inheres in Kingsley's novel which is *about* a working-class boy but is ostensibly directed *to* a middle-class child reader; in addition, many of *The Water-Babies'* references to topical mid-nineteenth-century scientific, social reform and educational debates were obviously directed to an adult *rather* than a child reader, thus further complicating the intended audience of the novel. I will argue that the complicated address of *The Water-Babies*, which is picked up and mirrored by Jamaica Kincaid in 'Wingless', is a function of the ways in which the figure of 'the child' – in imperialist *and* post-colonialist texts – is the site of overdetermined and often contradictory investments.

As many critics have noted, *The Water-Babies* is a novel which protests the continuing use of child labour, advocates improvements in working-class sanitation, and reworks Darwin's evolutionary theory to accommodate Kingsley's 'muscular Christianity'. The novel thus embodies Kingsley's responses to such topical issues as the 1859 publication of Darwin's *The Origin of Species* and the 1862 report of the Second Royal Commission on Employment of Children, which had heard testimony regarding the use of climbing-boys. *The Water-Babies* also contains a strong indictment – in the Isle of the Tomtoddies section[6] – of what Kingsley saw as the mindless proliferation of an examination system in English schools; this proliferation resulted in part from the 'trickle down' effect of changes in foreign civil service appointments, for 'in 1860 the

Commission on Civil Service had begun to make appointments on the basis of competitive examination' (Uffelman 1979: 81).[7] Thus, *The Water-Babies* reflects the domestic impact of changes in colonial administration.

However, it is also one of the few nineteenth-century novels for children to 'de-scribe', at least implicitly, the function of the specifically *working-class boy* in imperialist expansion. The story of *The Water-Babies* is well known: it traces the moral and even physical – for Kingsley believed that 'the soul secretes the body as a snail secretes its shell' – evolution of a working-class boy through the intercession of various female figures. Tom, the chimney-sweep, realizes the degree of his own physical and moral filth only when he happens upon the sleeping figure of Ellie, the young daughter of Sir John Harthover whose chimneys he has been cleaning. Coming down the wrong chimney, Tom finds himself in Ellie's bedroom, a room 'all dressed in white' (1863: 25):

> Looking round, he suddenly saw, standing close to him, a little ugly, black, ragged figure, with bleared eyes and grinning white teeth. He turned on it angrily. What did such a little black ape want in that sweet young lady's room? And behold, it was himself, reflected in a great mirror.
>
> (ibid.: 28)

In his desperate and feverish attempt to wash himself in a river, Tom falls in, drowns, and turns into a water-baby, a 'being about four inches . . . long, and having round the parotid region of his fauces a set of external gills . . . just like those of a sucking eft' (ibid.: 69). Ellie, who also dies in an attempt to convince a stubborn professor that there are such things as water-babies, is assigned by the ugly fairy, Mrs Bedonebyasyoudid, to be Tom's schoolmistress. Tom's long and difficult evolution eventually comes to an end and the reader is told that 'he is now a great man of science, and can plan railroads, and steam-engines, and electric telegraphs, and rifled guns, and so forth' (ibid.: 346). Tom is ready to take up the work of Empire. A long 'moral' is appended to the novel, the penultimate paragraph of which reads:

> Meanwhile, do you learn your lessons, and thank God that you have plenty of cold water to wash in; and wash in it, too, like a true English man. And then, if my story is not true,

something better is; and if I am not quite right, still you will be, as long as you stick to hard work and cold water.

(ibid.: 349–50)

As the 'moral' indicates, sanitation and moral evolution – or physical and spiritual salvation – were closely linked in Kingsley's mind. The question of what working-class children were to be saved *for* is addressed more explicitly in 'The Massacre of the Innocents', a speech Kingsley gave in 1859 on behalf of the Ladies' Sanitary Association in London. This speech in support of sanitary reform and legislation explicitly associates the improvement of working-class conditions and of the survival rate of working-class children with the promotion of imperial expansion. Kingsley claims that between 30 and 40 per cent of working-class children died before reaching their fifth year. Given the very real threat of overpopulation in England, what, Kingsley asks the Ladies' Sanitary Association, are they 'to do with all those children whom they are going to save alive?' (1880: 258). His answer is, send them to the colonies. The following passage is worth quoting in full because it so explicitly argues for the production and salvation of children for the sake of colonial imperialism:

if [the ladies of the Sanitary Association] believe . . . that of all races upon earth now, the English race is probably the finest, and that it gives not the slightest sign whatever of exhaustion; that it seems to be on the whole a young race, and to have very great capabilities in it which have not yet been developed, and above all, the most marvellous capability of adapting itself to every sort of climate and every form of life, which any race, except the old Roman, ever has had in the world; if they consider with me that it is worth the while of political economists and social philosophers to look at the map, and see that about four-fifths of the globe cannot be said as yet to be in anywise inhabited or cultivated, or in the state into which men could put it by a fair supply of population, and industry, and human intellect: then, perhaps, they may think with me that it is a duty, one of the noblest of duties, to help the increase of the English race as much as possible, and to see that every child that is born into this great nation of England be developed to the highest pitch to which we can develop him in physical strength and in beauty, as well as in intellect and in virtue.

(1880: 258–9)

This lecture – directed to middle-class women – makes absolutely explicit what *The Water-Babies* itself can only gesture towards: the fact that poor or working-class children were increasingly regarded as a kind of human capital to be carefully husbanded and invested in settler colonies abroad. What is *not* so clear is why, in *The Water-Babies*, this message was ostensibly addressed to middle-class children or why it was encoded in fantasy literature. I want to suggest here that the ambivalent address, together with the surround of 'the fantastic', point to some of the conflicting investments inherent in nineteenth-century constructions of 'the child' and of 'childhood'. Many of these conflicts also inhere in nineteenth-century constructions of the colonial project and of the native Other under imperialism: once again to quote Bhabha quoting Macaulay, 'Be the father and the oppressor' (1985a: 74). Thus although Kingsley signals – through his use of long verse epigraphs from Wordsworth, Coleridge and Longfellow – his commitment to Romantic constructions of 'the child' as close to a state of nature and thus to the divine, he also makes it clear that the condition of 'childhood' is not equally available to all children. By making 'the child' – both as implied reader and protagonist – the site of political, scientific, and educational debate, Kingsley (albeit unintentionally) clarifies the ways in which 'the child' is *produced* differently, though always ambivalently, by specific historical, material and class conditions. The intended middle-class, male, child reader – Kingsley's 'dear little man' – is clearly being prepared for *his* role in managing less fully evolved Others, whether the working classes of his domestic environment or the native Others of the colonies. However, if (as I am claiming here) an idea of 'the child' (whether British or native Other) as, to put it bluntly, human raw material, was the necessary precondition of colonialist imperialism, how does the figure of 'the child' circulate in *post*-colonialist texts and theory? To answer this question, I want to look at two texts: the abridged Puffin Classics edition of *The Water-Babies* and Jamaica Kincaid's 'Wingless'.

4

One of the most consistent tendencies in 'the West's' constructions of 'the child' has been to deny the constructedness of the figure. This denial has manifested itself as the drive to naturalize the construction, often by rewriting – putting under erasure – the history of 'the child'. This is nowhere more evident than in the Puffin abridgement of *The Water-Babies*. Excisions from this edition are of two basic (and often overlapping) orders: the first ostensibly brings the novel in line with current literary, linguistic, and moral standards *for children*; the second deletes all topical references, especially to nineteenth-century scientific and educational debates.

In terms of *literary* standards for children, the abridged edition eliminates much which may, by today's standards, be considered condescending and unnecessarily didactic in tone; omitted, for example, is the second of the novel's opening sentences: 'Once upon a time there was a little chimney-sweep, and his name was Tom. That is a short name, and you have heard it before, so you will not have much trouble in remembering it' (A9, U2).[8] Significantly, however, this version also eliminates much, though by no means all, of the direct authorial address in the novel and has the effect of generalizing the child reader and of making him less the focus of an explicitly pedagogic discourse. The abridged edition also eliminates what may be seen as lengthy and unnecessary digressions thus more efficiently furthering the narrative. But, again, a closer examination of deleted passages reveals the sacrifice of much historical and geographical specificity. For example, a long catalogue of place names (which, incidentally, also contains another example of direct authorial address) is deleted from the abridged edition; the passage, which is too long (and boring) to reproduce, concludes: 'and then, whether you have found Vendale or not, you will have found such a country, and such a people, as ought to make you proud of being a British boy' (A34, U46). Other more subtle references to English imperial expansion – what the British boy was constructed *for* – are also deleted. We are told, for example, that after passing beneath the 'great white gate' of the Shiny Wall on his journey to Mother Carey, Tom 'was not a bit frightened' (A154); the following sentences are deleted: 'Why should he be? He was a brave English lad, whose business is to go out and see all the world' (U278).

As is obvious from these few examples, it is impossible fully to distinguish literary from moral values; however, the Puffin edition also eliminates much obviously offensive or impolitic stereotyping. Kingsley's anti-American and anti-republican diatribes are eliminated as are lengthy passages lampooning the Irish as a race of inveterate but charmingly childlike liars.[9] Editorial sensitivity to Irish stereotyping also results in the elimination of all of Kingsley's unfriendly references to potatoes. Tom discovers through the history of the devolution of the Doasyoulikes that 'when people live on poor vegetables instead of roast beef and plum-pudding their jaws grow large, and their lips grow coarse'; 'like the poor Paddies who eat potatoes' is the deleted conclusion to this sentence (A135, U244). The Puffin edition also eliminates potatoes from Kingsley's list of the evils unleashed on the world from Pandora's box (A160, U288).

The intention of the Puffin edition seems fairly clear: to produce a text which today's child will find readable (hence the excision of any passages which do not immediately further the narrative) and to produce a text which reflects contemporary sensitivity to issues of class and race. However, I want to sidestep the question of what children *ought* to read or to be allowed to read – the question itself assumes a particular construction of childhood; instead I want to point out that the general effect of these excisions is both to dehistoricize and depoliticize the figure of 'the child' and to put under erasure a history of strategic colonialist investment in that figure. I want also to suggest that the Puffin edition of *The Water-Babies* is paradigmatic of 'the West's' continuing and contradictory investment in a vision of child*hood* as a universal unmarked by class, place, or history. For ironically, it is around representations of 'the child' – whether they are evoked by UNICEF or the Foster Parents' Plan or famine relief agencies – that post-colonialist 'guilt', like colonialist aspiration, circulates. Jamaica Kincaid's 'Wingless', however, disallows such a disavowal of historical and geographical specificity by returning both the text of *The Water-Babies* and the child reader to colonialist history. Significantly, this return is centred in the schoolhouse, in the classroom.

Kincaid's critique of the interpellative apparatus of colonialist education is articulated through an ambivalent identification between Kingsley's chimney-sweep and her own child-narrator, whose most intimate fantasies and aspirations have been thoroughly informed by her reading of such texts as *The Water-Babies*. Like Tom, Kincaid's child-narrator sees herself as under instruction and in evolution, in suspension between infancy and adulthood, vulnerable and long-suffering. However, as Althusser tells us, interpellation is never seamless: though both the nineteenth-century working-class boy and the twentieth-century colonial child-subject are marginalized within a discourse of empire, gender/class/race and historical differences fracture any possibility of full identification.

Rather, as the following passage indicates, the child-narrator appropriates the idea of 'the child' and mobilizes it to fuel her emancipatory fantasies of future empowerment:

> I shall grow up to be a tall, graceful, and altogether beautiful woman, and I shall impose on large numbers of people my will and also, for my own amusement, great pain.
>
> (Kincaid 1983: 22)

This passage – with its disconcertingly sadistic undertones – puts its finger on the unease with which, as Jacqueline Rose (1984) has discussed, 'the West' contemplates the uncontained and polymorphous perversity of 'the child', but it also puts its finger on the colonizer's fears of native retribution.

5

My conclusions are necessarily of a preliminary nature; however, I want to suggest that Jamaica Kincaid, like so many other post-colonial writers, returns to the autobiographical site of 'childhood' because it offers both an explanatory *and* an emancipatory potential. That is, it enables the writer to examine a trope and an apparatus of colonization – the schooling of 'the child' – and to imagine a future condition of empowerment.

NOTES

1 I am greatly indebted to Michelene Adams for bringing Jamaica Kincaid's story to my attention, and to Stephen Slemon for guidance in the field of post-colonial theory.
2 The 1853 India Act and the 1855 East India Company report recommended that 'the most lucrative and prestigious administrative posts in the empire' be decided by competitive examination (Baldick 1983: 70). Foremost among the subjects to be examined was English language and literature; as Baldick phrases it, the effect of the 1853 India Act was officially to encourage 'the study of English literature for the good of the empire' (ibid.).
3 Children's literature in English is usually dated back to the 1744 publication of John Newbery's *Little Pretty Pocket-Book*.
4 As these texts make clear, 'childhood' was not and never has been available to all children but has always been a site marked by gender and class. As Ariès points out, the 'particularization of children was limited for a long time to boys' of middle-class and aristocratic families (1962: 61). For this reason, when referring to children of the nineteenth century and earlier, I use the masculine pronoun throughout this paper.

5 See also Postman's (1982) argument that an idea of 'adulthood', and thus of 'childhood', comes into being with the invention of the printing press. The 'adult' is one who can read and who thereby has access to certain kinds of knowledge. Chambers points out that 'There are those who are denied the right of speech and who, in etymological terms (Latin *in-fans*, not speaking), are infantilized' (1990: 3). This denial can take the form of 'exclusion from the powerful discursive positions of "preexisting", socially derived authority (the media, including print; the professions, including in particular the profession of politics; and so forth)' (ibid.: 4). I am grateful to Alan Lawson for bringing this argument to my attention.

6 The Tomtoddies, 'all head and no body', have 'a song which they sing morning and evening, and all night too, to their great idol Examination – "I can't learn my lesson: the examiner is coming!"' (Kingsley 1863: 350).

7 Baldick (1983) and Viswanathan (1987) have discussed the effect of these examinations on the establishment of English studies.

8 Page references to the abridged Puffin edition will be preceded by 'A' while those to the unabridged Macmillan edition will be preceded by 'U'.

9 'Instead of being angry with him, you must remember that he is a poor Paddy, and knows no better; so you must just burst out laughing; and then he will burst out laughing too, and slave for you, and trot about after you . . . for he is an affectionate fellow' (U131). In a lengthy passage extending from pages 129 to 135 in the unabridged edition, and which ostensibly describes salmon streams throughout the British Isles, Kingsley clearly articulates a descending hierarchy of British 'races' – from the English to the Scottish to the Irish to the Welsh.

13

MODERNITY, VOICE, AND WINDOW-BREAKING

Jean Rhys's 'Let them call it jazz'

Sue Thomas

Like Mary Lou Emery's, my project on Rhys negotiates the 'tension between the two spaces or contexts of Rhys's writing – the West Indian colonial context and the modernist European – as it is inscribed in terms of sex/gender relations in her novels' (Emery 1990: xii). The translation of Rhys's fiction into an exclusively modernist European cultural and literary context – a characteristic move in Rhys criticism – exhibits the 'logic of translation-as-violation' discussed by Gayatri Chakravorty Spivak (1986) in 'Imperialism and sexual difference': such translations are inadequately informed by a sense of the 'subject-constitution of the social and gendered agents in question' (1986: 235), the author or her protagonists. The translation of Rhys's fiction into a West Indian or post-colonial context is an effort to read it 'other-wise', a term Molly Hite uses in her acute analysis of the refusal of 'the prevailing constructions of gender and genre' (1989: 6) by women writers. This effort is occasionally effected, as Emery suggests combined 'feminist and Third World' readings of Rhys are, by 'a structural analogy between colonial hierarchies and sexual oppression that still positions the protagonist as a victim who lacks agency and offers little or no resistance' (Emery 1990: xii). These strategies of translation, I have argued elsewhere, often insufficiently question the terms and ethics of exchange of gendered knowledges of women and colonialism (S. Thomas 1990b). My project historicizes Rhys's fiction in the gaps, contradictions, and hybridized improvizations of her West Indian colonial and modernist European cultural and literary contexts. Feminist ahistorical, indeed anti-historicizing, approaches to Rhys render 'ungrammatical'[1] her negotiation of first-wave British feminist discourse and European modernism; and effects which operate as implicit critique or ironizing commentary on modern European feminist tradition or European modernism have gone largely unnoticed in her fiction.

Rhys's 'Let them call it jazz', first published in *The London Magazine* in February 1962, and collected in *Tigers are Better-Looking* (1968), provides an appropriate point of departure. The history of Caribbean emigrations and the lack of legal restriction on the rental terms of a furnished bedsit in Notting Hill inscribed in the story establish its 1950s setting. Rhys alludes in 'Let them call it jazz' to two generic first-wave British feminist narratives – the militant suffragette as martyr and the perils of the working woman. The Caribbean voice cynically dismisses pre-existent generic plots because they do not inscribe her reality: 'I don't think it's at all like those books tell you' (Rhys 1972: 59). The intertextuality of Rhys's plot and these feminist narratives signals a commentary on the 'indifference' of British law, first-wave British feminist discourse, and the 'doxa of socialities' of plausible narratives. I use and extend Luce Irigaray's concept of indifference, but also proceed to undermine the unitary sign of 'the woman'. Indifference has been summarized as:

a) Within the masculine order, the woman is indifferent in the sense of non-different or undifferentiated because she has no right to her own sexual difference but must accept masculine definitions and appropriations of it.

b) As a consequence, she is indifferent in the sense of detached or remote because of the imposture of her position.

c) From a feminine perspective, however, she might experience difference differently, in relation to her resemblance to another woman rather than to a masculine standard.

(Irigaray 1985b: 220)

Rhys works to demaximize, that is to undermine the 'doxa of socialities' – the maxims – which render plausible[2] the unitary sign of the citizen in British law, the indifferent sign of the racial and class other in first-wave British feminist narratives, and the indifferent sign of blackness in the racial stereotype. Her strategy involves the adoption of a black Creole voice; 'stylized patois'[3] functions as the principal sign of the authenticity of Caribbean difference.

In 'Let them call it jazz' Selina Davis, a young seamstress who has emigrated from Martinique to London, tells her story of finding a home and job in Britain. That process is complicated by racial

discrimination and the disjunctive technological times of Martinique and London. Her Notting Hill landlady and her neighbours in
an unnamed suburb have the power to objectify her in terms of
racial stereotype; the police and the judiciary believe the evidence
of white Britons with property. After Selina is evicted from her
Notting Hill bedsit, she is offered protection by a shadowy Mr
Sims, who, it is implied, attempts to recruit her into prostitution.
Selina is arrested twice – once for being drunk and disorderly, and
once for unpremeditated window-breaking. On the second charge
she is sent to Holloway Prison. The walls of Holloway, made
analogous through allusion with the walls of the biblical Jericho, the
accursed city, make literal the imprisonment of Selina within racial
stereotype and lack of class prerogative. Acutely conscious of the
spectacle made by the 'different' motility of her body and quality of
her voice in front of the police and the judge, she does not feel she
can prove her counter-charges against the landlady and the racist
neighbours, and retreats into silence as a tactic to maintain integrity
in the face of such invalidation in the time of the story. In the time
of the narration of the reconstructed story Selina assumes authority
over the representations of her and her property by others.[4] 'So let
them call it jazz,' Selina thinks, specifically with reference to a
musician's appropriation and marketing as jazz of a precious song
she picked up in Holloway. The gift of the song, with words glossed
as 'cheerio and never say die' (Rhys 1972: 60), offered her a measure
of spiritual freedom. But the authority she gains over her experience by voicing her story allows her to shrug off other representations of her in terms of jazz. Jazz also means 'meaningless or
empty talk', 'sexual intercourse', and 'to move in a grotesque or
fantastic manner; to behave wildly' (OED). Selina can shrug off the
police and the judge's apparent perceptions of her efforts at
explanation as meaningless spectacle; the neighbours' looks, which
place her as a 'wild animal'; their complaints about the obscenity of
her Caribbean dancing; their construction of her as a 'tart'; and the
unspeakable of the italics of the wife's 'At least the other tarts that
crook installed here were *white* girls' (ibid.: 54) – the fear of
miscegenation – which structures their sense of the contamination
of cross-racial contact. The preservation of the song of solidarity
intact in memory is a metonym of the horizon of spiritual freedom,
but Selina acknowledges: 'Even if they played it on trumpets, even
if they played it just right, like I wanted – no walls would fall so
soon' (ibid.: 63).

After Rhys herself was briefly imprisoned in Holloway in 1949 – so that a psychiatric evaluation could be made after she had been convicted on charges of assault – she ironically remembered the sacrifices of the suffragettes (which have been read historically as the origin of feminist modernity) and planned to write a story called 'Black Castle',[5] words which are used of Holloway in 'Let them call it jazz' (ibid.: 57). However, one does not need such extra-textual support to justify a reading of 'Let them call it jazz' in the context of suffragette history. Appearance in a British court on charges of disorderly conduct and malicious damage to property (by window-breaking), and imprisonment in Holloway are staple elements of the first-wave feminist generic narrative of the suffragette as martyr. Disruptions of public meetings, demonstrations, and 'the political argument of the stone' (C. Pankhurst 1959: 97) to attack 'the secret idol of property' (E. Pankhurst 1914: 266)[6] were militant tactics of the Women's Social and Political Union (WSPU). Imprisonment in Holloway was an important rite of passage for WSPU members; it also became part of its iconography of martyrdom which Lisa Tickner (1987) has analysed brilliantly. Rhys alludes in constructions placed on Selina's behaviour by prison staff to aspects of suffragette experience: attempted suicide by throwing oneself over a railing (1972: 58); and hunger-striking (ibid.: 59). Emily Wilding Davison, who eventually succeeded in committing suicide for the cause in 1913 by colliding with the King's horse on the Derby course, had attempted suicide by throwing herself from a Holloway balcony in 1912; she was honoured with a large WSPU funeral cortège, bearing banners with, among others, the words 'Give me Liberty or Give me Death' (Tickner 1987: 138–40). By August 1909 hunger-striking was normal WSPU practice in Holloway. Given Selina's repeated claim that the police and the judiciary discriminate against those without material property, Rhys's choice of Selina's trade, seamstress, may also hint obliquely at the fate of 'Jane Warton', seamstress, the cross-class disguise assumed by Lady Constance Lytton to prove class discrimination in the treatment of suffragette prisoners. Lytton had a heart condition, the state of which is carefully documented in her *Prisons and Prisoners* (1914); Rhys's Selina makes several references to the condition of her heart – her emotional well-being – and the hard-heartedness of Britons. That Rhys may have read *Prisons and Prisoners* is also suggested by Selina's carrying of the song as a 'comforter', a belief in her 'own power to exist freely' when outside prison. This action replays and reinflects patronizing advice offered in Lytton's 'Dedication to Prisoners'. Lytton urges prisoners to seek 'release from all that is helpless, selfish, and unkind' in themselves.

> Unless you are able to keep alight within yourself the remembrance of acts and thoughts which were good, a belief in your own power to exist freely when you are once more out of prison, how can any other human being help you? . . . But if you have this comforter within you, hourly keeping up communication with all that you have known and loved of good in your life, with all the possibilities for good that you know of – in your hands, your mind, your heart – then when you are released from prison, however lonely you may be, or poor, or despised by your neighbours, you will have a friend who can really help you.
>
> (Lytton 1914: ix–x)

The generic narrative of suffragette prisoners as martyrs contested the authority of representations and constructions of them as criminals (in the eyes of the law) and as grotesques (in the eyes of anti-suffrage public opinion). These representations and constructions undermined the legitimacy of their constitution as 'politicized speaking subjects in the symbolic order' of a white, middle-class culture. Using and extending Kristeva's theorization of abjection, I have argued that in the hostile public opinion:

> As the borders between the proper and the improper, the clean and the unclean, order and disorder [of conventional femininity] are crossed by the suffragette . . . it is implied that the degeneracy and lawless licence of the demand for the vote may be read from the body and the voice.
>
> (S. Thomas 1990a)

Typically the body and voice are mapped as grotesque, as boundaries of sexual, racial, animal, or class difference are crossed. In telling their own stories as propaganda, as speeches from the dock, as autobiography, as history, suffragettes contested such stereotyping representations, attempting to regain authority over their own discourse on the 'battlefield of representations, on which the limits and coherence of any given set are constantly being fought for and regularly spoilt' (T.J. Clark, quoted in Tickner 1987: 151).

Rhys's Selina has available to her two of the same sites of

contestation of stereotyping and criminalizing representations which undermine her constitution as a politicized speaking subject in a patriarchal, white, middle-class culture – a dock speech and an autobiographical account of oppression – and on each of these sites the difference of her cultural capital, and the implications of that difference are marked. When the judge asks her if she has anything to say, she daydreams an account of provocation entailing class and racial discrimination, but is too self-conscious about the extravagance of her body and voice, an extravagance which maps her cultural capital, to articulate it fully publicly:

> I want to say this in decent quiet voice. But I hear myself talking too loud and I see my hands wave in the air. Too besides it's no use, they won't believe me, so I don't finish. I stop, and I feel the tears on my face.
>
> (Rhys 1972: 57)

She is overcome by a lack of self-confidence and a sense of her implausibility; she becomes the 'silent Other of gesture and failed speech' (Bhabha 1990b: 316). Her extravagance is, to adapt and fissure Nancy K. Miller's formulation of the function of implausibility in women's writing, a form of insistence about the relation of women and representation: a comment on the stakes of difference within the theoretical indifference of British law and of first-wave British feminism and feminist narratives.[7] The unreflective maxims of racial stereotype are rendered implausible by the demaximizing juxtaposition of Selina's point of view. This demaximization of the threatening carnival of the primitive is, to extend Mary Russo's analysis of the 'figure of the female transgressor as public spectacle', a stark reminder that the bodies and voices of certain women, not just unfeminine ones, 'in certain public framings, in certain public spaces, are always already transgressive – dangerous, and in danger' (Russo 1986: 217).

The theoretical indifference of British law in the 1950s is usefully discussed by Edward Pilkington in his study of the deteriorating race relations which led to white riots in Notting Hill in 1958:

> The established legal view held by government and the judiciary was that the law must be impartial, and should not distinguish between classes or types of people, including racial groups. The problem with this 'colour blind' approach was

that it left no legal grounds for prosecuting those who practised racial discrimination.

(Pilkington 1988: 47)

Or, by extension, those other blind spots of an old legal dream of symmetry, sexual or class discrimination.[8] British law also did not officially recognize discrimination – racial, sexual or class – as a defence in mitigation: Emmeline Pankhurst gives an example of the law (represented by the judge in a trial of Mr and Mrs Pethick Lawrence and herself) being out of step with public opinion (of a jury) on the issue of mitigating circumstances (1914: 228–48). In speeches from the dock, window-breaking middle- and upper-class British suffragettes offered the defence of sexual oppression and it was rejected. Mrs Leigh, the first suffragette to be imprisoned for window-breaking, said in the dock, indicating she would repeat the offence: 'We have no other course but to rebel against oppression' (quoted in E. Pankhurst 1914: 119). Selina justifies herself after she has broken the window (not in court): 'But if they treat you wrong over and over again the hour strike when you burst out that's what' (Rhys 1972: 55). The theoretical indifference of the law is destabilized by Selina's consciousness of the racism implicated in the responses to her extravagance. The symmetries of interest assumed in the British legal tradition also justified the refusal to extend the franchise to women: 'It was argued that the interests of all women and working-class men who did not meet the property qualification could be adequately represented by the votes of propertied men, whose interests were the same' (S. Thomas 1990a). Suffragettes challenged this economy of sameness in their self-representations and their demonstration that it was maintained by the physical violence of arrest, imprisonment and force-feeding in the last resort.

A paradigmatic and compressed contestation of the legitimacy of the asymmetry of interest is provided by Harold Bird's 'No Votes Thank You' produced for the National League for Opposing Women's Suffrage in February 1912 (Tickner 1987: 193; Figure 13.1), and Louise Jacobs's 'The Appeal of Womanhood' produced for the Suffrage Atelier in 1912 (Tickner 1987: 214; Figure 13.2). 'The foregrounded classical figure of womanhood' in Bird's poster 'represents the aspirations of bourgeois individualism (vide Bakhtin)' (S. Thomas 1990a). It is implied that the criminally licentious grotesque suffragette in the middle ground (armed for a

Figure 13.1 'No Votes Thank You' by Harold Bird. By courtesy of the Bodleian Library, University of Oxford. (John Johnson Collection: Woman's Suffrage Box 3.)

window-breaking raid) has crossed boundaries of racial and sexual difference. This same figure appears in a slightly earlier Bird poster with a feather in her hat ('Her Mother's Voice', Tickner 1987: 195). Her place is taken in Jacobs's reply

> by a women's parade of working-class misery and exploitation over which looms the darkness of Westminster. . . . It is implied the interests of these women are unrepresented or inadequately represented in the State; their plight is a sign of the degeneracy of the State. The abject in this representation of women is the non-nurturant State.
>
> (S. Thomas 1990a)

Suffragists and suffragettes stressed the ideally nurturant functions of the State in which their different interests as women would be incorporated (Holton 1986: 14). The underside of the State, and more specifically London, is the dark, feminized collective body of

Figure 13.2 'The Appeal of Womanhood' by Louise Jacobs. Courtesy of the Museum of London.

the working class, whose interests may be represented by the cross-class chivalry of bourgeois, feminist individualism symbolized in the foregrounded figure (S. Thomas 1990a).

The suffragist and suffragette generic narrative of the working-class woman's life represented her as negotiating a perilous course between sexual and economic exploitation, in their melodramatic vocabulary the White Slave Traffic and sweated labour. This narrative is codified and compressed in paradigmatic form in M. Hughes's postcard 'The Scylla and Charybdis of the Working Woman', produced for the Suffrage Atelier, c. 1912 (Tickner 1987: 182; Figure 13.3). In such narratives London is often orientalized as modern Babylon. The body and voice of the prostitute or the casually promiscuous woman are rendered other to those of the maiden chivalric warriors of the WSPU or the classically feminine suffragists. The motility of the body of the prostitute is so obscene that the body is literally unspeakable, and various metonyms take its place in the narrative – modern Babylon, venereal disease, the sick

Figure 13.3 'The Scylla and Charybdis of the Working Woman'
by M. Hughes. By courtesy of the Museum of London.

bodies of the respectable women and children infected with
venereal disease, 'dreadful trade' as in, for instance, Christabel
Pankhurst's *The Great Scourge and How to End It* (reprinted in Marcus
1987). As Lisa Tickner argues:

> The rhetoric of moral outrage required men to be venal and
> prostitutes to be victims. As articulated by the WSPU it
> sharpened sexual antagonism and disguised the circumstances
> in which prostitution in fact took place. . . . In that sim-
> plification, however, lay the strategic power of their argu-
> ments, which could then be fitted to an increasingly
> influential concern with the relation between moral behav-
> iour and social stability.
>
> (Tickner 1987: 225)

The first paragraph of 'Let them call it jazz' locates the story in a
very specific place (Notting Hill), time (1950s), and recently
acknowledged social problem (racketeering landlords abusing

uncontrolled tenancies of black Caribbean tenants in Notting Hill),
circumstances well documented by Edward Pilkington (1988: 40–
67); the narrative then moves to an apparently more timeless site.
Selina negotiates the working woman's perilous course between
prostitution and sweated labour, but she is not loosened into this
narrative channel by the venality of men. Her situation is more
complex, inflected by her racial difference, dispossession of money
and tenancy, disjunctive technological time, and her cultural
capital. Initially she cannot find even sweated work, but eventually
– after her imprisonment – imposes herself in the market through
anancy-style trickery. As she negotiates that perilous course,
deliberately under-melodramatized in Rhys's ironizing reinscription of it, she goes hungry, possibly becoming anorectic until the
intervention of the precious song. In the protection of the venal Mr
Sims, Selina has to choose between food and the alcohol which will
allow her to transcend the materiality of her body and release her
into a nurturant dreamspace of Caribbean and maternal memory –
in this space she dances, sings, remembers calypso heroes, and
imitates her feisty grandmother to produce carnivalesque laughter.
This dreamspace allows her to preserve her psychological and
cultural integrity. Rhys resolutely inscribes Selina's demaximizing
body and voice.

Selina is released into a hybrid narrative site of female and
immigrant Caribbean Gothic picaresque. On this site Rhys contests
both the hegemonic first-wave British feminist construction of the
working woman and the real circumstances of potential recruit-
ment into prostitution; and offers ironic commentary on the
symmetries of interest assumed in the cross-class chivalry of
bourgeois feminist individualism. Rhys often takes up and
improvizes on the seduction-betrayal-ruin paradigm of female
Gothic picaresque in her novels, abandoning the heavy moralism
characteristic of the genre. In one picaresque version of female
Gothic – inflected differently in 'Let them call it jazz' – the middle-
class white heroine, declassed (or whose middle-class dependence is
threatened), is called upon to resist sexual menace, often from
villains posing as protector figures, by displaying qualities of
resourcefulness and strength which run counter to the stereotypical
view that women are inherently passive. The preservation of
chastity is a metonym for preservation of integrity. Extending an
argument of V.S. Naipaul's, Ena V. Thomas (1990) argues that the
'typical picaroon environment of violence and brutality' was

reproduced socially for the black Caribbean person in colonial Trinidad and that that closed environment 'elicited picaroon responses from its most vulnerable citizens'; Caribbean picaresque does not imitate, but rather reinscribes and crucially reinflects, picaresque in a discordant literary historical time (1990: 211). Dispossessed of any Caribbean middle-class prerogative by the British labour market and racism in the 1950s, the non-white Caribbean immigrant generally entered a closed picaresque environment, in which the material and cultural capital to break down its walls was difficult to obtain or impose. The emerging Caribbean British literature of the 1950s – Samuel Selvon's *The Lonely Londoners* (1979) and George Lamming's *The Emigrants* (1980), for instance – reinflects the picaresque, marking the emergence of an authentic national cultural time with the imported Caribbean vernacular and hybridizing it with ironizing modernist set pieces or narrative strategies. In 1910, Rhys herself was dispossessed of Caribbean middle-class prerogative by a paucity of marketable skills and the impoverishing death of her father. The loosely autobiographical origins of her fiction are well known, but the discursive and narrative sense and meanings she gave that experience crucially reinflect and improvize on the female Gothic picaresque to stage her marginality. They mark the emergence of her unique hybrid modernist female Gothic and immigrant Caribbean picaresque, which ironizes the generic narratives of European cultural and literary modernity, inscribing the cultural vernaculars of her underclass. These reinflections and improvizations are examples of the hybridity Homi Bhabha writes of as

> the perplexity of the living as it interrupts the representation of the fullness of life; it is an instance of iteration, in the minority discourse, of the time of the arbitrary sign – 'the minus in the origin' – through which all forms of cultural meaning are open to translation because their enunciation resists totalization.

> (Bhabha 1990b: 314)

Rhys's reinscription and reinflection of two of the generic narratives of suffragette modernity in the time of the emergence of second-wave British feminist modernity may be read as her fear of the 'ghostly' repetition[9] of the indifferent sign of 'the woman' which gives sexualized racial and class others (among others) no rights to their own differences, forcing on them indifferent middle-class British feminist definitions and appropriations of those differences. The cumulation through time of suffragette autobiographies and histories also produced 'ghostly' recirculations of that first-wave British feminist sign of 'the woman' and of the generic narratives Rhys contests. The temporal gap also reminds us that certain women caught within the maxims of indifference experienced feminist time as recursive, not progressive. Further, Rhys's indifference to the British feminisms of her day may be read as crucially inflected by her imposture within their orders.[10] Rhys and her protagonists experience their difference differently from feminist maximizing constructions.

Part of that different sexual difference as Caribbean immigrant may be read through Rhys's adoption of a cross-racial voice in 'Let them call it jazz' and her representations of attachments to nurturant Caribbean dreamspace. Rhys tries to produce the stylized patois in good faith, with attention to detail of syntax, vocabulary and form. 'Let them call it jazz' is also a 'speakerly text' (Gates 1984: 296), true to the oral traditions of Caribbean folk language. The story caused Rhys considerable anxiety, but not over the ethics of cross-racial voicing. She posted the manuscript to her daughter Maryvonne for typing rather than give it to her regular typist, fearing the operation of the autobiographical fallacy in a local reading of it would confirm the worst suspicions 'people here' had of her. There is a danger in the voicing, but she also wrote the story 'as a holiday . . . A bit of a crazy story. For fun.'[11] Rhys's title, too, may mark her own shrugging off of any potential invalidation of her experiment with patois and cross-racial voicing as jazz, in a range of its meanings. In her autobiography and in her fiction the nurturant black Caribbean dreamspace of patois, calypso song, and a black maternal body are produced as the oceanic, not ungendered as the oceanic usually is (Torgovnick 1990: 165), but gendered feminine. For her white Caribbean female protagonists, Anna Morgan and Antoinette Cosway Mason, that oceanic is a *potentially* pleasurable site for the obliteration of racial difference, and *potentially* operates outside, but can never wholly escape the colonialist patriarchal law and its legacies which structure the maxims of power which repress the oceanic.

NOTES

1 I am using and applying in a new context Nancy K. Miller's notion of the 'ungrammaticalities' of women's fiction. Miller discusses the inability of a patriarchal critical paradigm to read aspects of women's fiction which 'violate a grammar of motives' informed by 'a certain ideology (of the text and its context)' (1988: 26–7).

2 In a 'translation-adaptation' of an essay by Genette, Nancy K. Miller affirms that

> the precondition of plausibility is the stamp of approval affixed by *public opinion* . . . the critical reaction to any given text is hermeneutically bound to another and preexistent text: the *doxa* of socialities. Plausibility then is an effect of reading through a grid of concordance:
>
>> What defines plausibility is the formal principle of respect for the norm, that is, the existence of a relation of implication between the particular conduct attributed to a given character, and a given, general, received and implicit maxim. . . . To understand the behavior of a character (for example), is to be able to refer it back to an approved maxim, and this reference is perceived as a demonstration of cause and effect.
>>
>> (G. Genette 1969: 174–5)
>
> If no maxim is available to account for a particular piece of behavior, that behavior is read as unmotivated and unconvincing.
>
> (Miller 1988: 26).

'Demaximization' is Miller's term; I use it in a wider range of contexts.

3 Jean Rhys, letter to Francis Wyndham, 6 December [1960] (Wyndham and Melly 1985: 197).

4 My argument here endorses and extends that of Paula Le Gallez (1990), who questions the validity of conventional constructions of Rhys's protagonists as passive victims. Le Gallez argues that:

> Where Rhys's heroines are concerned, the struggle [for authority] concerns itself not with a physical grouping together in solidarity against the oppressive forces, but rather in the more subtle way of each becoming her own maker of fiction. As such . . . the 'Rhys woman' has the power to build texts and to articulate her own narratives. In this respect, as the author of her own discourse, she sets herself against the suffocation of her spirit, a suffocation which the traditionally expected 'passivity' would surely bring her.
>
> (176)

5 Rhys writes of her Holloway experiences to Peggy Kirkaldy on 4 October [1949]: 'I did think about the Suffragettes. Result of all their sacrifices? The woman doctor!!! Really human effort is futile' (Wyndham and Melly 1985: 56). She mentions 'Black Castle', a projected story about Holloway, on Monday [1950] (Wyndham and Melly 1985: 76). Rhys was diagnosed as a hysteric (Angier 1992: 446). During Rhys's residence in Beckenham between 1946 and 1950, she was

convicted on charges of wilful and malicious damage to property, assault (several times), and being drunk and disorderly (Angier 1992: 442–54).

6 Emmeline Pankhurst writes in her ghosted autobiography, *My Own Story*:

> *There is something that governments care far more for than human life, and that is the security of property, and so it is through property that we shall strike the enemy.* From henceforward the women who agree with me will say, 'We disregard your laws, gentlemen, we set the liberty and the dignity and the welfare of women above all such considerations, and we shall continue this war, as we have done in the past; and what sacrifice of property, or what injury to property accrues will not be our fault.
>
> (1914: 265)

Amplifying her charge that courts discriminated against suffragette window-breakers, she comments:

> The smashing of windows is a time-honoured method of showing displeasure in a political situation. . . . Window-breaking, when Englishmen do it, is regarded as honest expression of political opinion. Window-breaking, when Englishwomen do it, is treated as a crime.
>
> (ibid.: 119)

7 Cf. N.K. Miller:

> I am arguing that the peculiar shape of a heroine's destiny in novels by women, the implausible twists of plot so common in these novels, is a form of insistence about the relation of women to writing: a comment on the stakes of difference within the theoretical indifference of literature itself.
>
> (1988: 39)

8 My formulation of arguments about symmetry and asymmetry of interests owes some debt to Luce Irigaray's 'The blind spot of an old dream of symmetry', *Speculum of the Other Woman* (1985a).

9 The term is borrowed from Homi Bhabha, who discusses the 'ghostly repetition' of the 'time and space' of black British peoples in the film *Handsworth Songs*: 'in the historic present of the [Handsworth] riots, emerge the ghostly repetition of other stories, other uprisings. . . . There are no stories in the riots, only the ghosts of other stories' (Bhabha 1990b: 306–7).

10 Accounts of Rhys's antipathy to feminism (Niesen de Abruña 1988: 327; Angier 1985: 121) usually uncritically recirculate David Plante's story:

> Letters from fans she asked me to read out to her and as I did she looked wistfully sad. If the letters enclosed reviews, she asked the title and the first line, then said, 'Tear it up.' When the title was 'The Dark Underworld of Women' or 'The Woes of Women' or had 'women' in it in any way, she'd grab the review from me and tear it up herself and throw it in the basket, laughing, and say, 'No, I've had enough of *that*!'
>
> (Plante 1983: 39)

This story can be read in many ways; it is usually only read as a confirmation of Rhys's anti-feminism.

11 Letter to Maryvonne Moerman, 22 June [1960] (Wyndham and Melly 1985: 187); letter to Francis Wyndham, 6 April [1960] (ibid.: 184).

14

SPEAKING THE UNSPEAKABLE

London, Cambridge and the Caribbean

Paul Sharrad

In this essay, I want to set up a dialogue between two works to generate readings of each that help both to describe and to question inscriptions of power and colonial history. I work on the idea that post-coloniality is a matter of textual structuring as well as reading strategy. Reading (and writing) 'against the grain' implies that there *is* a grain to work against. This entails the problem of counter-discourse, which preserves a binary opposition and perpetuates the privileging of one of the poles even as it seeks to complicate and dismantle the basis for discriminatory contrast. With Foucault's ideas on discourse in mind (1981), I explore the mutual exposure of opposing uses of silence in Dickens' *Oliver Twist* (1839) and Caryl Phillips's *Cambridge* (1991).[1]

Caryl Phillips's novel, *Cambridge*, is so understated in its arrangement of narrative, so plain in its prose style that its complex implications may be overlooked. But restraint, decorum and proper measure are ideas central to Phillips's story. The daughter of an absentee plantation-owner sails to the West Indies to inspect the family property and escape from an arranged marriage. Critical of her father's domineering but self-indulgent behaviour, Emily Cartwright finds the colonies equally excessive. Local whites live either in unwarranted extravagance – 'luxuries abounding where decencies are often found to be lacking' (Phillips 1991: 117) – or abject deprivation (ibid.: 107–8); blacks have no dress sense, wearing either nothing or a riot of colours, violating 'laws of taste which civilized peoples have spent many a century to establish' (ibid.: 66), and their behaviour swings from extreme lethargy to violent outbursts of activity, sullen silence to inexplicable merriment.

Emily loses her Spanish maid and companion to a fever on the voyage out and arrives alone as an equivocal figure. On the one hand she is upper-class, Home-grown, and a surrogate male, being a plantation owner's daughter. On the other hand she is an unaccompanied, and therefore vulnerable, female, and an ignorant newcomer. The plantation manager has been removed, apparently for over-sympathizing with his workers, and has been replaced by a man with little breeding but a capacity for brutal command of slaves. Emily's prim outlook and proper diary prose struggle to maintain a sense of balance and control.

> Without rank and order any society, no matter how sophisticated, is doomed to admit the worst kind of anarchy. In this West Indian sphere there is amongst the white people too little attention paid to differences of class. A white skin would appear passport enough to a life of privilege, without due regard to the grade of individuals within the range of that standing. The only exception I have so far observed was the modesty displayed by the book-keeper who first conveyed me here. However, sensible to propriety, he has subsequently maintained his distance. The other men, perhaps because I am a woman, have shown little courtesy in affording the attentions proper to my rank. They converse with me as freely and openly as they wish. This is barely tolerable amongst the whites, but when I find the blacks hereabouts behaving in the same manner I cannot abide it, and see no reason why I should accommodate myself to the lack of decorum which characterizes this local practice.
>
> (ibid.: 72)

None of the marks of civilized social order, as Emily understands it, are to be found. In fact, her own very English and respectable attitudes prove to be increasingly infected by the system she tries equably and rationally to analyse. The loaded terms used to describe slave speech – 'slobber', 'jabber', 'drawl', 'bray', 'the enervating yawl and drawl of the negro accent' (ibid.: 95)[2] – and her stereotypic reproduction of 'nigger talk' go hand-in-hand with her increasing personal distress and her inability to come to any consistent position about Emancipation. She begins by hoping to bring practical experience to the service of the abstract principles of the anti-slavery lobby and is troubled by the use of the word 'nigger', but with her shift to the 'we' of the local status quo, she increasingly uses terms like 'sambo' and depicts Wilberforce and his followers as deluded, finally admitting she does not know what she thinks (ibid.: 8, 16–17, 37, 86, 179). As her own restraint breaks down, we see that the only controls in her immediate society are imposed by sectarian prejudice, class privilege, patriarchal dominance, provincial backbiting, racist intolerance and the law of whip, gun and gallows.

This becomes patently evident when, two-thirds of the way through the book, we shift to the story of the recalcitrant but well-spoken slave, 'Cambridge'. From the anguished bewilderment of capture in West Africa, we follow Olumide (his original name) through his transportation to England as gentleman's house-servant, his evangelical Christian education, liberation and poverty-stricken marriage to a white servant, his activity as a preacher in the anti-slavery cause, his voyage back to Africa to convert his heathen brethren, his kidnapping, return to the Caribbean plantations and eventual death by hanging.

Cambridge's slave-narrative/gallows-confession story is a dramatic rupture in the fabric of the novel, made more potent by its conciseness and emotional restraint. It succinctly contradicts or undermines almost every confident observation Emily has made. (Her pronouncements on the extravagance of local fashions, black and white, are deprived of their authority, for example, when Cambridge notes in passing that the Englishwoman is 'a trifle over-dressed for the heat' (ibid.: 164).) His first encounter with whites reverses the stereotypic perceptions of black speech, cannibalism and lack of human feeling found in the rest of the book (ibid.: 135). He also, in describing his impressions of England, directly counters Emily's silly access of romantic exoticism when she asserts that the English worker would do well to swap places with the plantation slave (ibid.: 67, 150).

Cambridge's 'noble sufferer's' view of things is not allowed, however, to become a simple substitute for Emily's. There are at least three interpretations of his life on the island, and we can see in his own stilted prose how he has been mentally, as well as physically, enslaved by the discourse of civilization. He patronizes his African home-folk, lords it over his wife and, later, as a widower and reluctant 'trusty' on the plantation, he tries to control and convert his housemate, the feared *obeah* woman, Christiania. Because he claims a moral and intellectual authority superior to the physical control of the white overseer, Brown, Cambridge has to be removed, but it is questionable whether he was ever a real threat to anyone.

If he is killed off, Cambridge is none the less 'present' in the closing pages of the book. His memory is invoked by Emily, who is living proof of his influence. The apparent murder of Brown has freed her from an unwanted liaison while trapping her in a similar isolation to Cambridge's own privileged destitution at the edges of plantation society. Like the educated slave, Emily has 'refused to serve', and it is the memory of his passive resistance to Brown as well as of his death that she summons up in her closing delirium (ibid.: 183), where she is mentally and physically isolated, abandoned by lover, father and doctor friend. Her sole company, out of a generosity we only appreciate fully at the end of the story, is her negro servant-companion whose name supplies the last word of the book. The opening and closing female companions (Isabella and Stella) and the implied link between Emily and Cambridge are but two of the devices framing the several stories of the novel and implying its overriding message. The book opens with a composed observation of the 'perfectly chaotic world of men and freight', the product of 'much trafficking'. At its close, we find the observer socially disgraced and apparently demented, and we realize that she, and everyone on both sides of the Atlantic, and of the divides of class, gender, race and wealth, have been part of a chaotic, destructive trafficking whose infernal logic Phillips has masterfully delineated.

The reformist project of giving voice to the silent oppressed invites comparison with an earlier literary reformer. Though it has been argued that Dickens was driven by personal anxieties of being marginal to true respectability, and that his work of social analysis was more imitative than original, he has been seen as an icon of literary and cultural authenticity: the voice of London, Christian charity and middle-class gentility. This much is at least implied in Homi Bhabha's pairing his work with Naipaul's *A House for Mr Biswas* (Bhabha 1984b: 93) and is confirmed by Naipaul (1976) himself.[3]

One of the many anomalies in the work of Dickens is the appearance in a popular sentimental romance (serialized in parts or cheap newspapers with all the drama of dastardly deeds, salacious touches of low-life and suspenseful episode breaks) of a hero who does very little and says even less. The most famous scene of *Oliver Twist* is the one in which Oliver actually does and *says* something –

PAUL SHARRAD

he gets up (albeit under duress from his workhouse companions) and asks for more. The exaggerated horror and outrage with which this act is greeted seem to underline not only the author's satiric irony, but the unexpectedness of anyone from the ranks of the boys speaking up at all, and, when we have read most of the book, we feel there is cause for further amazement that it is Oliver who is their spokesman.

Elsewhere in the novel, Oliver is characterized in terms of his silent witnessing of events and the pitiful expression on his appealing features. (His face 'voices' his innocence and silently saves him from the suspicion of the morally upright, rescues him from an early grave as a chimney sweep, and makes him prey to the evil figures in the book). Oliver's face, in fact, speaks more than he does (just as the voiceless picture of his mother speaks forcefully to him). True, Oliver does escape Sowerberry's to 'seek his fortune' in London after turning on Noah Claypole, but it is a reaction to circumstances rather than a heroic decision, and it is significant, I think, that his primary employment is as an undertaker's *Mute*, again because of the expressive pathos of his slender frame and pale, refined features. Despite the sub-title, 'A Parish Boy's Progress', Oliver is no Dick Whittington, or Samuel Smiles; indeed, the suggestion of that legend behind the orphan's story only serves to heighten the contrast.

The experience of the individual caught up in the 'machine' of industrial and urban society has typically been one of *anomie* and victimhood. In terms of social realism, it is understandable that Dickens should have Oliver as a passive, somewhat bewildered stand-in for the hero. As a moral hero, Oliver also has to retain his natural innocence, and therefore he cannot afford to become embroiled in the unremittingly corrupt and corrupting world in which he moves. He remains always attached to the unworldly images of his mother's spirit and the Maylies' pastoral retreat, even though the world constantly reaches out to trap him in its plots and prisons. As such, he is the allegorical embodiment of Christian fortitude, a noble, but static virtue.[4] This inevitably means that it is the more active (and effective) agents of evil who appear as colourful centres of dramatic interest – Fagin being the most memorable character of Dickens' book. Another reason for Oliver's effacement, is of course, that he is, from the outset, a 'non-entity' because of the mystery of his mother's identity. The book is his story, but he cannot tell it for himself. Various people make up identities for him (mostly to his detriment) and at the denouement of the mystery plot, all these figures come together to provide him with a composite character: Nancy, Monks, Bumble and the crones from the workhouse all speak to Brownlow who delivers the full revelation to Oliver.

The Herculean slave, Cambridge, suffers from the same kind of strategy of literary representation. He is almost emblematically fixed as the kneeling supplicant of Josiah Wedgewood's 'Am I not a Man and Brother?' medallion. Like Oliver, Cambridge is given his name by others and can speak only at the end of his story. Unlike Oliver, though, he has a remembered original identity, Olumide, and a surfeit of other names – Black Tom, David Henderson, Cambridge, Hercules, 'the black Christian'. His problem is to speak through all these imposed guises, to shape them into a single narrative, just as we have to assemble a single narrative out of several versions and find the one tale of human black oppression amongst Emily's monstrous plethora of shape-changing labels: 'children of the sun, sons of Ham, negro, sambo, nigger, jetty woman, ape-woman, imp of satan, ebon community, sable freight', etc. When Oliver and Cambridge do begin to speak for themselves at the end of their stories, both are pushed into the background. Oliver is displaced by the usurping voice of the narrator/biographer (himself one of the several absent presences of the book whose intrusions serve to underline his otherwise 'silent' speaking). Cambridge is removed forcibly to be replaced by the official and sensationalist media account of his crime and hanging and then by Emily – not her narrating voice, this time, but a distanced view of her situation and thoughts. Amidst all the speaking out of Phillips's text, there is also a contradictory silence and silencing. Phillips solves this technical problem to some extent by his economical foregrounding of Cambridge and the selectively filtered presentation of the evil Brown. I would also argue that, overall, his ironic approach serves to make present the absences of history, to give motive force to the fixity of types and to allow the unspeakable truths of slavery to become compellingly eloquent.

In Dickens, on the other hand, the silence of Oliver can be seen as symptomatic of unspoken truth. Oliver's non-entity emphasizes the bustle and chatter of those around him, all of which is selectively stage-managed. Dickens speaks out on some social issues, leaving an uneasy sense of the unspeakable in hints of moral and social contradictions. Dickens' text dramatizes, but leaves unspoken until later work, Blake's point that charity without general social reform simply perpetuates inequality.

> Pity would be no more
> If we did not make somebody Poor;
> And mercy no more could be
> If all were as happy as we.
>
> (Blake 1957: 33)

Oliver can be saved only through the actions of Brownlow as benign father-figure; but Brownlow has built the fortune that allows him his generosity (and the leisure to play detective) within the very system that has oppressed Oliver. Dickens, the epitome of the Londoner and the figure who came to represent, through Pickwick, a vision of a comfortable, romantic England, constantly adverts to the basis of Britain's prosperity in colonial ventures. In *Great Expectations*, the felon makes his money in the colonies while Pip ends up in Egypt as part of Britain's imperial expansion. In *Oliver Twist*, it is the Artful Dodger who is shipped off to Botany Bay (1985: 390). The northern cotton mills in *Hard Times* imply the presence of the United States and the sweated labour of the slave plantation.

Comparison with Phillips's book, part of which is set in the south of England, allows us to explore this colonial underpinning to Dickens' world, and brings us to a new understanding of the dimensions of Oliver's silence. It is a marker of Dickens' own confrontation with the unspeakable at the heart of British gentility. While he opposed great missionary works and civilizing pro-grammes abroad on the grounds that social reform at home was a more pressing need, he championed the ideals of personal Christian charity that justified these imperial projects and dealt only with the symptoms of injustice. Whereas he satirized politicians and the law, he fought in his fiction for the social changes produced through parliamentary reforms that were used in a self-congratulatory way to justify Britain's interventionist role as global policeman. Under-lying all of this was the unexamined hypocrisy of its major contribution to international welfare, the abolition of the slave trade. Self-congratulation at this international humanitarianism served to obscure not only the appalling work and housing conditions at home, but also the fact that Britain had been the major developer of the slave trade in the first place.

In *Oliver Twist*, there are three significant mentions of the West

Indies. Mr Brownlow's housekeeper, who mothers Oliver, tells him a great many stories about her 'amiable and handsome' children, one of whom is 'clerk to a merchant in the West Indies' (Dickens 1985: 143). Later, when Oliver is rescued by the Maylies and returns to London to find Mr Brownlow and explain his protracted absence, he discovers that gentleman has 'sold off his goods and gone to the West Indies' (ibid.: 187). When the mystery of Oliver's identity and Monks's intrigue is resolved, we are told that the bastard step-brother quit Europe to live on an estate in the West Indies (ibid.: 438).

This shadowy but unarticulated presence of the West Indies signals a basic limitation to Dickens' reformist programme – a silencing that, if not explicitly conscious to him, none the less shared in a deliberate collective revisionism. Economically, politically and legally – Abolition Act 1807, Emancipation 1833 (Craton 1974) – and in literature (at least since Aphra Behn's *Oroonoko* 1688), slavery had been on the agenda for progressive English social thinkers for more than a hundred years, and the West Indies had become the standard example for the debate in England on the morality and economics of slavery. Dickens, however, makes no reference at all to slavery in his letters up to the publication of *Oliver Twist*. In fact he was prepared to use 'niggers' as a term of contempt, describing some police on one occasion as 'a rascally bunch of *Negurs!*' (Dickens 1965: 14). Yet, the manifestations of slavery were still very apparent.[5] Phillips's novel epitomizes them in a mention of pet shops selling black children along with parrots and monkeys (1991: 151), and allows an ironical voice to the black domestics:

> My master made it known that I was to consider myself his domestic, not his slave, and he spoke in a manner which suggested abhorrence of the trade which had occasioned his fortunes to increase. I soon came to understand that English law had recently decreed the trading in human flesh illegal, so I learned to perceive my master as a criminal. However, he was but one of a large multitude of contented plunderers happily accommodated in the bosom of English society.
>
> (ibid.: 141)

It may be that Dickens deliberately connected Monks with the West Indies to indicate moral degeneracy by association with the slave trade, but it is far more likely that he simply saw the tropics as a natural metonym for physical, mental and moral degeneration as Charlotte Bronte was to do later in the decade in *Jane Eyre*. Dickens' later condemnation of slavery (Dickens 1957) in the emotive tones with which he castigates the oppressors of London's deserving poor accuses his audience of double standards, but his basic rationale for opposing the barbarities of institutionalized slavery is that it corrupts the whites involved in it, and therefore demeans white civilization as a whole. This is the argument of the egregious plantation doctor McDonald in Phillips's novel and is consistent with the insular logic of social reform in *Oliver* which proclaims that if good gentlefolk keep their own hands clean, their consciences clear, and practise Christian benevolence, the world will inevitably become a better place.

Reading back onto Oliver's story with the West Indies and Phillips's novel in mind, however, highlights the limitation of this sentimental construction of social good which never really crosses lines of race and class. The sentimentalizing of the rural cottage, personal philanthropy and women, and the deferral of total happiness and justice to the life hereafter are all symptoms of repression of the extent of institutional enslavement and a confession that there are truths the social fabric depends upon to remain unspoken. Reading back from Phillips onto Dickens allows us to see the utopian vision of rural house and garden found in the Maylies' retreat as a gentrified miniature of the eighteenth-century pastoral celebrations of the West Indian plantation, i.e. as a transplanted model of the landscaped Great House.

> White peasant village embowered in trees,
> And gardened mansions dot the widespread map;
>
> . . .
>
> Plenty lies cradled in the isle's soft lap;
> Canes clothe with waving wealth the smiling land;
>
> . . .
>
> And towns, and bristling forts, emboss the silver sand.
> (Dunbar 1986: 121)

The fear and loathing of the London mob evident in Dickens' fiction, seen in the context of trafficking with the West Indies (and underlined by comparisons between the British working class and slaves in *Cambridge*) is a localized, urban and class-based analogue of the paranoia in colonized societies about the possibility of a convict uprising, a slave revolt or an Indian Mutiny. (One of the reasons the overseer Brown is able to displace the more benign Mr Wilson is that the latter refuses to take seriously a local white militia raised to prevent rebellion (Phillips 1991: 62).) The masses can be cheerfully patronized and celebrated for their 'colour' in speech, habits and dress just so long as they know their place in the order of things or so long as their wild outbursts can be channelled into the service of the status quo. Verbalized containment of the masses, however, is always accompanied by an unspoken fear of their strength. The textual restraint surrounding Cambridge's presence and personal narrative is matched by a sense of his restrained power: he is morally superior for his self-control, he is a physical giant, a Hercules in Emily's eyes, and his word carries much weight amongst the plantation workers: his fate represents their own. The London mob under Brownlow's direction, extirpates an outlaw; the island removes Cambridge, a disturbing element who appears to have made himself an outcast, like Sikes, by committing bloody murder.

Dickens displaces the tensions of his novel onto the sentimentalized figure of the 'fallen woman'. Oliver's mother mirrors the fate of the pivotal Nancy who both validates and disturbs the comforting story of Rose Maylie's adoption and Oliver's accession to social standing. Motherhood and womanhood as sources of innate goodness are the only real points of contact between the gutter and the cottage: an ambivalent sign of redemption and degradation, assertion and dependency. Dickens writes on behalf of the helpless sacrificial victim, and in doing so barely allows him or her (especially her) to speak. We can feel pity, respect, even admiration for the victim (orphan, fallen woman, slave) as long as he/she is kept at a distance, memorialized in safely conventional texts (like tombstones) that *speak for* rather than allow to speak.

Phillips sets up an interesting parallel here, in that Emily, while apparently speaking for herself from the dominant position of white, London-based plantation-owner's daughter, is also spoken *about* (by Cambridge and of course by the author), and *for* by all the males in the book, who take for granted her role as helpless newcomer, marriage-object, etc. Her mixed status means that she has no position from which to command unquestioning obedience; when she operates as a white, she is undermined by her status as ignorant newcomer, when she plays owner's daughter, her power is negated by her position as woman, though all of these roles allow her possibilities of strategic withdrawal as well, so that not until the very end is she completely stripped of authority.

This shifting set of roles and power relationships eventually speaks for the all-embracing polymorphism of hegemonic discourse. It frames Emily's personal ambivalence towards slavery, where she comes out with confused responses to both theory and practice depending on which role and what state of mind she is in. Cambridge is similarly caught in the tragic attempt to straddle a fence he has not asked to be placed on but cannot get off.[6] The only positions in Phillips's novel are uncomfortable ones, for characters and ultimately for readers too.

Dickens, on the other hand, delivers a spurious comfort by creating a reductive enclosure of gentility and good feelings, but it is always vulnerable to intrusion by contesting forces because its self-containment is illusory. Admitting that the fences are down between country and city, gentry and mob, God and man, morality and survival, in any form other than demonized, nightmarish (and therefore unnatural) visitations, is to negate the possibility of order and virtuous, secure social improvement.

Phillips calls into question Dickens' activist but limited notion of the writer as social conscience, adopting a more Brechtian approach that refuses sentimental self-gratification through emotional catharsis. Indeed, the comparison with Dickens and his times, reveals not only Phillips's tight restraint – both in narration and character – but his deliberate, even defiant, intertextuality. The text emphasizes the historicity and facticity of its material through its attention to late eighteenth-century style (phraseology and diction and a penchant for italicized words) and through generic parody. Not only do we find set pieces of description (the colonial house and table; the negro festival) and explanations of the plantation system (Dr McDonald's discourse on medical treatment for blacks and whites; the bookkeeper's speech on the creolization of the population post-Abolition), but also quoted slave songs and a parody of the colonial gutter press and the gallows confession. The very plot suggests a pastiche of eighteenth-century Enlightenment works of an abolitionist nature.[7] One of the terms used for the blacks is *Mungo* (Phillips 1991: 136) suggesting the lead character in a popular drama by Isaac Bickerstaff, *The Padlock* (1768, playing into the nineteenth century). Cambridge's story almost exactly parallels that of the protagonist in a well-known abolitionist poem, 'The Dying Slave'

(Thomas Day/John Bicknell, 1773), in which a London negro is baptized, marries a white servant and is then shanghaied onto a slave ship. Cambridge does not leap overboard to a watery grave, nor does he lead a slave revolt, as does the most famous of literary characters co-opted to the abolitionist cause, Oroonoko. There are suggestions, however, that he is fomenting unrest amongst the slaves, and like his literary forebear, he studies Christianity and is memorably flogged for his pains (Anstey 1975: 142–53).

An intertextual dialogue with a writer like Dickens makes clear Phillips's reluctance to comment via the particular, the topical and the sentimental. His allusions and parody, moreover, emerge not as impoverished imitation, but as subversive mimicry in a counter-discursive application of Homi Bhabha's concept of colonial ambivalence. Phillips's highlighting of the text's literariness as derivative pastiche resists mimetic interpretations of either a nationalist or ethnic essentialism or a neo-colonialist disparagement and containment. Comparison to this story shows that Oliver's eloquent muteness is entirely necessary and totally consistent with the project of both author and society. Dickens' novel implies that we can only ever have an unworldly purity, one that is matched by a hellish impurity. In the face of lurking manichean oppositions, average mortals are struck dumb and wander aimlessly through moral confusion hoping that there will be agents of providence to save them, but unable to name them or claim kin until true identity is recognized.

Such a text needs a benign author as the world needs a divinity to shape its ends, so that despite the proliferation of characters and the underlying unspoken tensions of *Oliver Twist*, it is a fundamentally monologic book. It speaks out of stereotype and satire and romance, all of which suggest a central, normative basis for judgement. Much of Dickens' social commentary arises from the ironic counterpointing of knowingness and naivety – without Oliver's silent passivity we would not have the primary index to the proper reading of 'the merry old gentleman's' perversion of family, industry and 'enlightened self-interest'. While there is a reversal of moral positioning in relation to the board of the workhouse and the judiciary as represented by magistrate Fang so that the reader condemns the abuses of thoughtless social theorizing and heartless legislation, there is no questioning of the basic social institutions; rogues remain irredeemable rogues; the law acts to curb the mob, to pursue the degenerate villain, and to keep the virtuous protected and pure, untainted by the system of which they are part. However, the nightmare scenes of mob retribution (encouraged by Brownlow) and the waking nightmare of Oliver by the Maylies' cottage window attest to Dickens' deeper suspicion that there is no protection, nor any safe retreat from the trafficking endemic to his world. To cope with his overwhelming involvement in the complexities of his world, Dickens resorts to a strategic reductiveness. Excess is finally subjected to decorum, human beings to names on tombstones; the narrator assumes all identities and ties all strings tidily, affecting to play slave while remaining the slave-master.

In Caryl Phillips's text irony works to turn monologue into dialogue, uniformity into contesting forms. Arnold Brown, of course, is white; Cambridge is Olumide; Christiania is resolutely pagan. White (but Spanish) Isabella is set against black Stella; the contrast qualifies the polite notion of 'ladies' companion' with which Emily frames her narrative ('Dear Stella': the last words of the book), but the similarity of names underlies their common status as servants and feeds back into our perception of Emily so that we are able to see the reversal of roles in which mistress becomes dependent and all three, as women, stand exposed as victims of another kind of trafficking, the kind that Dickens cannot deal with and attempts to cover over with sentimentality. By the time we reach the end of the book, the last words of the Prologue have been opened up for inspection: 'England./The truth' (1991: 4). The patriotic and conventional sentiments about England voiced by Emily are matched by the truth that she is escaping a country that condemns her with a life sentence of servitude and barren tedium and the reality of what lies at the end of the chain of British commerce. Is England the truth: the source of all proper judgement and homeland of the heart, or are the two terms placed in contradistinction? Where can Emily find the freedom she dreams of? (ibid.: 132).

It would seem, finally, that this book which speaks eloquently about the evils of slavery allows no authoritative position from which any of the characters or even the authorial persona can pass judgement: irony and sheer unreliability undermine everyone's perception of the truth.[8] The author confines himself principally to Emily's consciousness and we are left only with her realization that she has changed, and that we may take it that she is not sure of what she is, possibly at all, but definitely when it comes to questions of race and emancipation (ibid.: 179). This certainty that she is not sure of anything is a reversal of the self-assurance with which she has pronounced on the state of the colonies. Emily's confident but fallible speaking is itself framed by a contradiction: that all of her speaking out is in fact a silence, because it takes the form of an extended diary entry, and because we leave her at the close of the book 'voicing' her silent thoughts. A further aspect of the contradiction, and one explored by other Caribbean writers, is that real history, for a slave society, must perforce be an imaginative one (Naipaul 1969; Harris 1967). The 'document' in the novel most likely to survive in real life is the most 'official' and also the most unreliable – the sensationalist report of the murder of Brown, biased by white prejudice, 'yellow press' cliché and the report of an interested witness from a group otherwise repeatedly depicted as willing to say anything on oath. The rest is silence.

Silence, however, is a mark of many things, not all of them negative. For Emily it is a sign of civilized conduct, polite restraint. But while she castigates the negroes for their uncontrolled loquacity (Phillips 1991: 38–9), she herself prattles on obsessively in her diary and her eventual delirium (ibid.: 178, 183), unwittingly indicating a fear of falling silent that stems from her realization of the powerlessness of those unable to speak. If Emily initially has greater access to speech than the slave, it is increasingly circumscribed until at the end she has only a slave with whom to converse.

If silence can indicate lack of power, it is also a sign of liberation and resistance. At the outset of the book, she faces her father silently: 'Still she spoke no words. Papa I have buried feelings. She listened as her voice unspooled in silence' (ibid.: 4). The story also ends in her silent monologue, but in the interim she has quietly escaped servitude to her father, an arranged marriage, and an unfortunate affair. In contrast, Cambridge tries to speak out through the letter of European law and the law silences him because it does not recognize the authenticity of his claim upon it. Within the system of which he is a living criticism, but which, also, he ironically perpetuates, he can speak only within a constrained personal space. Emily is in the same situation.

Cambridge and Emily are also alike in both labelling the marginalized Christiania as mad. Emily interprets her behaviour as wilful insult and malign witchcraft. Cambridge knows that it is the pathetic result of her being brutalized since the age of ten by black and white alike, but even he loses patience with her when she starts to mock his unsustainable roles as her husband-protector, saintly sufferer, and plantation mediator. He withdraws into the ineffectual bombast of a domineering Christian patriarchy.

Christiania's 'madness' is figured as her rejection of words, her refusal of the Word. Her silent speech, which is at one level the pitiful ravings of a lunatic reduced to an animal scratching in dust and filth, is also a powerful menace when heard as *obeah* incantations. It is also a sign of resistance to containment in discourses of domination that entrap the other characters. It is, after all, Christiania who finally escapes. She, to quote Stella, 'has no use as such' (ibid.: 73) and as such is both the least and most liberated character of the book whose gesture of playing mistress of the Great House indicates the futility of talking within the system as well as the subversive power of silent mimicry of the unspeakable.

Here we arrive at the crux of Phillips's project in comparison with Dickens'. His strategy of indirection and escape through silence to reveal the unspeakable that Dickens seeks to control and silence through a surfeit of words is a double-edged one. The writer struggles to find a space from which to speak a truth that will not be selective or contained within the terms made available to it by the system it analyses. In a way, the writer's 'silent' refusal to pronounce or to privilege any voice is a more radical challenge, because it forces us to assemble the evidence and make judgement, to connect past and present, fiction and reality. It also resists any containment by disputes over historical fact, emphasizing the importance of the system and its textually-constructed discourse. Such a ploy, though, may allow us to read the text as merely a literary historical reconstruction, an intertextual play, with nothing helpful to say about contemporary life. The dilemmas of an ironic silence are elsewhere illustrated in the writings of Gayatri Spivak (1987, 1990). In struggling to find a position within history from which to speak critically about it, she circles her own 'subjectivity' and 'positionality'. The question of whether the subaltern can speak (or at least speak through her mediation) voices the unspoken but eloquent problematic at the heart of *Cambridge*'s cool detachment: not just whether the historical slave can be allowed to speak, but also how the modern post-colonial writer can speak objectively and with commitment about the hegemonic forces that shape his/her own life, language and literary production.

If a reading of Phillips opens up Dickens' position and ideological formation to analysis, it also shows that the British West Indian writes out of a project that includes David Dabydeen's work on the history and literary representation of blacks in England and the burgeoning and politicized recognition of 'ethnic' or minority writing in contemporary Britain, signalled in the appearance of journals like *Third World Quarterly*, *Third Text* and *Wasafiri*. In this context, Phillips's novel adopts a tactic of indirect symptomatic analysis in which a 'historical' text demonstrating the all-embracing traffic of a particular institution serves as an allegory that reaches out to attack the roots of modern racism. As such, it runs the danger of being too subtle to be effective – too distanced for its modern applicability to be recognized, so comprehensive in its exposé that it seems nihilistic, and too relativized by its ironies to admit a position from which to make judgements for committed action. But any silence resulting from Phillips's strategic choice is also a potent gesture that resists ready co-option onto narrow platforms of backward-looking Black Diaspora reverse essentialism. It also resists easy integration into the master culture, questioning the very bases of its ideological formations. Like Soekarno under house arrest, like the escaped Christiania, *Cambridge* is comprehensively 'silent in a thousand tongues' rather than shouting a partial message in only one.

One key marker of post-colonial literature is that it offers a more cogent description of Empire by *de-scribing* it – by allowing the unspeakable a space in which to speak, uncovering gaps in discourse and revealing hidden dialogue and intercourse. The colonial text, on the other hand, obscures and silences Empire by covering it over with inscription, by offering the impression of *total description*, papering over gaps, containing dialogue and denying intercourse. Dickens' text is constrained by discourses that are a piece with those of colonial narratives, and thus it works in quite different ways from Phillips's novel. Phillips's post-colonial textuality is partly constructed out of a *reading*, and therefore appropriation, of other texts. Such reading against the grain to investigate the ambiguous power of silence allows an instinctive interrelation of margins and centres, past and present, black and white, that offers no easy accommodation, but the possibility of discovering new co-ordinates for an enunciation of the unspeakable.

NOTES

1 Here I take the point of Mukherjee (1990: 1) that even within post-colonial critical debate the 'playing field' is not a level one. The other

ideas arise as responses to Ashcroft *et al.* (1989), and Tiffin (1987: 17).

2 The depiction of black speech is noted by Jaggi (1991).

3 Dickens, of course, was *within British academia* relegated to the margins of the Great Tradition, partly because, like so many post-colonial writers, he sought to expose the power structures of hegemony (and thus was not a 'pure' artist), and partly because, as defence against this, the public celebrated his sentimental side, thereby removing him from consideration as a 'serious' writer. See F.R. Leavis (1962).

4 This reading is generally anticipated by Angus Wilson (1972: 131–2). Dickens, of course, wanted Oliver to illustrate 'the principle of Good surviving through every adverse circumstance' as a part of a moralized realism that would distance his work from the 'Newgate novel' romances attacked by Thackeray. (See his Preface to the second edition.)

5 The celebrated inquiry into the case of Grace Jones revealed that slaves were still being traded in Britain as late as 1827, and black children were being exhibited in 'freak shows' at least to 1815. See Peter Fryer (1984).

6 This mobility of roles and ironized utterance provides a demonstration of Homi Bhabha's argument about the fundamental ambivalence of colonial stereotypes. See Bhabha (1983: 18–19).

7 The naming of Emily's arranged and rejected suitor in England (Thomas Lockwood) and the Heathcliffean representation of Brown suggests also a possible allusion to *Wuthering Heights*.

8 Again, we may refer to Bhabha's point that the complexity of subject formation in colonial discourse (and therefore in counter-discourse as well) does not admit of simple fixed reifications or dialectical representations that can be corrected by mere substitution or reversal. This creates problems for 'the *historical* enunciations of colonial discourse'. See Bhabha (1983: 24). On the matter of mimicry, see Bhabha (1984a, 1985c).

15

THE SPEAKING ABJECT
The impossible possible world of realized Empire

Howard McNaughton

In education, in legislation, in books ranging from the Bible to airline timetables, the textuality of the British Empire has written itself across the globe, to be internalized by its subjects. But such textuality is neither an objectified historical phenomenon 'back there' nor a univocal, uninterrupted monologic drone. Imperialism is a more pervasive phenomenon than its obvious geopolitical manifestations celebrated in movies of the Raj, or in royal tours to the colonies. As the power structures of the world realign, to construct possible power structures of possible worlds, and communications become on the one hand more popular and on the other more specialized, sophisticated and controlled, imperialism aspires to anonymity, and its textualities become increasingly subtle, amorphous, and rhizomic. This essay focuses on the deposition of 'abject' human remains as a marker or camouflage of the edge of Empire, to explore the nature and implications of textuality in two types of contemporary situation: a 'media drama' – the crash of an aeroplane while on a sightseeing trip to New Zealand's Antarctic 'dependency' – and stage plays in which theatre's richly polyphonic discourse enables the strategic exploration of the ironies of, and the impossible possibility of escaping from, the constructions of Empire.

On 28 November 1979, Air New Zealand TE 901 hit Mount Erebus, Antarctica, following exactly the flight co-ordinates with which its computer was erroneously – unknown to the captain – loaded. The flight path was a 'possible' one in the double sense that it was inscribed in the computer and that the crew read the sky ahead as accessible; it was 'impossible' in that this 'possible' route actually contained the highest mountain on the Antarctic continent, an impossibility apparently rendered possible in earlier publicity footage made by the New Zealand National Film Unit which seemed to show an aircraft flying into a mountain and out the other side.[1]

The *réalisation* of what had happened would come with the sighting of the wreckage, but in the lacuna before that, in which radio and radar contact dissolved, individual airline officials in Auckland realized what had happened; one of them even consulted *Scott's Last Expedition* to help him construct the possible scenario (Macfarlane 1991: 289). As with Scott, the devastation – both human and mechanical – became an ambiguous inscription of advance into the alien. While television repeatedly pictured the 'proud koru' still visible on the tail in the wreckage, the human remains were retrieved:

> Recovering the bodies was a nightmare. The aircraft shattered upon impact. Officials had to scoop up the bodies in a hostile environment. Skua gulls, scavengers by nature, pecked at the flesh; they even managed to get at the flesh when placed in polythene bags. One hundred and fourteen substantially intact bodies were recovered and there were another 133 bags containing human remains (in one case, three bags contained parts of one and the same person). Of the total 257 victims, 213 bodies were recovered and identified.
>
> (Suter 1991: 152)

Anthroposemiotics, it appears, is a discipline that will take some time to become established in Antarctica. But the smudge in the snow on all the front pages was not the only way Erebus was textualized:

> Probably no other major disaster in history has been so well photographed at the precise time of the tragedy. Virtually everyone on board had cameras and about 900 frames were eventually processed . . . . The photographs taken while the aircraft was heading straight for Mount Erebus showed everyone smiling and enjoying themselves. The most macabre photograph was taken as the photographer passed from life to death and his or her finger pressed the camera button.
>
> (Suter 1991: 152–3)

To these textualities might be added the cockpit voice recorder and the flight data recorder. But as legal proceedings looked for culpability, new erasing textualities emerged. The airline immediately imposed a 'news clamp', causing the many overseas journalists to complain 'that it was unprecedented for an airline which had lost a plane to control the dissemination of all news' (Macfarlane 1991: 293). Subsequently, records were systematically destroyed in an attempted cover-up which a Royal Commission described as a 'pre-determined plan of deception' and an 'orchestrated litany of lies'. From a different quarter came another erasing pressure, the ecologists' demand that New Zealand should clear its rubbish out of Antarctica.

The multi-voiced history of Erebus has an obvious hybridity in that the discourses of salvage, photography, and tape fuse together to grow into the various book accounts of the incident. But as well as a hybrid relationship there is also a palimpsestic one, most conspicuous in the 'cover-up' but also implicit in the call to keep Antarctica tidy: a hostile relationship in which concealment postures as revelation,[2] in which the superscription of a text attempts to blank out another. In addition, natural semiotics provides the erasing 'flat light' or 'white-out' conditions which allow an air crew to read a solid mountain as uninscribed. Inherently, the palimpsest engages a semiotic swivel of hostility: the 'litany' and the Commission report reciprocally contest each other's right to be read, as do the bits of bodies in the snow and the photographed overlay of smiles in the sky.

The whiteout, however, only realizes an erasing energy that is already present: reading Antarctica as a blank page is also a product of the narcissistic imperialistic desire[3] to read a world as available, empty, unfurnished, uninscribed. This was epitomized in the wall map of a virtually blank Antarctica with which Edmund Hillary promoted his 1956–8 polar expedition, a map of (his) absence, syntaxed only by the remains of the expeditionary forces that had staked their boundaries and destinies there: footsteps like the dotted lines up Everest, value-added footsteps sanctified by the body at the end. The persistent respect for this ethic, that abject bodily penetration rather than a fly-over is what marks a claim to a land, was articulated by a member of Hillary's 1969 polar expedition as part of the debate over the level of compensation for the Erebus victims: he emphasized that Antarctica is a dangerous continent, especially to those who want to drink champagne while flying over it, as opposed to those who have sweated on foot up its slopes. Hillary's own inscription is ambiguous, contributing to both layers of the palimpsest, in that he was scheduled as official commentator on the previous Antarctic flight a fortnight before the crash.

Three textualizing strategies may be distinguished in the Erebus history: that of 'scribing' or 'worlding' Erebus, that of 'superscribing' or 'reworlding', and that of 'de-scribing' or 'unworlding'.[4] Enmeshed in the practice of these are elements of camouflage, alibi, and 'cover'. The assumptions and suppositions implicit in an imperialist project of reading a text or a territory as uninscribed were amply realized at Erebus, in spite of the fact that the captain made a 'hobby' of collecting maps and on this flight used the *New Zealand Atlas*; among the last noises on the cockpit recorder were the sounds of pages being turned.

The hybrid and the palimpsestic may be sharply differentiated in the polyphony of theatrical discourse. Rudy Wiebe in interview (Keith 1981: 154) once discussed the Edward Bond aphorism: 'Every writer writes in other men's blood' (Bond 1974: 42). Wiebe was bending Bond for his own agenda, but the context parallels that of the de-scribed Antarctica. Bond's Shakespeare, the epitome of the self-authenticating writer, has given up the theatre because he perceives that it is simply colluding in the spread of oppression and capitalism. He gets drunk with Ben Jonson, and then heads off home from the pub to commit suicide. It has been snowing, and on the way home he finds himself in a de-scribed territory, with the hedges, paths, and ditches, the markers of capitalistic landownership, erased. Textuality has been voided, and so has Shakespeare's contribution to it. Exhilarated by release from the burden of textuality, he reads the snow as a blank page, inviting Shakespeare the child to write something on it: a new empire of textuality seems accessible to him.

> Writing in the snow – a child's hand fumbling in an old man's beard, and in the morning the old man dies, goes, taking the curls from the child's fingers into the grave, and the child laughs and plays under the dead man's window.
>
> (Bond 1974: 42)

As at Erebus, the palimpsestic overlay of laughter denies the grave the right to be read. But at that moment a shot is fired upstage, and in the first production blood was suddenly flung all over the snow. Shakespeare sprawls in the snow, writing not with the child's hand but with his own body, in the blood of the anonymous old man who has been shot. Shakespeare's voice continues, worlding the character of the old man:

> I didn't want to die. I could lie in this snow a whole life. I can think now, the thoughts come so easily over the snow and under my shroud. New worlds. Keys turning new locks – pushing the iron open like lion's teeth. Wolves will drag me through the snow . . . . I sit at the bottom and cry at my own death.

(Bond 1974: 42–3)

The snow is a conceit of nostalgia, a worlding textuality of its own, akin in its concealing, camouflage function to Edward Said's 'covering'. The empire of capitalism cannot be unworlded simply by humanist retreat.[5]

The reworlding cadaver in Bond or on Erebus is thus conceived – in semiotic terms – as a marker of the edge of Empire, the lines of white crosses in Flanders Fields that delineate the parameters of advance. The body site here is syntactic, marking the divides and cohesions of units of territorial meaning. Semiotically, it may be read as Empire's abject, the rubbish dumps of Empire, an ecological blot. At the other extreme, it may be seen as claiming 'some corner of a foreign field/That is forever England'. Whatever the subsequent remappings, the lines of crosses constitute a focus of pilgrimage for veterans for decades, veterans who reconstruct the possible absence of those crosses. But any ten-year-old will tell Rupert Brooke that Flanders Fields are *not* forever England, they never have been. This England is a possible England constructed by the body under the cross, a cross that is saying that that is an impossible possible England, as impossible as the flight path through Erebus. For the unfocused, however, the crosses have a purely syntactic function, a conjunction of two textual territories, a semiotic channel to the delineation of the edge of Empire.

If Flanders Fields are not forever England, neither does anyone want Erebus to be marked as forever New Zealand. The camouflage culture of the twentieth century, explicated in works like Teresa Hayter's (1971), has projected the textuality of imperium as one of erasure or alibi. In 1991, Saddam Hussein used trenches, minefields, and barbed wire to write Iraq across Kuwait. By mid-year, it was all being de-scribed, with British engineers working through the minefields and one burning well after another being extinguished by Red Adair. De-scribing like this, of course, does not leave the field uninscribed; the marks of erasure have a textuality of their own, even if only smoke in the sky or New Zealand wool being used to mop up the oil in the Gulf.

But what was America's initial scribal involvement in its notionally counter-imperialist capacity? When did the Gulf War start to be realized? When did it achieve *réalisation*? This question was frequently addressed, and the phrasing came echoing back from Vietnam: the war will be registered on the American consciousness when the first body-bags start coming home.

The marking function of the body-bag is clearly different from the Flanders grave. It gives no edge to Empire. Because – like the polythene bag punctured by the skua – it appears initially as a numbered shipment, whose only origin is an airport and whose only destiny is an airport, its lack of name-coding, place-coding, and destiny-coding constitutes an erasure of the sites of self and of Empire, a floating abjection. Legally, Air New Zealand TE 901 was simply an internal domestic flight from Auckland to Christchurch which happened to fly past 'various southern islands' en route. Erebus was in no sense timetabled as an available destiny, and even reading Erebus as a syntactic link between the two New Zealand cities is much more than reflexive: it is self-voiding, a denial of cohesion between the cities, a denial represented by the absurdity of the *New Zealand Atlas* in the cockpit. The originless, unworlded body-bag speaks Roland Barthes' alibi language: 'I am not where you think I am; I am where you think I am not' (Barthes 1973: 133). Or Lacan's camouflage language:

> Mimicry reveals something in so far as it is distinct from what might be called an *itself* that is behind. The effect of mimicry is camouflage, in the strictly technical sense. It is not a question of harmonizing with the background but, against a mottled background, of becoming mottled – exactly like the technique of camouflage practised in human warfare.
>
> (Lacan 1973: 99)

Instead of saying 'Kilroy was here', the body-bag says, 'Perhaps everyone except Kilroy was there.' And for the family of the possible Kilroy the bag becomes a site for (unworlding) desire: 'I hope that isn't Kilroy, I hope he's out there where the crosses should be.'

While the body-bags are being forklifted around Kuwait, other syntaxes are emerging. Empire is looking for 'command and control' locations, with the idea that power can be centred. Find the centre, and power may cease to exist. Hussein is speaking his own alibi language with inflatable tanks and missile launchers, and with his own persona as the Scarlet Pimpernel of Iraq. And at the same time General Powell is holding up his famous emptied maps, conceived on the Hillary model, effectively telling the press in his briefing sessions: 'These maps represent what isn't happening in Iraq. This is an impossible possible Iraq.' Through language strategies of alibi and camouflage, Empire is neither scribed nor described; it is disguised, it becomes semioclastic, or at least one of Spivak's 'fractured semiotic fields' (1990: 53). It becomes a complex arena of distortion in the Freudian double sense of both change of appearance and also displacement:

> When disaster befalls a company, or other corporate entity, or a department of state, there almost invariably commences a process of seeking a scapegoat for the occurrence. Each person with some apparent responsibility will seek to shed the burden and place it elsewhere.
>
> (Macfarlane 1991: 40)

This writing of an alibi text to Erebus is thus analogous to Empire itself. But, if the quantity of properties in any possible world is always finite, they may nevertheless be concealed or transposed. Like the continuous media speculation about the number, arming, and placement of Hussein's missiles, the Erebus judge read the airline's defence as a game: 'The cards were produced reluctantly, and at long intervals, and I have little doubt that there are one or two which still lie hidden in the pack' (Lambert and Palenski 1982: 335–6). The alibi text is thus neither fully legible nor fully erased, and its fracture is perceptible only to the actual world of the judge, the model audience.

In Australian stage drama, an elaborate synchronization and overlaying of temporal worlds occurs in Janis Balodis's *Too Young for Ghosts* (1985). Leichhardt the explorer is moving through Northern Queensland in 1845, syntaxing his travels by carving 'L' on a tree every time he camps. But he also marks his 'flight path' by leaving behind him a trail of dead Aboriginal people, comrades, and dingoes. As a sub-world to his necro-syntax, his accompanying naturalist, Gilbert, is gazing into the guts of dead animals. Balodis collates this with the world of wartime Stuttgart and the world of Latvian migrants in the canefields in 1948. This kind of collation is something that the necessarily polyphonic nature of theatrical discourse is peculiarly able to do: worldings can coexist, and their relationship may be anything from contrapuntal to simple doubling. Here, Balodis can set up the diachronic imperatives of colony, nation, and the post-colonial, all flowing through the synchronizing frame of the stage. Initially, the migrants are just another shipment, destinyless and now to the audience world originless, packed in a tin hut, a canned commodity for a world market, a mass body-bag. Their textuality is vestigial: they speak Latvian not as a mark of defence but as a mark of erasure because Latvian is a property that does not exist in the possible world of Northern Queensland.

For most of the play, these diachronic worlds are – formally at least – discrete, but towards the end of the play, Balodis reworlds it all with a technique like Bond's snow, a flood that seems to erase all writings on the land. As the water goes down, a remapping is generated, and the rules of trans-world access are contested. In the first half of the play, the present has invaded the past, a privilege we often accord it, as when *Scott's Last Expedition* reaches Erebus. But now the past begins invading the present, and the two worlds read each other with ostensibly symmetrical access, their separate possibilities multiplying out to generate an impossibility. The previous markers re-emerge as undefended textuality, to be radically reread. Through a semiotic swivel, the 'L' on the tree simply says that someone has been vandalizing eucalypts, and the bones of Leichhardt's botanist, Gilbert, are emptied, read just as 'Some old black feller's bones wrapped in bark' (Balodis 1985: 43).[6] The tree is chopped down, and the bones are tossed into the water. The markers, which previously gave an edge and a syntax to Empire, are now body-bags, floating abjections of a new empire.

The emptying of meaning-loading blurs the syntactic and the semantic in a manner noted by Julia Kristeva:

Where then lies the subjective value of those demarcations, exclusions, and prohibitions that establish the social organism as a 'symbolic system'? The anthropological analysis of these phenomena was for Mary Douglas essentially *syntactic* at first: defilement is an element connected with the boundary, the margin, etc., of an order. Henceforth she finds herself led to *semantic* problems: what is the *meaning* that such a border-element assumes in other psychological, economic, etc., systems?

(Kristeva 1982: 66)

But on the way to abjection Gilbert has found the position of Shakespeare crying at his own death. Leichhardt guns him down, with a subtlety of metaphor that might belong to John Wayne: 'Your time had come. There were no blank pages left in your journal' (Balodis 1985: 44). Gilbert relates what happened after Leichhardt shot him:

> I was scoured out by a flood. Some natives found me after the flood receded. Not having had so tame a spirit in their clutches before, they opened me up, as I would have liked, to learn my innermost secrets. How disappointed they were to learn the viney-viney was like them. They washed and wrapped my organs in aromatic leaves, filled my body and laid me to rest on a platform in the branches of a tree. Light and airy and warm. A kind of heaven. But the birds gave me no peace and my bones were carried off by wild pigs.
>
> (ibid.: 38–9)

Through the speaking abject, the Artaudian '"I" overcome by the corpse' (Kristeva 1982: 25),[7] the trans-world reading dynamics have also been inverted. Gilbert, who read Australia in the bowels of birds, is now being dissected and read by Australia. The flood, which has so far seemed a temporal fulcrum to the marking project, now becomes atemporal, and the erasure of Gilbert is a process rather then a single act of hostile textuality. And as he has been erased, by natives, pigs, birds, and floods, he has also been palimpsestically reinscribed in a body-bag that is neither name-coded, nor destiny-coded, nor origin-coded, but it *is* now culture-coded: the bark wrapping appropriates Gilbert, inviting the rereading by the canefields manager. But even there, access is further problematized since for the audience the bones retain a voice, the voice of Shakespeare crying at his own death, so that trans-world energies contest each other.

The Island, co-written by Athol Fugard, John Kani, and Winston Ntshona, is set in the island prison in which imperium seems to be totalized and textualized. But another textuality is also contained there, that of Sophocles' *Antigone*, which two prisoners (John and Winston) are rehearsing. The play seems particularly apt. Robben

Island is an arena of abjection, an off-shore rubbish dump. The body of Polynices, Antigone's brother, has been thrown over the walls of Thebes to be eaten by birds and animals, following the Greek legal principle of brushing away the 'impure':[8]

> the traitor Polynices, who had come back from exile intend-
> ing to burn and destroy his fatherland, to drink the blood of
> his masters, was to have no grave, no mourning. He was to lie
> on the open fields to rot, or at most be food for the jackals.
>
> (Fugard *et al.* 1974: 73)

But Antigone is an archetype of resistance: at night she goes out and buries her brother's body, which is uncovered again the next day. As such, the play was repositioned by Jean Anouilh within the context of occupied France, and became a focus for French resistance, with a Methuen blurb-writer speculating that 'the Germans allowed the play to be performed presumably because they found Creon's arguments for dictatorship convincing' (Anouilh 1960). But the question is implicit: what is the point of a rhetoric of resistance on Robben Island, itself a textuality of dictatorship? Or the Scott myth on Ross Island's Erebus? Or, to put it more succinctly in the words of one of the characters, 'Fuck legends' (Fugard *et al.* 1974: 62).

The prison environment, arena of much colonial and post-colonial drama, assumes macroscopic proportions within South African society, to the extent that a Bakhtinian 'context' is read as an irrelevant luxury (see Kristeva 1981: 64ff.). Similarly, the Workshop 71 *Survival*, another Robben Island play, abjects *Aida*, the imperialist tract of the Suez Canal opening. The end of Antigone, as of so much else on Robben Island, means that reading *Antigone* is just another discipline like those imposed by the unseen guard, Hodoshe: 'Learn to dig for Hodoshe, learn to run for Hodoshe, and what happens when I get back to the cell? Learn to read *Antigone*!' (Fugard *et al.* 1974: 52).

The interplay between world (the island) and subworld (*Antigone*), between the temporal and the atemporal, between pleading not guilty and pleading guilty (ibid.: 53), is reflexive and metatheatrical. Both worlds are stripped of possibilities and choice. When John's appeal is successful, he celebrates his release in three months by a worlding of freedom with the lexicon of incarceration that is almost as restrictive as the island (ibid.: 69).[9] The metatheatre becomes explicit on the last page, when Antigone is condemned. John, as Creon, addresses the audience:

> Take her from where she stands, straight to the Island! There wall her up in a cell for life, with enough food to acquit ourselves of the taint of her blood.

Winston (as Antigone) replies:

> I must leave the light of day forever, for the Island, strange and cold, to be lost between life and death. So, to my grave, my everlasting prison, condemned alive to solitary death.
>
> (ibid.: 77)

At that point, he tears off his women's clothes and breaks sub-role. As with Leichhardt and Gilbert, the past has invaded the present. But the present has also abjected the past: Antigone's final scene, in the cave with Haemon, and Creon's final peripeteia, are denied, and instead Antigone is dumped on Robben Island. But as Antigone is emptied, a new strength is articulated, which means that the supposedly totalized imperium of the island prison is penetrated and its realization is contested. On the island, imperium is written on the supposedly uninscribed territory of the prisoners. Cross-dressing from text to 'context' is just a counter-investment in an oppressive order, acceptance of the possibility of an impossible world. *Réalisation* through role-breaking asserts the power of the oppressed and articulates the impossibility of the possible world of realized erasure, the 'uninscribed'. If destinies are as yet uncoded, scavengers and salvagers are denied the chance to just 'scoop up the bodies in a hostile environment'.

Such a dissolution of role and agency parallels the final recorded dialogue on the flight deck at Erebus:

> *Unidentified speaker*: Bit thick here eh Bert?
> *Flight Engineer Maloney*: Yeah my . . . oath.
> *Maloney*: You're really a long while on . . . instruments at this time.
>
> (Macfarlane 1991: 329)

Initially, this was presented as evidence that responsibility for the crash lay with the cockpit crew. But the name-coding or role-casting is an editorial overlay. Maloney was not called Bert, and there was no one of that name on the crew.

NOTES

1 This motif was used as the cover photo for Macfarlane (1991).
2 This notion is implicit in the ambiguity Edward Said found in the journalistic term 'covering'. See Said (1981).
3 The relation between narcissism and emptiness is developed by Julia Kristeva (Kristeva 1987: 21–4). She dodges the Pausanian Narcissus discussed by Jenijoy La Belle (La Belle 1988: 24).
4 This develops the terminology used by Gayatri Spivak (1990: 1): 'the notion of textuality should be related to the notion of the worlding of a world on a supposedly uninscribed territory . . . . The imperialist project . . . had to assume that the earth that it territorialized was in fact previously uninscribed.'
5 With characteristic naiveté, Bond himself read the play as an imperialist tract, entitling a *Sunday Times* article 'Beating barbarism' (25 November 1973: 37): 'We are, in fact, a society committed to not understanding itself, and that is barbarism.'
6 The echo of Henry Lawson's story, 'The bush undertaker' is obvious, but the situation is wittily inverted in Jack Davis's claim that he is 'the only Aborigine who has kept a European skull' (Chesson 1988: 106).
7 As well as her cited references, Kristeva is clearly alluding to Artaud's 'Theatre and the plague' (in Artaud 1974), a very popular text among post-structuralists.
8 Cf. Kristeva's 'Semiotics of biblical abomination', in *Powers of Horror* (Kristeva 1982).
9 This irony is also realized in *Survival*, when a character experiences 'freedom'.

CONCLUSION
Reading difference
Alan Lawson and Chris Tiffin

It is one of the apparent paradoxes of the field that, as Stephen Slemon argues above, post-colonialism is often seen to attempt to construct and analyse colonialism as an overarching, transhistorical practice, whereas at all levels its constitutive marker is one of heterogeneity. Post-colonial textual reading and cultural analysis have been grounded in a phenomenology, a heuristics, and a hermeneutics of *difference*. Like the political process of decolonization with which it shares much of its ground and motivation, post-colonial studies seeks to identify, valorize, and empower what colonialist discourses label the barbarous, the primitive, the provincial. Thus, 'difference', which in colonialist discourse connotes a remove from normative European practice, and hence functions as a marker of subordination, is for post-colonial analysis the correspondent marker of identity, voice, and hence empowerment. Difference is not the measure by which the voiceless alien fails to be European; it is the measure by which the European episteme fails to comprehend the actual self-naming and articulate subject. Moreover, difference demands deference and self-location. Post-colonial projects must be both careful and clear about the nature of the differences which they seek to establish or recuperate or demobilize: not all differences are the same. Even as they speak of difference, the essays in this volume are concerned to identify a further difference – that between the subjects they discuss and the positions from which the essayists themselves speak.

These essays share the belief that the (post-)colonial subject – races as well as individuals – continues to be interpellated by a range of imperial mechanisms just as effectively as they were previously coerced by the more overt and formal institutions of Empire. This too must be historicized: it is necessary to reaffirm that imperialism and its practices continue, but equally necessary to notice that they do not continue to take the same form and to register the historical, cultural, and geographical specificities of both their deployment and its effects. Hollywood interpellates colonized peoples in a way comparable to, for example, the way missionaries and their texts once did at moments of contact. At the end of the twentieth century, however, the methods of control are not quite the same, and the colonized has greater access to textuality to rebut normative external paradigms with alternative maps of the power relationship. Post-colonial analysis of imperial texts is thus at least a double process: it analyses imperial texts to expose the ideological valency of trope and narrative (as in the essays by Jo-Ann Wallace and Robert Dixon), and it resituates them with other texts to neutralize the power of their privileged voice (as in the essays by Paul Sharrad and Howard McNaughton). But post-colonial readings also often take advantage of the 'readability' of texts in order to redeploy their '*acquired* authority' (Chambers 1990: 3) in the service of decolonization. The texts of Empire need to be described as part of the anatomy of Empire, but they also need to be de-scribed as part of the liquidation of Empire's effects.

The invasive difference of colonial experience is observed nowhere more acutely than in that ambivalent figure, the settler subject. Situated at the very site of the operation of colonial power, the male settler is part of the imperial enterprise, its agent, and its beneficiary, without ever acquiring more than associate member-ship of the imperial club. He is both mediator and mediated, excluded from the unmediated authority of Empire and from the unmediated authenticity of the indigene. From this half-empowered limbo he fetishizes yet disparages a Europe which in turn depreciates him while envying his energy, innocence, and enter-prise. Simultaneously he infantilizes, displaces, and desires the indigene completing the hierarchy of parallel loathing and desire.

The position of the female settler subject is, if anything, even more complex as the essays by Chris Prentice, Fiona Giles, and Bridget Orr demonstrate. The female settler subject is a site upon which contending, but also mutually affirming, systems of domi-nance meet: the female settler is simultaneously an object of patriarchy and an agent of imperial racism. Other power structures may intersect with these and it becomes necessary to register the precise organization of multiple systems of difference and interpellation. As Paul Sharrad notes, the imperial status of Emily, one of the characters in Caryl Phillips's novel, *Cambridge*, is complexly equivocal: 'on the one hand she is upper-class, Home-grown, and a surrogate male, being a plantation owner's daughter. On the other hand she is an unaccompanied, and therefore vulnerable, female, and an ignorant newcomer.' Markers of this political and psychic ambiguity are shared between historical event and its textual record. It is not surprising that the analyses by Dixon, Giles, Orr, and Sharrad all remark upon colonial dress as a site of ambiguity and ambivalence.

Dress, argues Fiona Giles, was for Jessie Couvreur a declaration of speaking position. Speaking position has been, and continues to be, a problem for post-colonial writers, because of the intimate connection of their medium, the English language, with the structures of power they seek to expose and dismantle. This may lead to paralysis – how can I escape and unmask imperialism if all I have is an episteme inflected by the imperial language? – or it may lead to a self-destructive negativity if one comes to believe one's post-colonial discursive options are limited simply 'to know[ing] how to curse'. It may also, however, lead to unsightly and often factitious squabbles among post-colonial critics precisely because questions of language and speaking position are often really contentions over domains of ambiguous authority. The very diversity of colonial experience with its Eurocentred hierarchies has fathered a shadowy counter-hierarchy in which he or she who can most plausibly claim the kiss of the whip is accorded the pre-eminent speaking position. Like the settler subject, a majority of post-colonial critics find themselves uncomfortably inside the residue of power structures they profess to oppose, and ambivalent beneficiaries of those structures. These questions of speaking position have a particular, though often unapprehended, resonance for the growing number of US critics who have begun to speak in and of this field of inquiry. Imperialism is a cultural effect of comprehensive power in the transmission and consumption of ideology that is not adequately registered by colours on a map. The globalizing effects of US monologia and its frequent disavowal of its own power in a variety of intellectual debates are core signifiers of neo-imperialism. The complicity of the US academy in the exercise and circulation of that power remains substantially unexamined.

But as Gareth Griffiths and Terry Collits argue, these are questions that should not be resolved with a spurious claim (or capitulation) to 'native' authenticity since this has the effect of itself foreclosing on difference. It also risks a terrifying return to the arithmetic of racial purity as practised in the plantation economies of the Americas, economies that produced precise lexicons of racial gradation in order to define the subject as property. It also tends to produce a 'native' subject locked in a prehistoric and hence apolitical authentic *past*. The 'problem' of speaking in colonial space is never solved in a transcendent theorem of colonial relations. The treaties will always be subject to renegotiation.

Much of the difference in subjectivity and interpellation we have been discussing is grounded in a difference in historical specifics. While some of the preconditions for Empire were certainly founded in Europe and its economic, social, and intellectual traditions (and Jo-Ann Wallace identifies a proto-colonial subject in the European child), the establishment and maintenance of the Empire was constantly modified by the geographies, resources, societies, and epistemes it encountered, deprecated, assimilated, or appropriated. As has been widely recognized (Low 1964; Ashcroft, Griffiths, and Tiffin 1989; McClintock 1992), each new imperial enterprise produced different forms for the management of colonial relations. Thus it is ultimately not adequate to speak of a homogeneous, unspecified 'Empire' or 'imperialism'; and neither can we adequately speak of an unspecified and undifferentiated post-colonialism. Indeed, we generalize at the risk of dehistoricizing the Empire, as well as disempowering the imperialized world and its own originary agency. As Homi Bhabha has argued (1983; 1984a; 1984b; 1985b; 1991), Western modernity itself was utterly deflected by its encounter with its Other or, more emphatically, with the whole bewildering array of its Others. For Bhabha (and for S.P. Mohanty 1989) the 'Other' ceases to be the impenetrable, insular 'that which is not self' and is seen to have already been rather an agent with 'relative', specifiable interests, powers, knowledges; Bill Ashcroft, in his essay, describes the recognition of this as 'a process in which the marginal, the excess, is becoming the actual'. In Bhabha's words, 'the project of modernity is itself rendered . . . contradictory and unresolved through the insertion of the "time-lag" in which colonial and postcolonial moments emerge *as sign and as history*' (Bhabha 1991: 195, emphasis added). It is this emergence of the (post-)colonial moment as sign (as text) which opens up the space *between* subjectivities, a space in which the enunciation (and the agency, the subjectivity, the signification) of colonial space can perform the essential *interruption* that brings about the transformation of modernity and its narratives.

Empire may have been constituted by sharp difference born of hard specifics, but this does not obviate problems of delineation and demarcation. As Dixon, McNaughton, and Slemon argue, the boundaries of Empire are pervious at the level of discourse, text, and discipline. These border-lands are the 'region where the control of representation can be contested' (Ashcroft p. 42). Boundary-drawing around colonial space(s), then, is less an exercise in taxonomy than a politics of representation. Boundary-marking produces effects on races, subjects, narratives, and the academy. Demarcating the perimeters of colonial space also configures and regulates its 'internal' structures of power. It is a recognition of this 'double movement', centripetal and centrifugal, which makes descriptive readings such as those by McNaughton and Sharrad so effective.

Both McNaughton and Sharrad offer what might be termed adjunctive readings. Each chooses contemporary post-colonial texts, Phillips's *Cambridge*, Balodis's *Too Young for Ghosts* and Fugard, Kani, and Ntshona's *The Island*, and reads them in the light of other texts. The aim of the interrogation is neither to demonstrate a deliberate, intentional reply by post-colonial to imperial (which might tend to preserve rather than dislocate the circumferential model of Empire) nor to identify a specific homology in the grouped texts in order to reveal psycho-social patterns in the authoring societies (which might tend to preserve a simply reflective model of textuality). Rather, each critic allows the adjunction of other texts to generate metaphors, to reveal absences, to expose the scribal power of Empire even when it denies or deprecates its control of utterance. Sharrad's demonstration of the essential monologia of Dickens' novel uses *Cambridge* to ask the question, 'what is absent from the novel and what is the implication of that absence?' This is neither a wilful nor an arbitrary question, because it focuses attention on the imperial system which energizes the values of the novel and determines their strengths and limitations. *Cambridge* thus reads back to *Oliver Twist* neither as parody nor reply, but as a cognate text offering direct but powerfully-incisive windows for critique.

If Sharrad explores the censorship and controlling silences of Empire, McNaughton explores Empire's astonishing prolixity. Newspaper reports, Greek plays, official inquests, even the detritus of exploration, travel, and war are constituted by, or themselves constitute, languages with authorizing power structures. The result is a dazzling excess of textualities within which to situate the post-colonial text, and, as J.M. Coetzee has shown, the resilience and ingenuity of textuality in eluding forms of constraint and control is almost 'limitless'. Again, the technique is an adjunctive one, but the process offers less a window for critique than a sense of systemic and polyphonic resonance in which the text is embedded. Both techniques proceed by indirection to amplify the contexts in which post-colonial texts can be read and deployed to recognize, describe, and de-scribe Empire.

BIBLIOGRAPHY

Achebe, C. (1964) *Arrow of God*, London: Heinemann.

—— (1975) 'An image of Africa: racism in Conrad's *Heart of Darkness*', the Second Chancellor's Lecture at the University of Massachusetts, Amherst, 18 February; reprinted in amended form in R. Kimbrough (ed.) *Joseph Conrad: Heart of Darkness*, Norton Critical Edition, 3rd edn, New York: Norton, 1988.

Alpers, A. (1982) *The Life of Katherine Mansfield*, Oxford: Oxford University Press.

Angier, C. (1985) *Jean Rhys*, Harmondsworth: Penguin.

—— (1992) *Jean Rhys: Life and Work*, Harmondsworth: Penguin.

Anouilh, J. (1960) *Antigone*, trans. L. Galantière, London: Methuen.

Anstey, R. (1975) *The Atlantic Slave Trade and British Abolition 1760–1810*, London: Macmillan.

Ariès, P. (1962) *Centuries of Childhood: A History of Family Life*, trans. R. Baldick, New York: Vintage Books.

Artaud, A. (1974) 'Theatre and the plague', *Collected Works*, vol. 4, trans. V. Corti, London: Calder & Boyars.

Arthur, K.O. (1989) 'Neither here nor there: towards nomadic reading', *New Literatures Review* 17: 31–42.

—— (1990) 'Beyond orality: Canada and Australia', *ARIEL* 21, 3: 23–36.

Asad, T. (1973) *Anthropology and the Colonial Encounter*, London: Ithaca Press.

Ashcroft, B. (1989) 'Constitutive graphonomy: a post-colonial theory of literary writing', *Kunapipi* 11, 1: 58–73.

Ashcroft B., Griffiths, G., and Tiffin, H. (1989) *The Empire Writes Back: Theory and Practice in Post-Colonial Literatures*, London: Routledge.

Bakhtin, M. (1981) *The Dialogic Imagination*, ed. M. Holquist, trans. C. Emerson and M. Holquist, Austin: University of Texas Press.

—— (1984) *Problems of Dostoevsky's Poetics*, ed. and trans. C. Emerson, Minneapolis: University of Minnesota Press.

Baldick, C. (1983) *The Social Mission of English Criticism 1848–1932*, Oxford: Clarendon Press.

Balodis, J. (1985) *Too Young For Ghosts*, Sydney: Currency Press.

Barthes, R. (1973) *Mythologies*, trans. A. Lavers, London: Paladin.

Bataille, G. (1956) Preface to *My Mother; Madame Edwarda; and the Dead Man*, trans. A. Wainhouse, 1989, London: Marion Boyars.

—— (1967) *The Accursed Share: An Essay on General Economy*, 3 vols; Vol. 1, *Consumption*, trans. R. Hurley, 1988, New York: Zone.

—— (1985) *Visions of Excess: Selected Writings, 1927–1939*, ed. A. Stoekl, trans. A. Stoekl, C.R. Lovitts, and D.M. Leslie, Jr., Minneapolis: University of Minnesota Press.

Beazley, C. (1897–1906) *The Dawn of Modern Geography*, 3 vols, London: Frowde.

Becke, L. (1908) *The Pearl Divers of Roncador Reef and Other Stories*, London: James Clarke.

Beilby, R., and Hadgraft, C. (1979) *Ada Cambridge, Tasma and Rosa Praed*, Melbourne: Oxford University Press.

Benedict, R. (1983) *Race and Racism*, with a Foreword by J. Rex, London: Routledge & Kegan Paul.

Benterrak, K., Muecke, S., and Roe, P. (1984) *Reading the Country*, Fremantle: Fremantle Arts Centre Press.

Berkeley, G. (1948) *The Works of George Berkeley Bishop of Cloyne*, ed. A.A. Luce and T.E. Jessop, London: Thomas Nelson.

Bhabha, H.K. (1983) 'The Other question: the stereotype and colonial discourse', *Screen* 24, 6: 18–36.

—— (1984a) 'Of mimicry and man: the ambivalence of colonial discourse', *October* 28: 125–33.

—— (1984b) 'Representation and the colonial text: a critical exploration of some forms of mimeticism', in F. Gloversmith (ed.) *The Theory of Reading*, Brighton: Harvester.

—— (1985a) 'Sly civility', *October* 34: 71–80.

—— (1985b) 'Signs taken for wonders: questions of ambivalence and authority under a tree outside Delhi, May 1817', *Critical Inquiry* 12, 1: 144–65.

—— (1985c) 'Signs taken for wonders: questions of ambivalence and authority under a tree outside Delhi, May 1817', in F. Barker *et al.* (eds) *Europe and Its Others: Proceedings of the Essex Conference on the Sociology of Literature, July 1984*, vol. 1, Colchester: University of Essex.

—— (1990a) 'Introduction: narrating the nation', in H.K. Bhabha (ed.) *Nation and Narration*, London: Routledge.

—— (1990b) 'DissemiNation: time, narrative, and the margins of the modern nation', in *Nation and Narration*, London: Routledge.

—— (1990c) 'Interrogating identity: the postcolonial prerogative', in D.T. Goldberg (ed.) *Anatomy of Racism*, Minneapolis: University of Minnesota Press.

—— (1991) '"Race", time and the revision of modernity', *Oxford Literary Review* 13: 193–219.

—— (1991b) 'The postcolonial critic: Homi Bhabba interviewed by David Bennett and Terry Collits', *Arena* 96 (Spring): 47–63.

Bishop, A. (1990) 'Western mathematics: the secret weapon of cultural imperialism', *Race and Class* 32, 2: 51–65.

Blake, W. (1957) 'The human abstract', in F. Bateson (ed.) *Selected Poems of William Blake*, London: Heinemann.

Bond, E. (1974) *Bingo*, London: Eyre Methuen.

Brantlinger, P. (1988) *Rule of Darkness: British Literature and Imperialism, 1830–1914*, Ithaca: Cornell University Press.

Breytenbach, B. (1964) *Die ysterkoei moet sweet*, Johannesburg: Afrikaanse Pers Boekhandel.

—— (1972) *Skryt*, Amsterdam: Meulenhoff.

—— (1983) *Eklips*, Johannesburg: Taurus.

—— (1984) *Buffalo Bill*, Johannesburg: Taurus.

—— (1985a) *True Confessions of an Albino Terrorist*, New York: Farrar, Straus, Giroux.

—— (1985b) *Lewendood*, Johannesburg: Taurus.

—— (1985c) *Mouroir*, New York: Farrar, Straus, Giroux.

—— (1986) *End Papers*, London: Faber & Faber.

—— (1988) *Judas Eye*, London: Faber & Faber.

Brink, A.P. (1980) 'Die vreemde bekende', in A.J. Coetzee (ed.) *Woorde teen die wolk*, Johannesburg: Taurus.

Brome, R. (1967) *The Antipodes*, London: Edward Arnold.

Brown, I. (1969) 'Dickens as social reformer', in E.W.F. Tomlin (ed.) *Charles Dickens 1812–1870*, London: Weidenfeld & Nicholson.

Brydon, D. (1991) 'The white Inuit speaks: contamination as literary strategy', in I. Adam and H. Tiffin (eds) *Past the Last Post: Theorizing Post-colonialism and Post-modernism*, Hemel Hempstead: Harvester Wheatsheaf.

Carpenter, H. (1985) *Secret Gardens: The Golden Age of Children's Literature*, London: George Allen & Unwin.

Carter, P. (1987) *The Road to Botany Bay: An Essay in Spatial History*, London: Faber & Faber.

Chambers, R. (1990) *Room for Maneuver: Reading (the) Oppositional (in) Narrative*, Chicago: University of Chicago Press.

Chesson, K. (1988) *Jack Davis: A Life Story*, Melbourne: Dent.

Chi, J., and Kuckles (1991) *Bran Nue Dae: A Musical Journey*, Sydney: Currency/Broome: Magabala Books.

Christian, B. (1987) 'The race for theory', *Cultural Critique* 6: 51–64.

Collingridge, G. (1983) *The Discovery of Australia: A Critical, Documentary and Historic Investigation Concerning the Priority of Discovery in Australia by Europeans Before the Arrival of Lieutenant James Cook, in the 'Endeavour', in 1770*, Gladesville, NSW: Golden Press.

Conrad, J. (1902) 'Heart of Darkness', in *Youth, Heart of Darkness, The End of the Tether*, Collected Edition, London: Dent, 1946.

—— (1924) 'Geography and some explorers', in Joseph Conrad, *Tales of Hearsay and Last Essays*, Collected Edition, London: Dent, 1955.

Cosmas (Indicopleustes) (1967) *Christianike Topographia: The Christian Topography of Cosmas, An Egyptian Monk*, ed. and trans. W. McCrindle, New York: Burt Franklin.

Craton, M. (1974) *Sinews of Empire: A Short History of British Slavery*, London: Temple Smith.

Crone, G.R. (1978) *Maps and Their Makers: An Introduction to the History of Cartography*, Hamden: Archon.

Davis, J. (1982) *Kullark/The Dreamers*, Sydney: Currency.

—— (1986) *No Sugar*, Sydney: Currency.

—— (1989) *Barungin*, Sydney: Currency.

de Lauretis, T. (1984) *Alice Doesn't: Feminism Semiotics Cinema*, Bloomington: Indiana University Press.

Debacco, R.E. (1980) 'Dickens and the mercantile hero', unpublished Ph.D. thesis, University of Pennsylvania.

Derrida, J. (1976) *Of Grammatology*, trans. G.C. Spivak, Baltimore: Johns Hopkins University Press.

Dickens, C. (1957) 'Slavery', *American Notes and Pictures of Italy*, London: Oxford University Press.

—— (1965) *The Letters of Charles Dickens*, Vol. 1, 1820–1839, Oxford: Clarendon Press.

—— (1985) *Oliver Twist*, 1839, ed. A. Wilson, Harmondsworth: Penguin.

Dixon, R. (1986) 'Rolf Boldrewood's *War to the Knife*: narrative form and ideology in the historical novel', *Australian Literary Studies* 12, 3: 324–34.

—— (1993) 'The New Woman and the Coming Man: gender and genre in the lost-race romance', in S. Magarey, S. Rowley and S. Sheridan (eds) *Debutante Nation: Feminism Contests the 1890s*, Sydney: Allen & Unwin.

Duffy, J. (1991) 'Divided Aborigines in call for mine enquiry', *West Australian*, 12 August: 9.

Dumont, J. (1696) *A New Voyage to the Levant*, 2nd edn, London.

Dunbar, R. (1986) 'The cruise', in P. Burnett (ed.) *The Penguin Book of Caribbean Verse*, Harmondsworth: Penguin.

During, S. (1985) 'Postmodernism or postcolonialism?', *Landfall* 39, 3: 366–80.

—— (1990) 'Literature: nationalism's other? The case for revision', in H.K. Bhabha (ed.) *Nation and Narration*, London: Routledge.

Elam, K. (1980) *The Semiotics of Theatre and Drama*, London: Methuen.

Eldershaw, F.S. (ed.) (1938) *The Peaceful Army: A Memorial to the Pioneer Women of Australia*, Sydney: Women's Executive Committee and Advisory Council of Australia's 150th Anniversary Celebrations.

Elliott, B. (1966) 'Antipodes: an essay in attitudes', *Australian Letters* 7: 51–75.

Emery, M.L. (1990) *Jean Rhys at 'World's End': Novels of Colonial and Sexual Exile*, Austin: University of Texas Press.

Fairclough, N.L. (1985) 'Critical and descriptive goals in discourse analysis', *Journal of Pragmatics* 9: 739–63.

Fanon, F. (1986) *Black Skin, White Masks*, with a Foreword by Homi K. Bhabha, London: Pluto Press.

Finnegan, R. (1976) *Oral Literature in Africa*, London: Oxford University Press.

Foss, P. (1986) 'Meridian of apathy', *Art and Text* 6: 74–88.

Foster, W.C. (1985) *Sir Thomas Livingston Mitchell and His World 1792–1855: Surveyor General of New South Wales 1828–1855*, Sydney: The Institution of Surveyors.

Foucault, M. (1969) 'What is an author?', trans. J.V. Harari, in J.V. Harari (ed.) *Textual Strategies: Perspectives in Post-Structuralist Criticism*, 1980, London: Methuen.

—— (1979) *Discipline and Punish: The Birth of the Prison*, trans. A. Sheridan, New York: Vintage Books.

—— (1981) 'The Order of Discourse', in R. Young (ed.) *Untying the Text*, London: Routledge & Kegan Paul.

Friederich, W.P. (1967) *Australia in Western Imaginative Prose Writings 1600–1960: An Anthology and a History of Literature*, Chapel Hill, North Carolina: University of North Carolina Press.

Fryer, P. (1984) *Staying Power*, London: Verso.

Fugard, A., Kani, J., and Ntshona, W. (1974) 'The Island', *Statements*, Oxford: Oxford University Press.

Gallop, J. (1982) *The Daughter's Seduction: Feminism and Psychoanalysis*, New York: Cornell University Press.

Gates, H.L., Jr. (1984) 'The blackness of blackness: a critique of the sign and the signifying monkey', in H.L. Gates, Jr. (ed.) *Black Literature and Literary Theory*, New York: Methuen.

—— (1991) 'Critical Fanonism', *Critical Inquiry* 17: 457–70.

Genette, G. (1969) *Figures II*, Paris: Seuil.

George, D.E.R. (1989) 'Quantum theatre – potential theatre: a new paradigm?' *New Theatre Quarterly* 18, 5: 171–9.

Gilbert, H. (1990) 'Historical re-presentation: performance and counter-discourse in Jack Davis' plays', *New Literatures Review* 19: 91–101.

—— (1992) 'The dance as text in contemporary Australian drama: movement and resistance politics', *ARIEL* 23, 1: 133–47.

Gilbert, K. (1988) *The Cherry Pickers*, Canberra: Burrambinga Books.

Giles, E. (1889) *Australia Twice Traversed: the Romance of Exploration: Being a Narrative Compiled From the Journals of Five Exploring Expeditions Into and Through Central South Australia and Western Australia, from 1872 to 1876*, 2 vols, London: Sampson Low.

Giles, F. (1988) 'Romance: an embarrassing subject', in L. Hergenhan (ed.) *The Penguin New Literary History of Australia*, Ringwood, Victoria: Penguin.

—— (1989) 'Finding a shiftingness: situating the nineteenth-century Anglo-Australian female subject', *New Literatures Review*, 'The Postcolonial Revision of Australian Literature', Special Issue, 18: 10–19.

Goldberg, D.T. (ed.) (1990) *Anatomy of Racism*, Minneapolis: University of Minnesota Press.

Goldie, T. (1988) 'Signifier resignified: Aborigines in Australian literature', *Aboriginal Culture Today*, Special Issue of *Kunapipi* 10, 1–2: 59–75.

Green, H.M. (1961) *A History of Australian Literature, Pure and Applied*, Vol. 1, 1789–1923, Sydney: Angus & Robertson.

Green, M. (1980) *Dreams of Adventure, Deeds of Empire*, London: Routledge & Kegan Paul.

Grey, G. (1841) *Journals of Two Expeditions of Discovery in North-west and Western Australia, during the Years 1837, 38, and 39, under the Authority of Her Majesty's Government Describing Many Newly Discovered, Important, and Fertile Districts, with Observations on the Moral and Physical Conditions of the Aboriginal Inhabitants*, 2 vols, London: T. & W. Boone.

Grosz, E. (1989) *Sexual Subversions*, Sydney: Allen & Unwin.

Gunew, S. (1985) 'Migrant women writers: who's on whose margins?' in Carole Ferrier (ed.) *Gender, Politics and Fiction: Twentieth Century Australian*

Women's Novels, 2nd edn 1992, St Lucia, Queensland: University of Queensland Press.

Hall, J. (1605) *Another World and Yet the Same: Bishop Joseph Hall's Mundus Alter et Idem*, trans. and ed. J. M. Wands, New Haven: Yale University Press, 1981.

Halsband, R. (1978) '"Condemned to petticoats": Lady Mary Wortley Montagu as feminist and writer', in R.B. White Jr. (ed.) *The Dress of Words: Essays on Restoration and Eighteenth Century Literature in Honour of Richmond P. Bond*, Lawrence, Kansas: University of Kansas Libraries.

Harley, J.B. (1988) 'Maps, knowledge, and power', *The Iconography of Landscape: Essays on the Symbolic Representation, Design, and Use of Past Environments*, Melbourne: Cambridge University Press.

Harley, J.B., and Woodward, D. (eds) (1987) *The History of Cartography* Vol. 1: *Cartography in Prehistoric, Ancient, and Medieval Europe and the Mediterranean*, Chicago: University of Chicago Press.

Harlow, B. (1987) *Resistance Literature*, New York and London: Methuen.

Harris, W. (1967) 'Tradition and the West Indian novel', in *Tradition, the Writer and Society*, London: New Beacon.

Hayter, T. (1971) *Aid as Imperialism*, Harmondsworth: Penguin.

Hite, M. (1989) *The Other Side of the Story: Structures and Strategies of Contemporary Feminist Narrative*, Ithaca: Cornell University Press.

Hodge, B., and Mishra, V. (1990) *The Dark Side of the Dream: Australian Literature and the Postcolonial Mind*, Sydney: Allen & Unwin.

Holton, S.S. (1986) *Feminism and Democracy: Women's Suffrage and Reform Politics in Britain 1900–1918*, Cambridge: Cambridge University Press.

Hulme, P. (1985) 'Polytropic man: tropes of sexuality and mobility in early colonial discourse', in F. Barker *et al.* (eds) *Europe and Its Others: Proceedings of the Essex Conference on the Sociology of Literature, July 1984*, vol. 2, Colchester: University of Essex.

—— (1986) *Colonial Encounters: Europe and the Native Caribbean 1492–1797*, London: Methuen.

Husserl, E. (1913) *Ideas: General Introduction to Pure Phenomenology*, trans. W.R. Boyce Gibson, 1931, London: Allen & Unwin.

Hutcheon, L. (1988) *A Poetics of Postmodernism: History, Theory, Fiction*, London: Routledge.

—— (1991) '"Circling the Downspout of Empire"', in I. Adam and H. Tiffin (eds) *Past the Last Post: Theorizing Post-Colonialism and Post-Modernism*, Hemel Hempstead: Harvester Wheatsheaf. An earlier version of this essay was published as '"Circling the Downspout of Empire": Post-Colonialism and Postmodernism', *ARIEL* 20, 4 (1989): 149–75.

Ihimaera, W. (1989) *Dear Miss Mansfield*, Auckland: Viking-Penguin.

Irigaray, L. (1985a) *Speculum of the Other Woman*, trans. G.C. Gill, 1974, Ithaca, New York: Cornell University Press.

—— (1985b) *This Sex Which Is Not One*, trans. C. Porter with C. Burke, 1977, Ithaca, New York: Cornell University Press.

Jaggi, M. (1991) 'Society and its slaves', *Times Literary Supplement* 15 March: 10.

James, L. (1988–89) 'Reflections, and the bottom of the river: the transformation of Caribbean experience in the fiction of Jamaica Kincaid', *Wasafiri* 9: 15–17.

Jardine, A. (1985) *Gynesis: Configurations of Women and Modernity*, Ithaca: Cornell University Press.

Johnson, B. (1987) Interview in I. Salusinszky, *Criticism in Society*, New York: Methuen.

Jones, R. (1985) 'Ordering the landscape', in I. and T. Donaldson (eds) *Seeing the First Australians*, Sydney: Allen & Unwin, 181–209.

Keith, W. (ed.) (1981) *A Voice in the Land: Essays by and About Rudy Wiebe*, Edmonton: NeWest Press.

Kincaid, J. (1983) *At the Bottom of the River*, New York: Farrar, Straus, Giroux.

—— (1985) *Annie John*, New York: Plume/New American Library.

Kingsley, C. (1863) *The Water-Babies*, London: Macmillan.

—— (1880) 'The massacre of the innocents', in *The Works of Charles Kingsley*, Vol. 18, *Sanitary and Social Lectures and Essays*, London: Macmillan.

—— (1984) *The Water-Babies*, Harmondsworth: Puffin Classics.

Kingston, B. (1977) *The World Moves Slowly: A Documentary History of Australian Women*, Melbourne: Cassell.

Kovel, J. (1988) *White Racism: A Psychohistory*, introd. by I. Ward, London: Free Association Books.

Kristeva, J. (1981) *Desire in Language: A Semiotic Approach to Literature and Art*, ed. L. S. Roudiez, trans. T. Gora, A. Jardine, and L.S. Roudiez, Oxford: Basil Blackwell.

—— (1982) *Powers of Horror: An Essay on Abjection*, trans. L. S. Roudiez, New York: Columbia University Press.

—— (1984) *Revolution in Poetic Language*, trans. M. Waller, New York: Columbia University Press.

—— (1987) 'Narcissism: a screen for emptiness', *Tales of Love*, trans. L.S. Roudiez, New York: Columbia University Press.

Kroetsch, R. (1989) *The Lovely Treachery of Words: Essays Selected and New*, Toronto: Oxford University Press.

La Belle, J. (1988) *Herself Beheld: The Literature of the Looking Glass*, Ithaca: Cornell University Press.

Lacan, J. (1973) *The Four Fundamental Concepts of Psycho-analysis*, ed. J.-A. Miller, trans. A. Sheridan, Harmondsworth: Penguin, 1979.

Lake, M. (1986) 'The politics of respectability: identifying the masculinist context', *Historical Studies* 22: 116–31.

Lambert, M., and Palenski, R. (1982) *The New Zealand Almanac*, Wellington: Moa Almanac Press, with Air New Zealand.

Lamming, G. (1980) *The Emigrants*, 1954, London: Allison & Busby.

Lawrence, D.H. (1950) *Kangaroo*, Penguin: Harmondsworth.

Lawson, A. (1993) 'Un/settling colonies', in C. Worth, P. Nestor, and M. Pavlyshyn (eds) *Literature & Opposition*, Monash University, Clayton, Vic: Centre for Comparative Literature and Cultural Studies.

Le Gallez, P. (1990) *The Rhys Woman*, Basingstoke: Macmillan.

Leavis, F.R. (1962) *The Great Tradition*, Harmondsworth: Penguin/Peregrine.

LeClair, T. (1989) *The Art of Excess: Mastery in Contemporary American Fiction*, Urbana: University of Illinois Press.

Locke, J. (1934) *Some Thoughts Concerning Education*, 1693, Cambridge: Cambridge University Press.

Low, D.A. (1964) 'Lion rampant', *Journal of Commonwealth Political Studies* 2, 3: 235–52.

Low, G.C.-L. (1990) 'His stories?: narratives and images of imperialism', *New Formations* 12: 97–123.

Lowenthal, C. (1990) 'The veil of romance: Lady Mary's embassy letters', *Eighteenth Century Life* 14: 62–82.

Lucretius (1947) *De Rerum Natura*, ed. C. Bailey, 2 vols, Oxford: Clarendon Press.

Lytton, C. (1914) *Prisons and Prisoners: Some Personal Experiences*, London: William Heinemann.

Macaulay, T.B. (1972) 'Minute on Indian education [1835]', in J. Clive and T. Pinney (eds) *Selected Writings*, Chicago: University of Chicago Press.

McClintock, A. (1992) 'The angel of progress: pitfalls of the term "post-colonialism"', *Social Text* 31–2: 84–98.

MacDonald, A. (1909) *The Island Traders*, London and Glasgow: Blackie.

Macfarlane, S. (ed.) (1991) *The Erebus Papers*, Auckland: Avon Press.

McIntyre, K. (1977) *The Secret Discovery of Australia*, Medindie: Souvenir Press.

Mackay, J., and Thane, P. (1986) 'The Englishwoman', in R. Colls and P. Dodd (eds) *Englishness: Politics and Culture, 1880–1920*, London: Croom Helm.

Macrobius (1952) *Commentary on the Dream of Scipio*, trans. H. Stahl, New York: Columbia University Press.

Malouf, D. (1985) *12 Edmonstone Street*, London: Chatto & Windus.

Mansfield, K. (1978) *The Urewera Notebook*, ed. I.A. Gordon, Wellington: Oxford University Press.

—— (1984) *The Collected Letters of Katherine Mansfield*, ed. V. O'Sullivan and M. Scott, vol. 1, Oxford: Clarendon Press.

Marcus, J. (ed.) (1987) *Suffrage and the Pankhursts*, London: Routledge & Kegan Paul.

Markus, A. (1990) *Governing Savages*, Sydney: Allen & Unwin.

Marlowe, C.(1981) *Tamburlaine the Great*, ed. J.S. Cunningham, Manchester: Manchester University Press.

Martin, C. (1890) *An Australian Girl*, 3 vols, London: Bentley.

Maza, B. (1989) *The Keepers*, in *Plays From Black Australia*, introd. J. Saunders, Sydney: Currency. 167–229.

Meaney, N. (1976) *The Search for Security in the Pacific, 1901–1914*, Sydney: Sydney University Press.

Memmi, A. (1965) *The Colonizer and the Colonized*, introd. by J.-P. Sartre, New York: Souvenir Press.

Merritt, R. (1978) *The Cake Man*, Sydney: Currency.

Miller, N.K. (1988) 'Emphasis added: plots and plausibilities in women's fiction', in *Subject to Change: Reading Feminist Writing*, New York: Columbia University Press.

Mishra, V., and Hodge, B. (1991) 'What is post(-)colonialism?', *Textual Practice* 5, 3: 399–413.

Mitchell, T. (1988) *Colonising Egypt*, Cambridge: Cambridge University Press.

Mitchell, T.L. (1839) *Three Expeditions into the Interior of Eastern Australia: with Descriptions of the Recently Explored Region of Australia Felix and of the Present Colony of New South Wales*, 2nd edn, 2 vols, London: T. & W. Boone.

Mohanty, C. (1988) 'Under western eyes: feminist scholarship and colonial discourses', *Feminist Review* 30: 61–88.

Mohanty, C., Russo, A., and Torres, L. (eds) (1991) *Third World Women and the Politics of Feminism*, Bloomington: Indiana University Press.

Mohanty, S.P. (1989) 'Us and them: on the philosophical bases of political criticism', *New Formations* 8: 55–80; *Yale Journal of Criticism* 2, 2: 1–32.

Morgan, S. (1987) *My Place*, Fremantle: Fremantle Arts Centre Press.

Morton, W.L. (1972) *The Canadian Identity*, 2nd edn, Madison: University of Wisconsin Press.

Mudrooroo (Narogin) Nyoongah (1990) *Writing from the Fringe: A Study of Modern Aboriginal Literature*, Melbourne: Hyland House.

—— (1991) *Master of the Ghost Dreaming*, Sydney: Collins.

Muecke, S. (1983a) 'Ideology reiterated: the uses of Aboriginal oral narrative', *Southern Review* (Adelaide) 16, 1: 86–101.

—— (1983b) 'Discourse, history, fiction: language and Aboriginal history', *Australian Journal of Cultural Studies* 1, 1: 71–80.

—— (1988) 'Body, inscription, epistemology: knowing Aboriginal texts', in E.S. Nelson (ed.) *Connections: Essays on Black Literatures*, Canberra: Aboriginal Studies Press.

Mukherjee, A. (1990) 'Whose post-colonialism and whose postmodernism?', *World Literature Written in English* 30, 2: 1–9.

—— (1991) 'The exclusions of postcolonial theory and Mulk Raj Anand's *Untouchable*: a case study', *ARIEL* 22, 3: 27–48.

Mulvey, L. (1986) 'Magnificent obsession', *Parachute* 42: 7–12.

Naipaul, V.S. (1969) *The Loss of El Dorado*, Harmondsworth: Penguin.

—— (1976) *The Overcrowded Barracoon*, Harmondsworth: Penguin.

Nelson, E.S. (1990) 'Literature against history: an approach to Australian Aboriginal writing', *World Literature Today* 64, 1: 30–4.

New, W.H. (1987) *Dreams of Speech and Violence: The Art of the Short Story in New Zealand and Canada*, Toronto: University of Toronto Press.

Newman, K. (1987) '"And wash the Ethiop white": femininity and the monstrous in *Othello*', in J.E. Howard and M.F. O'Connor (eds) *Shakespeare Reproduced: The Text in History and Ideology*, New York: Methuen.

Niesen de Abruña, L. (1988) 'Jean Rhys's feminism: theory against practice', *World Literature Written in English* 28, 2: 326–36.

Nowra, L. (1988) *Capricornia*, Sydney: Currency.

O'Sullivan, V. (1989) *Finding the Pattern, Solving the Problem: Katherine Mansfield and the New Zealand European*, Wellington: Victoria University Press.

Okpewho, I. (1979) *The Epic in Africa: Towards a Poetics of the Oral Performance*, New York: Columbia University Press.

Ong, W.J. (1982) *Orality and Literacy: The Technologizing of the Word*, London: Methuen.

Orkin, M. (1991) *Drama and the South African State*, Manchester: Manchester University Press.

Orr, B. (1989) 'Reading with the taint of the pioneer: Katherine Mansfield and settler criticism', *Landfall* 43, 4: 447–61.

Oxley, J. (1820) *Journal of Two Expeditions into the Interior of New South Wales, Undertaken by Order of the British Government in the Years 1817–18*, London: John Murray.

Pankhurst, C. (1959) *Unshackled: The Story of How We Won the Vote*, ed. Lord Pethick-Lawrence of Peaslake, London: Hutchinson.

Pankhurst, E. (1914) *My Own Story*, London: Eveleigh Nash.

Parry, B. (1987) 'Problems in current theories of colonial discourse', *Oxford Literary Review* 9, 1–2: 27–58.

Pêcheux, M. (1982) *Language, Semantics and Ideology*, trans. H. Nagpal, London: Macmillan.

Péron, M.F. (1809) *A Voyage of Discovery to the Southern Hemisphere Performed by Order of the Emperor Napoleon During the Years 1801, 1802, 1803, and 1804*, London: Phillips.

Phillips, C. (1991) *Cambridge*, London: Bloomsbury.

Pilkington, E. (1988) *Beyond the Mother Country: West Indians and the Notting Hill White Riots*, London: I.B. Tauris.

Plante, D. (1983) *Difficult Women: A Memoir of Three*, London: Victor Gollancz.

Porter, J.C. (1979) *The Inconstant Savage: England and the North American Indian, 1500–1660*, London: Duckworth.

Postman, N. (1982) *The Disappearance of Childhood*, New York: Dell.

Pratt, A. (1911) *The Big Five*, London: Ward, Lock.

Price, A.G. (1945) *Australia Comes of Age: A Study of Growth to Nationhood and of External Relations*, Melbourne: Georgian House.

Revel, J. (1989) 'The uses of civility', in R. Chartier (ed.) *A History of Private Life* Vol. 3: *Passions of the Renaissance*, trans. A. Goldhammer, Cambridge, Mass.: The Belknap Press of Harvard University Press.

Rhys, J. (1972) 'Let them call it jazz', *Tigers are Better-Looking: With a Selection from The Left Bank*, 1968, Harmondsworth: Penguin.

Robinson, A.H. (1982) *Early Thematic Mapping in the History of Cartography*, Chicago: University of Chicago Press.

Rosaldo, R. (1989) *Culture and Truth: The Remaking of Social Analysis*, Boston: Beacon Press.

Rose, J. (1984) *The Case of Peter Pan, or The Impossibility of Children's Fiction*, London: Macmillan.

Rousseau, G.S., and Porter, K. (1990) *Exoticism in the Enlightenment*, Manchester: Manchester University Press.

Rousseau, J.-J. (1984) *Emile*, 1762, trans. B. Foxley, London: Dent/Everyman's Library.

Rubin, M.L. (1988) 'Adolescence and autobiographical fiction: teaching *Annie John* by Jamaica Kincaid', *Wasafiri* 8: 11–14.

Russo, M. (1986) 'Female grotesques: carnival and theory', in T. de Lauretis (ed.) *Feminist Studies/Critical Studies*, Bloomington: Indiana University Press.

Rycaut, P. (1668) *The Present State of the Ottoman Empire*, 2nd edn, London:

Starkey & Brome.

Said, E. (1979) *Orientalism*, New York: Random House-Vintage.

—— (1981) *Covering Islam: How the Media and the Experts Determine How We See the Rest of the World*, New York: Pantheon Books.

—— (1989) *After the Last Sky: Palestinian Lives*, New York: Pantheon.

Sarvan, C. and Marhama, H. (1991) 'The fictional works of Caryl Phillips: an introduction', *World Literature Today* 65, 1: 35–40.

Schaffer, K. (1988) *Women and the Bush: Forces of Desire in the Australian Cultural Tradition*, Melbourne: Cambridge University Press.

—— (1993) 'Captivity narratives and the idea of "nation"', in K. Darian-Smith (ed.) *Captured Lives*, London: Robert Menzies Centre for Australian Studies, University of London.

Scott, M. (1990) 'Karbarra: the new Aboriginal drama and its audience', *Span* 30: 127–40.

Selvon, S. (1979) *The Lonely Londoners*, 1956, Harlow: Longman.

Serle, G. (1973) *From Deserts the Prophets Come: The Creative Spirit in Australia 1788–1972*, Melbourne: Heinemann.

Sharpe, J. (1989) 'Figures of colonial resistance', *Modern Fiction Studies* 35, 1: 137–55.

Sheridan, S. (1985) '"Temper democratic; bias, offensively feminine": Australian women writers and literary nationalism', *Kunapipi* 7: 49–58.

Shoemaker, A. (1989) *Black Words, White Page: Aboriginal Literature 1929–1988*, St Lucia: University of Queensland Press.

Showalter, E. (1981) 'Feminist criticism in the wilderness', *Critical Inquiry* 8, 2: 179–205.

Sigmond, J.P., and Zunderbaan, L.H. (1979) *Dutch Discoveries of Australia: Shipwrecks, Treasures and Early Voyages Off the West Coast*, Adelaide: Rigby.

Sinclair, K. (1969) *A History of New Zealand*, 1959, 2nd edn, Auckland: Penguin.

Skelton, R.A. (1958) *Explorers' Maps: Chapters in the Cartographic Record of Geographical Discovery*, London: Routledge & Kegan Paul.

Slemon, S. (1988) '"Carnival" and the canon', *ARIEL* 19, 3: 59–75.

—— (1989) 'Modernism's last post', *ARIEL* 20, 4: 3–17.

—— (1990) 'Unsettling the empire: resistance theory for the Second World', *World Literature Written in English* 30, 2: 30–41.

—— (1991) 'Modernism's last post', in I. Adam and H. Tiffin (eds) *Past the Last Post: Theorizing Post-Colonialism and Post-Modernism*, Hemel Hempstead: Harvester Wheatsheaf. An earlier version of this essay was published in *ARIEL* 20, 4: 3–17.

Smith, P. (1988) *Discerning the Subject*, Minneapolis: University of Minnesota Press.

Spacks, P.M. (1984) 'Imaginations warm and tender: Pope and Lady Mary', *South Atlantic Quarterly* 83, 2: 207–15.

Spillers, H. (1990) 'Metathesis: reading the future, future reading', paper given at the Modern Language Association convention, Chicago, December.

Spivak, G.C. (1985a) 'Can the subaltern speak? Speculations on widow-sacrifice', *Wedge* 7–8: 120–30.

—— (1985b) 'The Rani of Sirmur', in F. Barker *et al.* (eds) *Europe and Its*

Others: Proceedings of the Essex Conference on the Sociology of Literature, July 1984, vol.1, Colchester: University of Essex.

—— (1986) 'Imperialism and sexual difference', *Oxford Literary Review* 8, 1–2: 225–40.

—— (1987) *In Other Worlds: Essays in Cultural Politics*, London: Methuen.

—— (1990) *The Post-colonial Critic*, ed. S. Harasym, London: Routledge.

Stuart, J. McD. (1865) *The Journals of John McDouall Stuart During the Years 1858, 1860, 1861, & 1862, When He Fixed the Centre of the Continent and Successfully Crossed It from Sea to Sea*, 2nd edn, London: Saunders.

Sturt, C. (1833) *Two Expeditions into the Interior of Southern Australia, During the Years 1828, 1829, 1830, and 1831: with Observations on the Soil, Climate, and General Resources of the Colony of New South Wales*, 2 vols, London: Smith & Elder.

—— (1849) *Narrative of an Expedition into Central Australia, Performed under the Authority of Her Majesty's Government, during the years 1844, 5 and 6 together with a Notice of the Province of South Australia, in 1847*, 2 vols, London: T.& W. Boone.

Suter, K. (1991) *Antarctica: Private Property or Public Heritage?*, Leichhardt, NSW: Pluto Press.

Swift, J. (1983) 'On poetry: a rhapsody', *Jonathan Swift: The Complete Poems*, ed. P. Rogers, Harmondsworth: Penguin.

Tapping, C. (1989a) 'Oral cultures and the empire of literature', *Kunapipi* 11, 1: 86–96.

—— (1989b) 'Children and history in the Caribbean novel: George Lamming's *In the Castle of My Skin* and Jamaica Kincaid's *Annie John*', *Kunapipi* 11, 2: 51–9.

—— (1990) 'Voices off: models of orality in African literature and literary criticism', *ARIEL* 21, 3: 73–86.

'Tasma' [Jessie Couvreur] (1891) *The Penance of Portia James*, London: Heinemann.

Taussig, M. (1987) *Shamanism, Colonialism, and the Wild Man: A Study in Terror and Healing*, Chicago: University of Chicago Press.

Thomas, E.V. (1990) '*Crick Crack Monkey*: a picaresque perspective', in S.R. Cudjoe (ed.) *Caribbean Women Writers: Essays from the First International Conference*, Wellesley, Massachusetts: Calaloux Publications.

Thomas, S. (1990a) 'Mobilising women: representations of British women's relationship with the state 1905–1918', paper given at the La Trobe University Women's Studies Research Seminar series, Melbourne.

—— (1990b) 'Reading Antoinette's sexual desire in *Wide Sargasso Sea*', paper given at the Post-colonial Women's Writing Conference, Macquarie University, Sydney, September.

Thompson, R.C. (1980) *Australian Imperialism in the Pacific: The Expansionist Era, 1820–1920*, Melbourne: Melbourne University Press.

Tickner, L. (1987) *The Spectacle of Women: Imagery of the Suffrage Campaign 1907–14*, London: Chatto & Windus.

Tiffin, C. (1992) 'The voyage of the good ship "Commonwealth"', *Kunapipi* 14, 2: 12–21.

Tiffin, H. (1987) 'Post-colonial literatures and counter-discourse', *Kunapipi* 9, 3: 17–38.

—— (1988) 'Post-colonialism, post-modernism and the rehabilitation of post-colonial history', *Journal of Commonwealth Literature* 23, 1: 169–81.

—— (1991) 'Decolonization and audience: Erna Brodber's *Myal* and Jamaica Kincaid's *A Small Place*', in W. McGaw (ed.) *A Sense of Audience*, Wollongong: SPACLALS.

Tompkins, J. (1993) 'History/history/histories: resisting the binary in Aboriginal drama', *Kunapipi* 15.1 (1993): 6–14.

Tooley, R. (1979) *The Mapping of Australia*, London: Holland.

Torgovnick, M. (1990) *Gone Primitive: Savage Intellects, Modern Lives*, Chicago: University of Chicago Press.

Townsend, J.R. (1974) *Written for Children: An Outline of English-language Children's Literature*, Boston: The Horn Book.

Turner, G. (1986) *National Fictions: Literature, Film, and the Construction of Australian Narrative*, Sydney: Allen & Unwin.

Uffelman, L.K. (1979) *Charles Kingsley*, Boston: Twayne.

Van Toorn, P. (1990) 'Discourse/patron discourse: how minority texts command the attention of majority audiences', *Span* 30: 102–15.

Visel, R. (1988) 'A half-colonisation: the problem of the white colonial woman writer', *Kunapipi* 10, 3: 39–45.

Viswanathan, G. (1987) 'The beginnings of English literary study in British India', *Oxford Literary Review* 9: 2–26.

—— (1989) *Masks of Conquest: Literary Study and British Rule in India*, London: Faber & Faber.

Viviers, J. (1978) *Breytenbach*, Cape Town: Tafelberg.

Weil, S. (1952) *Gravity and Grace*, ed. G. Thibon, London: Routledge.

Weiss, A.S. (1989) *The Aesthetics of Excess*, Albany: State University of New York Press.

Wevers, L. (1988) 'How Kathleen Beauchamp was kidnapped', *Women's Studies Journal* 4, 2: 5–17.

White, R. (1981) *Inventing Australia: Images and Identity, 1688–1980*, Sydney: Allen & Unwin.

Wight, J.K. (1965) *The Geographical Lore of the Time of the Crusaders: A Study in the History of Medieval Science and Tradition in Western Europe*, 2nd edn, New York: Dover.

Williams, R. (1983) *Keywords: A Vocabulary of Culture and Society*, 1976, 2nd edn, London: Fontana.

Williams, G., and Frost, A. (1988) *Terra Australis to Australia*, Melbourne: Oxford University Press.

Willmott, B. (1989) 'Introduction: culture and national identity', in D. Novitz and B. Willmott (eds) *Culture and Identity in New Zealand*, Wellington: GP Books.

Wilson, A. (1972) *The World of Charles Dickens*, Harmondsworth: Penguin.

Withers, J. (1650) *A Description of the Grand Signor's Seraglio*, London.

Wittgenstein, L. (1976) *Tractatus Logico Philosophicas*, 1921, trans. D.F. Pears and B.F. McGuiness, London: Routledge & Kegan Paul.

Wood, G. (1922) *The Discovery of Australia*, London: Macmillan.

Woods, D. and Fels, J. (1986) 'Designs on signs: myth and meaning in maps', *Cartographica* 23, 3: 54–103.

Woodward, D. (ed.) (1987) *Art and Cartography: Six Historical Essays*, Chicago: University of Chicago Press.

Wortley Montagu, Lady M. (1965) *The Complete Letters of Lady Mary Wortley Montagu*, ed. R. Halsband, vol. 1, Oxford: Clarendon Press.

Wyndham, F., and Melly, D. (eds) (1985) *Jean Rhys: Letters 1931–1966*, Harmondsworth: Penguin.

Young, R. (1990) *White Mythologies: Writing History and the West*, London and New York: Routledge.

INDEX